D1173489

SHARING
THE TRUTH
IN LOVE

Royalties from the sale of this book will be designated for
Christian literature and education projects in Sri Lanka.

Discovery House Publishers

Books, music, and videos that feed the soul with the Word of God

Box 3566 Grand Rapids, MI 49501

SHARING
THE TRUTH
IN LOVE

HOW TO RELATE TO
PEOPLE OF OTHER FAITHS

Ajith Fernando

Sharing the Truth in Love:
How to relate to people of other faiths
by Ajith Fernando
Copyright © 2001 by Ajith Fernando

Discovery House Publishers is affiliated with RBC Ministries,
Grand Rapids Michigan 49512.

Discovery house books are distributed to the trade exclusively by
Barbour Publishing, Inc., Uhrichsville, Ohio 44683.

Cover design by Jim Connelly, Jenison, Michigan.

Library of Congress Cataloging-in-Publication Data

Fernando, Ajith.
    sharing the truth in love : how to relate to people of other faiths /
by Ajith Fernando.
        p. cm.
    Includes bibliographical references (p.).
    ISBN 1-57293-054-3
    1. Evangelistic work. 2. christianity and other religions. I. Title.

BV3793 .F47 2001
261.2--dc21   00-065916

Printed in the United States of America.

01 02 03 04 05 06 07 / CHG / 7 6 5 4 3 2 1

CONTENTS

PREFACE

When Dr. Robert de Vries of Discovery House Publishers invited me to update my book, *The Christian's Attitude Toward World Religions,* I did not realize that the scene in the church and in society had changed so much in the 15 years since I wrote it. I discovered that a completely new book was needed. Although a few sections from my earlier work have been retained, this is essentially a new effort. It is in some ways a companion to my other book, *The Supremacy of Christ.* These two books, along with my book *Crucial Questions about Hell,* will combine to provide a comprehensive theological base for Christian witnessing.

When I was in my late teens I heard a preacher who argued that not only those who receive Christ have salvation. Before the sermon was over, I walked out of the church in disgust. My mother, who is a convert from Buddhism and is much bolder than I, gave the preacher a piece of her mind after the service.

Around that time I was at another service on what was called Evangelism Sunday. The preacher claimed that Christ has saved the whole world. Evangelism is nothing more than telling these people that they are saved and now can live like saved people. I realized that we must give an intelligent response to these views that are growing in our churches. But being of a shy disposition and therefore unable to engage in effective debate, I believed that the way to unleash this burden was by writing. This book is an expression of that realization.

I am grateful that the Lord has given me opportunities to interact with those of other faiths from my childhood. Within three houses of the home where I grew up in Colombo, Sri Lanka, we had a Buddhist temple, a Buddhist family, a Hindu family, a Sunni Muslim family, a Shiite Muslim family, and a single person with New Age beliefs.

We were friendly with all these people. As a child I would go to the Buddhist temple and chat with the monks there. In my late teens and early twenties I met almost every Saturday night with a group of seven people, all except two of whom were Muslim. Another was an atheist and a fan of Bertrand Russell. We spent hours talking about various issues, including religion and philosophy.

I studied at a university that had only recently been converted from a Buddhist seminary to a university. The vice-chancellor there was a Buddhist monk. I stayed in a Buddhist home while I was there. And our ministry in Youth for Christ (YFC) has been predominantly with those of other faiths. Few joys on earth exceed the thrill of strategizing for such ministry and then going into the fields God has prepared for us to harvest.

I have been a youth worker for almost 25 years. The primary audience of my regular teaching ministry is teen-agers and the young volunteers and staff who work with them in the ministry of YFC in Sri Lanka. I have tried to teach the Bible and Christian doctrine to them. I have done this teaching alongside our evangelistic ministry among unreached youth. I have been active in the "theologizing" process that YFC has engaged in as we decide on what truths to communicate in our evangelistic programs and how best to communicate them. I have talked with many Christians and non-Christians about the issues addressed in this book.

What I learn through my ministry with YFC, and also at our church, I try to share with a wider audience through my itinerant ministry and writings. When I minister outside YFC, Christian laypeople and workers who have no time to consult technical works, have, I think (perhaps I should say, "I hope"), found my basic explanations of theological and exegetical matters helpful. This book is an extension of that ministry. I share with you the results of our attempts to theologize about relating to people of other faiths from the multi-faith context in which we have been called to serve.

This is not intended to be a groundbreaking work of scholarship, though I hope you will find fresh insights here. I have depended on the work of many scholars. Generalists such as I rely on the specialist scholars of the church, and I laud their efforts with deep gratitude to God.

I usually spend two weeks a year teaching in a seminary in Sri Lanka or abroad. One of the reasons I do so is that I gain the privilege of interacting with scholars. I have written for laypersons and busy Christian workers who do not have the time to read the more specialized books of the scholars.

Extensive endnotes are included to help the reader who wants to delve further into the issues discussed here. When choosing what material to include, I asked, "What should my readers know about this topic?" and "What are the questions they are asking?"

My ministry would be empty and ineffective without the colleagues God has given me. It is my joy to dedicate this book to some of them with whom I have partnered closely. Kumar Abraham and Noel Berman are former YFC staff and continue to be close friends. Mayukha Perera, Rajadurai Rajeevan, and Nadarajah Satchithanandakumar are my present colleagues. Working with each one of these brothers has been a great blessing and joy to me.

(John) Indrasiri Wijebahu is from the Sinhala congregation of the Nugegoda Methodist Church. I will never forget the day I went to preach there, taking John and his wife, Dalreen, as singers. Only the church custodian was there, and we were told that no one had come to worship for about three months. They were new believers at the time and had not yet joined a church. Not only did they join this church, but they also persuaded my wife and me to transfer our membership there. It was John's hard work (aided perhaps by the reluctant involvement of my wife and me) that enabled us to restart this congregation and see it grow and flourish. This is all the more remarkable considering that John is paralyzed from his waist down. Most of the members of this congregation are from other faiths. It is a great joy for us as a family to serve there under our own gifted pastor.

My hope is that this book will help its readers to understand and relate more wisely and lovingly with those of other faiths. But more importantly I hope it will convince them of the uniqueness of the Christian gospel and spur them to effective witness among those of other faiths.

To

Kumar Abraham
Noel Berman
Mayukha Perera
Nadarajah Satchithanandakumar
Rajadurai Rajeevan
(John) Indrasiri Wijebahu

celebrating the joy of
partnership in evangelism

1

THE CURRENT SCENARIO

Ⓐ missionary about to return home after twenty-eight years in Sri Lanka was interviewed by that country's leading English-language Sunday paper. He explained how he had changed after coming to a multi-religious country.

"I was rather intolerant of other religions at the time and thought that mine was the only true one," he said. "But all that changed during a visit to Anuradhapura" (a Buddhist holy place).

The missionary said he experienced such a sense of peace that he felt he was truly in the presence of God. The difference in faiths did not matter. From that experience this missionary said he learned "the lesson that all religions, lived up to their highest ideals, have the common threads of love and compassion in them. So," he said, "from that moment my ministry became not creed but need."[1]

This missionary reflects an attitude that is rapidly gaining popularity in the church today. Many Christians are living in an environment that is not conducive to maintaining the old belief in the uniqueness of Christ, and many are giving it up. A Sri Lankan church leader said that when he sees Buddhist devotees worshiping at the Bodhi tree, which is the tree sacred to Buddhists, he sees the Holy Spirit at work there.

Grappling with the Uniqueness of Christ

Yet we have many texts in the Bible that proclaim that Christ is the only way to salvation. Here are just a few.

- "Whoever believes in the Son has eternal life, but whoever rejects the Son will not see life, for God's wrath remains on him" (John 3:36).
- "I am the way and the truth and the life. No one comes to the Father except through me" (John 14:6).
- "Salvation is found in no one else, for there is no other name under heaven given to men by which we must be saved" (Acts 4:12).
- "For there is one God and one mediator between God and men, the man Christ Jesus" (1 Timothy 2:5).
- "He who has the Son has life; he who does not have the Son of God does not have life" (1 John 5:12).

Sustaining these beliefs today is a challenge, especially when we meet such nice people who belong to other faiths. Some are at a loss to know what to do when they work close to a non-Christian. A Christian musician who came to minister in Sri Lanka stayed in the home of a missionary who was away on furlough. At the time, the home was occupied only by a Buddhist worker. The believer was uneasy about the prospect of living under the same roof with this person. He was unfamiliar with the idea of relating so closely with a person of another faith.

Some years ago our ministry started a work in unreached villages. Ultimately this became a separate church-planting movement. Soon our staff workers and the believers in one of the villages were coming under attack. On one occasion, the staff workers were badly beaten.

We knew that the monks in the Buddhist temple nearby were behind this persecution. When I visited the village the believers persuaded me to visit the temple and explain to the monks what we were doing. The monks reluctantly agreed to meet with me.

Prior to my visit, I asked the former Buddhists in our ministry to tutor me about how I should address the monks. From their suggestions, I chose words which I felt did not compromise my convictions. When I went to the temple, I removed my shoes at the gate, as is the custom when one enters a Buddhist temple. I sat on the floor while the monk, who was younger than I, sat on a chair. This too is an accepted custom that expresses the respect the layperson should have for the monk.

I was simply following the customs of the people. This was part of the etiquette of the village, which I needed to respect. But some Christians felt that I had compromised my faith by acting in this way.

In today's society Christians must have guiding principles about how they should interact with non-Christians. We must also have convictions about how to respond to other beliefs. Christians in both the East and the West are faced with a special challenge as the environment is not conducive to maintaining the traditional belief in the uniqueness of Christ.

Religious Pluralism

The dominant philosophy regarding religious truth in the world today is *pluralism*. This has always been the approach to truth in Eastern religions like Hinduism and many forms of Buddhism.[2] Recently pluralism has become the dominant philosophy in the West as well.

Biblical Christians have correctly accepted pluralism over the centuries when it applies to other areas. For example, in the political sphere it is healthy to have different parties in competition with each other. In the sphere of Christian worship it is necessary to have different forms of worship according to the culture of the people worshiping. It is preferable to have different forms of sports and recreation to offer to students in a given school. We left-handers are grateful that we were not forced to write with our right hand as left-handed children were forced to do in an earlier generation.

Religious pluralism, however, can be held only by rejecting the Christian claim to possess absolute truth. This claim implies that the gospel has the ultimate truth that all people everywhere need to accept. We believe that God has revealed truth to humanity in the Scriptures and supremely in Jesus. This truth is without error and is the only way for the salvation of all peoples all over the world.

We accept that there is truth in other religions,[3] but not absolute truth in the sense that we just described. Religious pluralism says that there is no such thing as absolute truth. Therefore the different religions are "equals in the universe of faiths," as John Hick, the foremost pluralist in the church, said.

A Copernican Revolution?

Hick called for a Copernican revolution in our theology of religions. Copernicus realized that the sun, not the earth, is at the center of the solar system and that the other heavenly bodies including the earth revolve around it. In the same way, Hick says, "We have to realize that the universe of faiths centers upon God, and not upon Christianity or upon any other religion. He is the sun, the originative source of light and life, whom all religions reflect in their own different ways."[4] In his later writings Hick modified his position to include the Theravada Buddhists who do not include God in their system of beliefs. Instead of God, therefore, he placed what he called "the Real" in the center of his universe of faiths. He even included dedicated secularists, such as Marxists, as reflecting the Real.[5]

A key to understanding pluralism is to understand its view of truth. Biblical Christians have always believed much truth can be discovered by observation and experience without God's direct revelation. This is called general revelation, and it is discussed in chapter 5. But Christians also believe that God has revealed His truth to us ultimately and definitively through direct inspiration of the Scriptures and through Jesus Christ. Pluralists deny this. They say that if God speaks at all, He does it through the different religions. Each religion contains facets of truth that come from the particular experience that followers of these religions have. So the holy books of Hinduism contain truths about God that are discovered through the unique experiences that the Hindus have had. The Christian, Jewish, Muslim, and Taoist Scriptures contain truths discovered through the unique experiences of the people of those faiths.

Essentially then, in pluralism truth is discovered by people, or, as Hick would say, truth is human responses to the Real. In Christianity truth is something disclosed by God. Of course, Christians also discover truth, but this is truth that has its origin in God's disclosure and depends on the illuminating grace of God.

So the focus of truth is taken away from objective realities like God or the Bible. The Christian says, "I believe the Bible," and the Muslim says, "I believe the Qur'an." "I" is the subject and "Bible" and "Qur'an" are the objects. In the objective approach to truth, which is the approach in orthodox forms of Islam, Judaism, and Christianity, the focus is on the object and not the subject—that is, primarily on what the Bible or the Qur'an says and not on what I believe.

Pluralism adopts a more subjective approach to truth. The focus is placed on the subject, the individual, not on the object (the Bible or the Qur'an). So, "You have your truth and I have mine. If your truth is good for you, that's great! My truth is good for me." There is no truth that should be universally accepted by all because there is no such thing as absolute truth. In Athens, Paul said, "In the past God overlooked such ignorance, but now he commands all people everywhere to repent" (Acts 17:30). Such a statement would have no place in the pluralist scheme.

In pluralism, then, there is no such thing as absolute truth. Rather, all people are engaged in a common quest for more truth. So we learn from each other. Conversion is unnecessary, though it may take place if I come to feel that a certain religion is better for me than my previous religion. That is fine for me, but I must not insist that everyone needs to be converted to my new religion.

I once spoke in a seminar in Sri Lanka on the topic of Christian mission, and I tried to show that we must be involved in evangelism with conversion as a goal. The speaker who followed me presented another view: "If a Buddhist comes to me and says he wants to become a Christian, I discourage him from doing so," he said. "I tell him, 'You have a great religion for which I have the highest respect. Go and study your religion and try to be a good Buddhist.'"

Some people are even saying that the new mission of the church is to help create a harmonious society where everyone appreciates the other's religion and where we learn from each other.[6] They are calling this the new ecumenism. Indian churchman Stanley Samartha speaks of "new Christological insights" which "go far beyond the narrow confines of Christians to a deeper and larger ecumenism that embraces the whole of humanity."[7] The teaching of Jesus that He came to bring not peace but a sword is interpreted to refer not to the uniqueness of Christ but to Christ's opposition to things like materialism, greed, and exploitation. The various religions must unite, we are told, to combat these dangerous trends in society.

Modernism and Postmodernism

The philosophy of religious pluralism has harmonized well with another phenomenon that has swept the Western world: *postmodernism*. Many of the features of postmodernism were already part of life in the so-called Third World. But in recent times these features have become part of life in the West in a big way. Postmodernism from the West has harmonized well with the thinking of trendsetters in the Third World, and the postmodern influence is very evident in the media in places like Sri Lanka. In fact some are saying that many Third World nations are going to skip the modern era and go straight from a premodern era to a postmodern era.

To understand postmodernism we must first understand the distinctive features of what was known as the *modern era*. This is because postmodernism is a reaction to some of the excesses of the modern era. There is no unanimity about the dating of these eras, but generally the modern era is dated from around the late eighteenth century to the mid to late twentieth century.

The distinctive feature of the modern era was its emphasis on the rational. It was heavily influenced by the Enlightenment, the eighteenth-century European movement that emphasized the reliability of reason. The extreme expressions of this movement held that truth could be reached only through reason, observation, and experiment. Science was the supreme field of study during this era.

Some of the characteristic products of the modern era will help us to understand it. Darwin's evolutionary theory looked at nature as a completely self-contained system. Its emphasis on logically explained progression was extended beyond science to other fields too. Applied to the field of religion, people held that religions evolved from primitive forms such as polytheism to the more advanced forms such as monotheism.[8] Because practicality was the most important criterion in making moral decisions, the pragmatic idea grew: "If it works it must be good."

In such an environment stealing became wrong not because the Ten Commandments said so but because it interfered with the economic functioning of society. Euthanasia and abortion on demand became popular in the closing years of the modern era, as practical considerations were allowed to overcome moral objections to these practices.

Marxism is considered one of the fullest expressions of this era. It gave materialistic and economic causes for all human problems. Some date the beginning of the postmodern era from the fall of the Berlin Wall in 1989.[9] And the heavily rational expressions of evangelical Christianity, which do not value emotions and experience, are also considered typical expressions of the features of modernism.

Postmodernism is a reaction to some of the excesses of the modern era.[10] Scientific developments in the twentieth century contributed to the loss of trust in objective facts. Einstein's theory of relativity caused a revolution in science, which the development of quantum physics continued. Both these trends turned people's faith away from trust in the primacy of objective truth—that is, truth which can be arrived at through the "absolute" laws of science.[11] Similarly, developments in the field of philosophy began to emphasize what is in our minds rather than on the objective facts "out there."[12]

Postmoderns complained that, with so much emphasis on science and objective facts outside of us, people were dehumanized. No longer did they have the opportunity to express their feelings and instincts. So the postmodern generation has been called "an instinctually stimulated generation" where "people prefer to feel than to think."[13] The Nike motto, "Just Do It," or the Sprite advertisement, "Obey Your Thirst," are good expressions of this approach to life.

Laurence Wood has helpfully described the three eras by suggesting three representative bumper stickers. The premodern bumper sticker would say, "Let the church think for you." The modern would say, "Dare to think for yourself." And the postmodern would read, "Don't think! Just let it happen."[14]

Postmodern ideas seem to have penetrated every facet of Western society. Recently I met the former director of a key postgraduate institute for management studies in Singapore, who told me that the most cutting-edge management studies are heavily influenced by postmodern thought.

So postmoderns were revolting against the idea that people were being tyrannized by objective realities, like rules and beliefs, and objectives and goals, without a proper place being given to their feelings and instincts. In this environment we can see how postmoderns would embrace the subjective approach to truth, with its focus on me, "the subject." This is the approach of pluralism too. So pluralism has found a fertile breeding ground in postmodern culture.

The importance of feelings and instincts—"the inner life and experience"—has also resulted in a new interest in spirituality. About 25 years ago secular humanism, which devalued the place of the religious, was very popular in the West. Now it has been replaced by a more spiritual approach to life. Unfortunately, most present expressions of this spirituality are New Age and occultic. In chapter 11, we will show that Christian spirituality alone can fulfill the deep yearnings of the heart that are finding expression in postmodern spirituality.

Some forms of postmodernism are hailing the death of the individual subject in favor of the communally-based self. We are seeing a new interest in community and in what Doug Groothuis describes as "cultural constructs of meaning."[15]

The explosion of the charismatic movement is one expression of the postmodern thirst for a spiritual experience to replace dry, ultra-rationalistic religion.[16]

The yearnings that lie at the heart of postmodernism can be fulfilled adequately only by Christ. The world may not want this at the moment, as the Christian way includes things they may detest, such as submission to the teachings of Scripture and to the will of God. But without throwing up our hands in despair, we must ask how we can best communicate the gospel to postmoderns. And we will do so with the conviction that Jesus is the only One who can fill the void in the heart of the human being.

Various Christian thinkers and churches have attempted to respond to postmodernism with contextualized[17] theology[18] and ministry.[19]

"Fundamentalism" and the Persecution of Christians

If pluralism represents one end of the scale on the issue of tolerance of other faiths, what is now being called "fundamentalism" represents the other. But both approaches are united in their hostility to evangelism that seeks to convert people to Christianity.

The word *fundamentalism* seems to have become popular after a book entitled *The Fundamentals* was published in 1909.[20] This book was actually an affirmation of the fundamentals of the historic Christian faith in response to the modernism and theological liberalism that were sweeping the churches. Christians committed to these fundamentals became known as fundamentalists. More recently this word has been used in a more restricted sense to refer to evangelicals in the USA who have rightist political leanings.

But this word is now also being used to identify extremist Buddhists, Hindus, Orthodox Jews, and Muslims who are asserting the rights of their religion in such a way as to deny an equal place in society for those of other faiths. These fundamentalists wish to prohibit the conversion of their own people to another religion.

If we look at the root of the word *fundamentalism,* the use we are discussing here is incorrect. The word suggests that these people are trying to return to the fundamentals of their religions, but what many of these people espouse may not be in keeping with the fundamentals of the religions themselves![21] In Sri Lanka, some people who would be called Buddhist fundamentalists are using violence in their efforts to stamp out Christian evangelistic efforts, even though tolerance is a fundamental tenet of Buddhism. A more accurate way to describe what are called Hindu and Islamic fundamentalists are Hindutva advocates and Islamists respectively.[22]

Words often take their meaning from their roots. However, words also may take meanings ascribed to them through popular use. This is what has happened to the word *fundamentalism*. It has come to mean something that contradicts its root meaning. I will use it in this popular sense here.

This type of fundamentalism often equates a religion with a national identity. For this reason, some people say that if you are a true Indian you should be a Hindu. Ethnicity may be included in this form of nationalism. So in Sri Lanka some people say that only Buddhists from the Sinhala race are true Sri Lankans. Christians therefore would be considered second-class citizens. That is not such a big problem. What *is* a serious problem is that Christian evangelism is considered a foreign threat to the nation's security and integrity.

Our evangelistic efforts are often associated with Western expansionist designs. It is alleged that because the West cannot control the Third World through the old imperialism, it has resorted to economic and religious imperialism. By pushing the Western style of market economy and by converting people of other faiths to Christianity the West is said to be continuing its design of controlling our nations. Efforts are being made in many countries to outlaw conversion. In many Muslim countries it is illegal for Muslims to convert to Christianity, though Christians can convert to Islam.

I believe that when Western countries give devotees of Eastern religions the freedom to practice and propagate their faiths, they make a strong statement to the rest of the world. Those of us who live in non-Western countries are grateful that this is the case in most Western countries. Every time a Muslim mosque or a Hindu temple comes up in a neighborhood in the West, Christians living nearby express their dismay with statements like, "What is happening to our country?" But we here are grateful that Western Christians give others this freedom.

Though these religions make use of this freedom in the West, many of them do not give a corresponding freedom to Christians in their countries. The tolerant Western example could well help us in the Third World as we seek to practice and propagate our faith today.

We are grateful for the concern shown by Westerners when we are under attack, and we hope this concern will act as a warning and a deterrent to those who are attacking Christians. The president of a Muslim country in our region, under pressure from Islamists, banned a new version of the Bible just before it was released. Shortly after that he visited the USA. Some senators asked him about the recent banning of the Bible. Then a prominent religious leader informed him that he was the first national leader in history to ban a Bible. He promptly lifted the ban upon his return home!

You will recall the village where I visited the temple after the Christians there had been attacked. After several years of worshiping in temporary structures, these Christians were preparing to build a permanent church building. A Buddhist monk found out about it and set up a Buddhist temple next to the church. A few days later the church's temporary building was burned down.

The leader of this ministry, Adrian de Visser, made some important observations. He said that we must not stop our work because of this attack. We may need to be careful about programs that are too provocative to the Buddhists. But this is not a time to leave the area. After some years of violent opposition, the Buddhist leaders will be forced to recognize that this church is a permanent entity in the area, and the persecution will die down. This is a sequence of events seen often in church history.

Second, it may be necessary to ask some of our foreign friends to write to relevant authorities in Sri Lanka about human rights violations against Christians. We saw this in action when the village pastor of the work just mentioned was severely assaulted (and saved from possible death by his Buddhist neighbors). At the time, the police took little notice. But this time, after the burning, the police were much more supportive of this same worker and even severely warned the monk of legal action. Foreign pressure helps these authorities do what they are supposed to do—protect innocent, law-abiding citizens!

Buddhist and Hindu extremists become agitated when they realize that a church building is being constructed. For this reason some strategists suggest that churches should refrain from putting up large buildings. Instead they suggest that the Christians meet in houses, possibly in different locations on different Sundays. This may be the best option in many cases. It worked well with the house churches of China that thrived despite the brutal Cultural Revolution of Mao Zedong.

Yet converts to Christianity from religions like Islam, Buddhism, and Hinduism desire to have a place of worship to call their own. This reflects the importance of the mosque or temple in their former religions.

"Liberal Fundamentalism"

While non-Christians have the freedom to practice and propagate their faiths in the West, sometimes the Christians are actually denied this freedom in the West. This is also a form of fundamentalism, according to the "popular use" definition. We may call it "liberal fundamentalism."

It is a rapidly growing trend in the West today. The fact that many are reacting so excessively against "traditional values" may be an indication of an uneasy conscience in the West after the mass rejection of its spiritual heritage. Perhaps we in the non-Western world could help out by speaking up for our brothers and sisters in the West when "liberal fundamentalist" authorities discriminate against them.

The situation recalls Paul's statement: "Everyone who wants to live a godly life in Christ Jesus will be persecuted" (2 Timothy 3:12). True Christianity has never been popular in any society for very long. The gospel is too radical a message to maintain popular acclaim. Perhaps after an unusual revival people will be impressed for a duration. But after the initial glow passes, society will find it difficult to tolerate some of the implications of the gospel, especially its uncompromising attitude to unbelief, immorality, and injustice. And it will turn against the true followers of Christ.

Whether we live in the East or the West, the North or the South, if we are truly faithful to the call of God we will be persecuted. Again, without lifting up our hands in helpless resignation, let us like the early church use our wisdom and respond to the prompting of the Spirit to continue faithfully with a wise and bold witness for Christ in the world.

Inclusivism

Inclusivism is a significant development that has recently gained prominence in the church. Pluralist theologian John Hick says inclusivism "represents the nearest approach to a consensus among Christian thinkers today."[23] We respond to inclusivism in the last chapter of this book.

Inclusivism's ascension came first in the Roman Catholic Church, gaining momentum after the Vatican II Council of the 1960s. Unlike the pluralists, the inclusivists believe that Christ is absolutely unique. But they say that the salvation He gives may be mediated without the hearing of the gospel. In other words, those outside the Christian religion can also be included in Christ's saving work.

Some of the more radical forms of this view are still found among Roman Catholic theologians. The Catholic Church has had a "sacramental view" of salvation. They believe that salvation is mediated through the sacraments, like baptism and the Eucharist, which they regard as means of saving grace. Catholic inclusivists extend their understanding of sacraments to the rites of non-Christian religions and say that non-Christians could receive salvation through the rites of their own religions, though it is Christ who saves them.[24] These "saved" people of other faiths are sometimes called "anonymous Christians" because, even though they don't call themselves Christians, they are recipients of Christ's salvation.[25]

Perhaps the most famous presentation of this view is in the book, *The Unknown Christ of Hinduism,* by Catholic priest Raymond Panikkar. He says, "In the wake of St. Paul we believe we may speak not only of the unknown God of the Greeks, but also of the hidden Christ of Hinduism—hidden and unknown and yet present and at work because he is not far from any of us."[26] Panikkar wrote:

> The good and bona fide Hindu as well as the good and *bona fide* Christian are saved by Christ—not by Hinduism and Christianity per se, but through their sacraments, and, ultimately, through the *mysterion* active within the two religions. This amounts to saying that Hinduism also has a place in the universal saving providence of God and cannot therefore be considered as negative in relation to Christianity.[27]

The controversial Catholic theologian Hans Küng refers to the non-Christian religions as the "ordinary" way to salvation, whereas Christianity is a "very special and extraordinary" way.[28] Because of this belief in the special place that the Christian gospel has, I expect that people like Küng would encourage some sort of proclamation of the gospel to non-Christians.

We could say that these Roman Catholics represent one extreme of the inclusivist position. On the other extreme are evangelical inclusivists, like Sir Norman Anderson. In their attempt to answer the difficult question of the fate of those who have not heard the gospel they have come up with another form of inclusivism. These inclusivists say that those who respond in repentance and faith to what they know of the supreme God can be saved even though they may not have heard the gospel of Christ.[29] They do not say that Christ saves people through other religions as the Catholic inclusivists claim. Instead they focus on the type of response similar to that described in the Bible as saving faith. Others, especially Clark Pinnock and John Sanders, are less restrictive in their exposition of inclusivism than Norman Anderson.[30]

The traditional view that one must hear and respond to the gospel of Christ in order to be saved is called *exclusivism* or *particularism* or *restrictivism*.[31] Some evangelical scholars would have previously been described as inclusivists but now prefer to call themselves exclusivists. They leave the door open to salvation only to those who exercise saving faith as described in the Bible, even though those doing so may not know Jesus. This is presented as a possibility rather than a dogmatic certainty. Their emphasis is placed on the saving work of Christ and its efficacy as the exclusive way by which people may be saved.[32] Others prefer to remain agnostic on the issue.[33] Clark Pinnock criticizes this approach, calling it "a cop-out to avoid answering a fair and urgent question in a responsible way."[34]

Affirming Uniqueness in This Environment

The trends described above have combined to cause significant problems for Christians who affirm the uniqueness of Christ, especially in nations where they are a minority. During the writing of this book I was constantly made aware that the people in my nation will intensely dislike what I am writing. They have angry memories of the colonial period when Westerners considered themselves superior to us.[35] Most of our religions have a pluralistic approach to truth. Sri Lankans know that we affirm that salvation is only through Christ. This makes them angry, especially when they associate us with the colonial rulers who came from supposedly Christian countries.

Each week over the past few months letters and articles critical of Christians and Christianity have been published in the newspapers in Sri Lanka. Some of them are written in an angry tone. Almost always at the heart of the anger is their revulsion to the doctrine of the uniqueness of Christ.

For us this opposition has been difficult to endure. We love our people and seek to be their humble servants, refusing to leave our mission regardless of what happens. We cannot be bitter about their anger against us. Instead we must approach them with respect, love, and graciousness. We desire the best for them, but the best thing we can do for them is to tell them about the God who can grant them eternal salvation. They view us as arrogant traitors for doing that. We need grace and wisdom to respond appropriately. We also need courage and perseverance to remain faithful to the task.

What we are experiencing in Sri Lanka, every Christian will experience to some extent. The whole world is growing in its hostility to the doctrine of the uniqueness of Christ. So I trust that what I say will be of help to all who read it.

Paul's Example

Paul's ministry is extremely helpful in learning how to relate to people of other faiths. His ministry in Athens, recorded in Acts 17:16–34, is particularly instructive. It is a fairly detailed description of ministry with people whose religious background was completely different than Paul's. We will glean many principles from this passage to be applied to our contemporary situations. There are those who believe that Paul was a failure in Athens. But there is no hint in the text to suggest that Luke did not intend his readers to use this passage as a model of effective evangelism.[36]

Chapter 1 endnotes

[1] Alfreda de Silva, "Change of Heart after Anuradhapura Visit," The *Sunday Observer,* March 18, 1984.

[2] In practice, Buddhists and Hindus hold to certain religious tenets that they consider true (such as the Four Noble Truths of Buddhism).

[3] See chapter 5.

[4] John Hick, "Whatever Path Men Choose Is Mind," in *Christianity and Other Religions,* John Hick and Brian Hebblethwaite, editors (Glasgow: Collins: Fount Paperbacks, 1980). See also John Hick, *God and the Universe of Faiths* (London: Macmillan, 1973). For evangelical responses to Hick, see Ronald H. Nash, *Is Jesus the Only Savior?* (Grand Rapids, MI: Zondervan Publishing House, 1994); and Harold Netland, *Dissonant Voices: Religious Pluralism and the Question of Truth* (Grand Rapids, MI: Wm. B. Eerdmans Publishing Co.; and Leicester: Apollos, 1991).

[5] John Hick, *An Interpretation of Religion* (New Haven, CT: Yale University Press, 1988).

[6] This was the thrust of a speech given a few years ago at the conference of evangelism of one of the larger denominations in Sri Lanka.

[7] Stanley J. Samartha, "The Cross and the Rainbow," in *The Myth of Christian Uniqueness: Toward a Pluralistic Theology of Religions,* John Hick and Paul F. Knitter, editors (Maryknoll, NY: Orbis Books, 1987), 79. See also Raymond Panikkar, "Toward an Ecumenical Ecumenism," in *Classic Texts in Mission and World Christianity,* Norman E. Thomas, editor (Maryknoll, NY: Orbis Books, 1995), 273–275; and Paul F. Knitter, *No*

Other Name? A Critical Survey of Christian Attitudes Toward the World Religions (Maryknoll, NY: Orbis Books, 1985), 153–54.

[8] See "The Origins of Religion" in chapter 7.

[9] For this description of modernism I have relied heavily on Gene Edward Veith Jr., *Postmodern Times: A Christian Guide to Contemporary Thought and Culture* (Wheaton, IL: Crossway Books, 1994).

[10] Postmodernism is described in *The Challenge of Postmodernism: An Evangelical Engagement,* David S. Dockery, editor (Grand Rapids, MI: Baker Book House, 1995); Stanley J. Grenz, *A Primer on Postmodernism* (Grand Rapids, MI: Wm. B. Eerdmans Publishing Co., 1996); J. Richard Middleton and Brian Walsh, *Truth Is Stranger Than It Used to Be: Biblical Faith in a Postmodern Age* (Downers Grove, IL: InterVarsity Press, 1995); and Veith, *Postmodern Times.*

[11] Nancy R. Pearcey and Charles B. Thaxton, *The Soul of Science: Christian Faith and Natural Philosophy* (Wheaton, IL: Crossway Books, 1994).

[12] See Veith, *Postmodern Times,* chapter 2: "From the Modern to the Postmodern."

[13] Laurence W. Wood, "Telling the Old, Old Story in the Postmodern Age," *The Asbury Herald,* Autumn 1996, 3.

[14] Wood, "Telling the Old, Old Story," 4.

[15] In a personal letter to me.

[16] This idea was presented to me by Canadian church leader Dr. Brian Stiller.

[17] I have discussed contextualized ministry in chapter 4.

[18] Millard J. Erickson critiques evangelical theologians who respond to the postmodern challenge in *Postmodernizing the Faith: Evangelical Responses to the Challenge of Postmodernism* (Grand Rapids, MI: Baker Book House, 1998). Under negative responses to postmodernism he lists David Wells, Thomas Oden, and Francis Schaeffer. Under positive responses he lists Stanley Grenz, J. Richard Middleton, Brian J. Walsh, and B. Keith Putt. D. A. Carson presents a balanced approach in *The Gagging of God: Christianity Confronts Pluralism* (Grand Rapids, MI: Zondervan Publishing House; and Leicester: Apollos, InterVarsity Press, 1996). In Britain, Dave Tomlins believes that evangelicalism is too closely tied to modernism. See his book, *The Post-Evangelical* (Triangle, 1995). David Hilborn responds to this proposal in *Picking up the Pieces: Can Evangelicals Adapt to Contemporary Culture?* (London: Hodder and

Stoughton, 1997). Douglas Groothuis' book, *Truth Decay: Defending Christianity against the Challenges of Postmodernism* (Downers Grove, IL: InterVarsity Press, 2000), is also worthwhile.

[19] See Hilborn, *Picking up the Pieces*; Jimmy Long, *Generating Hope: A Strategy for Reaching the Postmodern Generation* (Downers Grove, IL: InterVarsity Press, l997); Timothy R. Phillips and Dennis L. Ockholm, *Christian Apologetics in the Postmodern World* (Downers Grove, IL: InterVarsity Press, 1995); Charles Strohmer, *The Gospel and the New Spirituality: Communicating the Truth in a World of Spiritual Seekers* (Nashville: Thomas Nelson Publishers, 1996); Leonard Sweet, *SoulTsunami: Sink or Swim in New Millennium* Culture (Grand Rapids, MI: Zondervan Publishing House, 1999).

[20] See Bruce L. Shelley, "Fundamentalism," in *The New International Dictionary of the Christian Church*, J. D. Douglas, editor (Grand Rapids, MI: Zondervan Publishing House, 1978), 396–97.

[21] See Vinoth Ramachandra, *Faiths in Conflict: Christian Integrity in a Multicultural World* (Leicester: InterVarsity Press, 1999). A penetrating analysis of Islamic and Hindu extremism.

[22] These are the terms used in Ramachandra, *Faiths in Conflict*.

[23] John Hick, *The Metaphor of God Incarnate: Christology in a Pluralistic Age* (Louisville: Westminster John Knox, 1993), 88. Quoted in Clark H. Pinnock, "An Inclusivist View," *Four Views of Salvation in a Pluralistic World*, Dennis L. Ockholm and Timothy R. Phillips, editors (Grand Rapids, MI: Zondervan Publishing House, 1995), 101.

[24] See Nihal Abeysingha, *A Theological Evaluation of Non-Christian Rites* (Bangalore Theological Publications in India, 1979). See also Patrick Kililombe, "The Salvific Value of African Religions," in *Mission Trends, no. 5: Faith Meets Faith,* Gerald H. Anderson and Thomas F. Stransky, editors (New York: Paulist Press; and Grand Rapids, MI, Wm. B. Eerdmans Publishing Co., 1981), 50–68; and Raymond Panikkar, *The Unknown Christ of Hinduism: Toward an Ecumenical Christophany,* revised and enlarged edition (Maryknoll, NY: Orbis Books, 1981), 84–85.

[25] Karl Rahner, "Christianity and the Non-Christian Religions," in *Christianity and Other Religions*, 75–77.

[26] Panikkar, *The Unknown Christ,* 168 (italics his).

[27] Panikkar, *The Unknown Christ,* 85–86. Roman Catholic theologian

Gavin D'Costa says his view "affirms the salvific presence of God in non-Christian religions while still maintaining that Christ is the definitive and authoritative revelation of God," in *Theology and Religious Pluralism: The Challenge of Other Religions* (New York: Basil Blackwell, 1986), 80.

[28] Hans Küng, in *Christian Revelation and World Religions,* Joseph Neuner, editor (London: Burns and Oats, 1967), 52–53.

[29] J. N. D. Anderson, *Christianity and the World Religions: The Challenge of Pluralism* (Leicester and Downers Grove, IL: InterVarsity Press, 1984), chapter 5.

[30] Clark H. Pinnock, "The Finality of Christ in a World of Religions," in *Christian Faith and Practice in the Modern World,* Mark A. Noll and David F. Wells, editors (Grand Rapids, MI: Wm. B. Eerdmans Publishing Co., 1988); Clark H. Pinnock, *A Wideness in God's Mercy* (Grand Rapids, MI: Zondervan Publishing House, 1992); and John Sanders, *No Other Name?* (Grand Rapids, MI: Wm. B. Eerdmans Publishing Co., 1992).

[31] See Dick Dowsett, *God, That's Not Fair!* (Sevenoaks: OMF Books and Bromley, Kent: STL, 1982); Hywel R. Jones, *Only One Way* (Bromley, Kent: *Day One Publications,* 1996); Erwin Lutzer, *Christ Among Other Gods: A Defense of Christ in an Age of Tolerance* (Chicago: Moody Press, 1994); Ronald H. Nash, *Is Jesus the Only Savior?* (Grand Rapids, MI: Zondervan Publishing House, 1994); Ramesh P. Richard, *The Population of Heaven* (Moody Press, 1994); and J. Oswald Sanders, *How Lost Are the Heathen?* (also published as *What of the Unevangelized?* Chicago: Moody Press, 1972).

[32] Chris Wright, *Thinking Clearly about the Uniqueness of Christ* (East Sussex: Monarch, 1997), 51.

[33] Lesslie Newbigin, *The Open Secret: Sketches for a Missionary Theology* (Grand Rapids, MI: Wm. B. Eerdmans Publishing Co., 1978), 88, 196; Calvin Shenk, *Who Do You Say That l Am? Christians Encounter Other Religions* (Scottdale, PA: Herald Press, 1997); John Stott in David L. Edwards and John Stott, *Essentials: A Liberal-Evangelical Dialogue* (London: Hodder and Stoughton, 1988), 327–329.

[34] Pinnock, *A Wideness in God's Mercy,* 152.

[35] See chapter 3 for a response to the charge of intolerance and arrogance made against those who affirm the uniqueness of Christ.

[36] Ajith Fernando, *The NlV Application Commentary: Acts* (Grand Rapids, MI: Zondervan Publishing House, 1998), 477–78.

2

DIALOGUE AND PERSUASION

To many people the title of this chapter expresses two incompatible approaches to inter-religious relations. The pluralistic mood of the day pushes the view that there is no such thing as absolute truth. Therefore there is no need to try to persuade people to go through so radical a change as conversion, which is the aim of Christian evangelism. Christian evangelists often encounter bitter opposition and other forms of resistance in their efforts to persuade others.

Dialogue and persuasion *are* difficult to hold together. Yet Christianity is a religion full of paradoxes. A paradox is not a contradiction but presents two sides of the same truth. Many like to live in a safe world that does not attempt the difficult task of reconciling paradoxes. Christians are called to do this. And Paul's ministry in Athens clearly shows this.

Distress, Restraint, and a Passion for People

The very first verse in the passage describing Paul's ministry in Athens (Acts 17:16–34) shows Paul with "a spirit provoked." Luke wrote, "He was greatly distressed to see that the city was full of idols" (17:16). The idols and the temples that housed them were beautiful works of art, reflecting the height of Greek cultural achievement. But Paul was more impressed by the wrongs of idolatry than by the beauty of the idols. So he was "greatly distressed."

The Greek word *paroxuneō,* translated "greatly distressed," is a strong word from which we get the English word *paroxysm,* which is another word for fit or convulsion. It is often translated "provoked" (NAS). G. Campbell Morgan described the situation well: "In the midst of the beauty and the glory and the art and the philosophy and the history of Athens, proud and wonderful Athens, this man was in a rage, was provoked."[1] Paul was reflecting here the same attitude to idols that his Scriptures, the Old Testament, reflected. It is the normal inward reaction of those whose hearts beat to the pulse of God. The chief aim in life of such persons is the glory of God. Idols are an affront to God's glory; so idols provoke them.

Actually Paul was similarly provoked by the unbelief of the Jews who, even though they did not worship idols, missed out on God's salvation because they rejected their Messiah. He expresses this vividly in Romans 9:2–3: "I have great sorrow and unceasing anguish in my heart. For I could wish that I myself were cursed and cut off from Christ for the sake of my brothers, those of my own race." I am reminded of a statement by Bob Pierce, the founder of the Christian humanitarian organization World Vision: "Let my heart be broken by the things that break the heart of God."

A similar reaction is recorded in the diaries of Henry Martyn, a missionary to India and Persia (Iran). Shortly after his arrival in Calcutta he wrote in his diary, "Let me burn out for thee." He once viewed a worship ceremony at a Hindu temple. He saw the worshipers prostrating themselves before the images and striking the ground with their foreheads. He did not view this with an attitude of academic interest as a typical foreigner would. Neither was he impressed by the devotion of these Hindus, as we described in the previous chapter. Martyn wrote, "This excited more horror in me than I can well express." His reaction to this horror is most significant. He said, "I thought that if I had words I would preach to the multitudes all day if I lost my life for it."[2]

Paul's reaction to his distress was similar. But unlike Henry Martyn, he "had words," for Paul knew Greek, the language of Athens. Luke records, "So he reasoned in the synagogue . . . as well as in the marketplace day by day with those who happened to be there" (17:17). While the first verse in this section described "a spirit provoked," the rest of the passage describes "a spirit restrained." As we observe the ministry of Paul in Athens, we see that even though the idols provoked him, he did not show his provocation outwardly. Even when he mentions in his speech that he "walked around and observed [their] objects of worship" (17:23), he did not mention the provocation this observation aroused within him. Instead, he said that he concluded from the observation that "in every way [they] are very religious" (17:22). His speech was a controlled, carefully reasoned defense of Christianity (17:22–31).

In this Paul differed greatly from the prophets of the Old Testament. When the prophets observed idols, they, like Paul, were provoked. But they reacted to this provocation by thundering angrily against idolatry. This was owing to the difference between the audiences of Paul and the prophets. The prophets were speaking to wayward Jews who had received God's special revelation and knew that idolatry was wrong. They needed to be upbraided for disobedience to God's revelation that they already knew.

The Athenians, on the other hand, had no special revelation like the Jews, though according to Romans 1:18–32 they should have known the futility of worshiping idols. They needed to be convinced of the futility of idolatry and the advisability of handing their lives over to God, the Father of Jesus Christ. If Paul had thundered angrily against idolatry he would have lost his audience. The sophisticated Athenians would have viewed Paul as an eccentric fanatic and disregarded his message. So Paul used the method of reasoning carefully against idolatry and in support of the Christian view of God.

Both Paul's and the prophets' aim was repentance from idolatry (see 17:30). Both were provoked by idols. The prophets saw fit to express this provocation with righteous anger. Paul restrained his anger and expressed himself with reasoned arguments.

Paul had a twofold attitude toward other religions. He firmly believed the wrongness of life apart from Christ. On the other hand, he maintained a deep respect for all individuals as intelligent human beings endowed by God with the privilege and responsibility of choosing to accept or reject the gospel. This caused Paul to reason with them about the truth of God. His strong conviction about absolute truth, combined with his respect for the individual, form one of the foundational principles for our attitude toward people of other faiths.

Straddling this provocation and respect was Paul's love for people. This too caused distress in his heart. "I have great sorrow and unceasing anguish in my heart," he said. "For I could wish that I myself were cursed and cut off from Christ for the sake of my brothers, those of my own race" (Romans 9:2–3).

In an earlier era this was called a "passion for souls." The phrase has fallen into some disfavor as the evangelical church rediscovered the social aspects of her call in the world. This may be due to a misinterpretation of the word *soul,* which has a variety of meanings in the Bible.[3] The phrase retains its vividness, but perhaps we should modify it to something like a "passion for people."

We must be known as lovers of people just as Jesus was. When our non-Christian neighbors are sick or facing other needs may they see us as genuinely concerned for them. There may be many things about their beliefs and lifestyle that provoke us to anger. They may be practicing homosexuals, alcoholics, idol worshipers, or people who dabble in the occult, but they are also our neighbors. And the command in the Scriptures is, "Love your neighbor as yourself." While there are many places where we are told to love our neighbors, the wording that includes "as yourself" appears nine times in the Bible, indicating how important deeply committed love is.[4]

We may think that these texts do not refer to people we have trouble with, but another text eliminates that interpretation: "You have heard that it was said, 'Love your neighbor and hate your enemy.' But I tell you: Love your enemies and pray for those who persecute you" (Matthew 5:43–44). The primary response of Christians to non-Christians is love. Perhaps this is where we have gone wrong in our reaction to things that repel us in society. We must wisely and clearly oppose the wrong, but we must also clearly express our love for those we oppose. One could write many books with stories of the conversion to Christianity of non-Christians who were first attracted to Christianity by the love shown to them by Christians.

Jesus' handling of the Samaritan woman is a model for us (John 4). He clearly did not accept her sinful lifestyle. But He treated her with respect.

He exercised patience when she used diversionary tactics to avoid facing up to the implications of what Jesus was saying. The end result was a transformed life. This approach could be a model to us of how we deal with people whose lifestyle and ideologies are different from ours.

Dialogue

The Greek word *dialegomai*, translated "reasoned," describes Paul's initial reaction to being provoked in Athens. It occurs ten times in Acts 17–24 in reference to Paul's ministry.[5] We get the English word *dialogue* from *dialegomai*.

There has been much discussion and no unanimity among scholars about *dialegomai*.[6] Paul spoke as if he were giving a speech and anticipating a discussion, with questions to be asked and objections raised. A recent study of Paul's preaching by D. W. Kemmler concludes the apostle employed formal and continuous discourse in Acts 17–24 but interspersed dialogue throughout.

Regardless of whether the word *dialegomai* implies a discussion, Paul's evangelistic activity shows that the viewpoints of the hearers were given due weight in his ministry (Acts 17:2–3). Yet *dialegomai* is not used in Acts in the philosophical sense in which it is used in classical Greek. G. Schrenk, in Kittel's *Theological Dictionary of the New Testament,* explains, "In the sphere of revelation there is no question of reaching an idea through dialectic."[8] But that is what the classical use of *dialegomai* implies. The classical use of *dialegomai* attempts to arrive at truth through discussion. We, however, believe that God has spoken, and we are called to proclaim that message by expounding it. In our proclamation we will face objections and questions that must be carefully answered so that we can persuade people of the validity of the Christian gospel. This is discussed under the topic of *persuasion* below.

The philosophical idea of *dialegomai* in classical Greek (reaching an idea through dialectic) is closer to the way many view evangelistic proclamation today. It fits with the pluralistic philosophy that has swept through much of contemporary society. Pluralist writers are calling for apologetics to be replaced by dialogue. But the dialogue they speak of is a meeting of minds, with no attempt to cause another to change religions. Rather, each one seeks to enrich the other without conversion in view.[9]

John Stott represents a more biblical approach when he says, "Although there is an important place for 'dialogue' with men of other faiths . . . , there is also a need for 'encounter' with them, and even for 'confrontation,' in which we seek both to disclose the inadequacies and falsities of non-Christian religion and to demonstrate the adequacy and truth, absoluteness and finality of the Lord Jesus Christ."[10]

Receiving feedback from our hearers through questions, observations, or objections is a necessary part of evangelism. It enables us to find out how they have understood what we have communicated. After giving an evangelistic message on John 3:16 at a Youth for Christ meeting I spoke to a Buddhist youth who had been in the audience. He told me that his religion says the same thing as I had said. I had thought my message should have clearly shown him the difference between Christianity and Buddhism. But he had processed my Christian terms through his Buddhist way of thinking and emerged with a Buddhist message from my Christian talk!

Commitment to proclamation also includes a commitment to listen to others. An opportunity to witness may require us to listen rather than talk. When people describe their views we must give them full attention. We do not want to interrupt. We are servants, and it should not bother us if our acquaintance dominates a conversation.

Of course, love for others will cause us to look for every opportunity to share the liberating news of Jesus. Part of our listening may involve reading what non-Christian writers have to say about their religion, rather than reading only apologetic material written by Christians. Paul's Areopagus address shows that he was well-versed in the religion of the Athenians.[11]

There is another type of dialogue that often takes place between Christians and those of other faiths. This should not be classed under the term *evangelism* but nevertheless is a valid activity. It is a natural expression of what Jesus meant when He said of His disciples, "My prayer is not that you take them out of the world but that you protect them from the evil one. They are not of the world, even as I am not of it. . . . As you sent me into the world, I have sent them into the world" (John 17:16, 18).

Though we are not of the world, we go into the world and participate in its activities. Jesus ate with tax collectors and sinners and earned the criticism: "Here is a glutton and a drunkard, a friend of tax collectors and 'sinners'" (Matthew 11:19). We meet with people who are quite different from us, but we talk and socialize with them. Among the things we talk about is religion.

When I was in my late teens and early twenties I regularly shared my views with a group of students in our neighborhood. We met in a Muslim home on Saturday nights, and the majority of those who met were Muslims. There was one atheist, a disciple of Bertrand Russell, and another somewhat nominal Christian. We discussed many things, including politics, sport, world affairs, philosophy, and religion. I always went there as a witness of Christ and often talked about my faith. I yearned for the salvation of these people, and they knew that. (Only the nominal Christian came to faith in Christ.) Our meetings could not be called evangelistic events. Yet what I learned from those meetings has been very important in my own pilgrimage.

Evangelicals have shied away from this type of dialogue as many of the liberal persuasion have substituted such dialogue for evangelism. But this is not evangelism at all. It is an exercise in community living and learning and no different from discussions of marketing, management, sport, politics, or technology.

These dialogues may be conducted in formal or informal settings.[12] In our hearts we long for the conversion of these people. But the rules of the discussion may prevent us from using persuasion in the way we understand it as practiced in evangelism. Such discussions become a *means to understanding* other faiths in a richer way than through general study. Our newfound understanding will enhance our proclamation and prepare people to receive the Christian message.[13]

Persuasion

Part of our task as witnesses is to persuade people of the truth of the gospel. The verb "to persuade" (*peithö*) is used seven times in Acts to describe Paul's evangelism.[14] In 2 Corinthians 5:11 Paul himself said, "We try to persuade men."

Peithö has been defined as the attempt "to convince someone to believe something and to act on the basis of what is recommended."[15] This confidence in our message derives from the conviction that we are bearers of the definitive revelation from God to the human race. If the Creator and Lord of the universe has given a final message to the human race and we know it, then we must do everything in our power and within our principles to bring people to accept that message.

I was once traveling by train to a predominantly Buddhist area where we had a ministry. Seated next to me was a Buddhist government official with whom I struck up a conversation. When he realized that I was a Christian worker going to a Buddhist area, he asked me a question that is in the minds of many in our religiously pluralistic nation. Why do Christians go to Buddhist areas and try to convert them? He pointed to the disruption that takes place in these villages because of our evangelism.

I told him that we believe in the God who created this world. And we believe He has provided an answer to the deep problems that plague the world. And, I said, we have discovered this answer. Now that we know it, we must share it. It would be selfish and unloving for us not to share it with others.

I do not know what his ultimate response to my answer was. But I think he came to understand why Christians are so eager to share their faith. Evangelism, then, aims at a response that is so comprehensive that it must be called a conversion.

Part of the task of persuasion is to show where others are wrong in their beliefs. Paul does this in his description of God to the Athenians. He said that God "does not live in temples built by hands" (v. 24). This statement is a "bold denial of the validity of the famous temples clustered round him."[16] Paul's next statement also denied the truth of the Athenian religious practices: "He is not served by human hands, as if he needed anything. Because he himself gives all men life and breath and everything else" (17:25). The Athenians had been trying to supply the needs of God through their offerings. But actually it is He who supplies all their needs. This, of course, is a major distinction between God and idols. God is self-existent; He needs nothing.

After describing more about God, Paul shows how it is impossible to represent Him by an idol. "Therefore since we are God's offspring, we should not think that the divine being is like gold or silver or stone—an image made by man's design and skill" (17:29). Paul even describes idolatry as ignorance and calls the people to repent of this way of life: "In the past God overlooked such ignorance, but now he commands all people everywhere to repent" (v. 30).

Paul was not afraid to clash with the thinking of his audience. If he was to bring the Athenians to accept the good news of the gospel, he first had to debunk their beliefs that could not co-exist with the gospel. In another context Paul said, "We demolish arguments and every pretension that sets itself up against the knowledge of God, and we take captive every thought to make it obedient to Christ" (2 Corinthians 10:5). Paul had earlier found points of contact with the Athenians. He did so later too. He was not afraid to agree with his audience when he could, for his sharing of the gospel was not a competitive argument he was having with them. His aim was to direct them to accept the truth. He affirmed whatever glimmerings of truth they already had. But he knew that when he presented truth, he also had to expose the things opposed to the truth.

Chapter 2 endnotes

[1] G. Campbell Morgan, *The Acts of the Apostles* (1924; reprint, Old Tappan, NJ: Fleming H. Revell Co., 1979), 411.

[2] Constance E. Padwick, *Henry Martyn: Confessor of the Faith* (New York: George H. Doran Company, n.d.), 167.

[3] See Carl Schultz, "Soul," *Evangelical Dictionary of Biblical Theology*, Walter A. Elwell, editor (Grand Rapids, MI: Baker Book House, 1996), 743–44.

[4] Leviticus 19:18; Matthew 19:19; 22:39; Mark 12:31, 33; Luke 10:27; Romans 13:9; Galatians 5:14; James 2:8.

[5] 17:2, 17; 18:4, 19; 19:8, 9; 20:7, 9; 24:12, 25.

[6] For a summary see my *NIV Application Commentary: Acts* (Grand Rapids, MI: Zondervan Publishing House, 1998), 460–61. Several points in this discussion on dialogue appeared originally in this book.

[7] D. W. Kemmler, *Faith and Human Reason: A Study of Paul's Method of Preaching as Illustrated by 1-2 Thessalonians and Acts 17, 24* (Leiden: Brill, 1975), 35; cited in William J. Larkin, Jr., Acts, *IVP New Testament Commentary Series* (Downers Grove, IL: InterVarsity Press, 1995), 245.

8 G. Schrenk, *The Theological Dictionary of the New Testament,* vol. 2, Gerard Kittel, editor, Geoffrey W. Bromiley, translator (Grand Rapids, MI: Wm. B. Eerdmans Publishing Co., 1964), 94.

9 See Wesley Ariarajah, *The Bible and People of Other Faiths* (Geneva: World Council of Churches; and Maryknoll, NY: Orbis Books, 1985), 61–71. For a defense of the validity of apologetics within inter-religious dialogue, see Paul J. Griffiths, *An Apology for Apologetics: A Study in the Logic of Interreligious Dialogue* (Maryknoll, NY: Orbis Books, 1991).

10 John R. W. Stott, *Christian Mission in the Modern World* (Downers Grove, IL: InterVarsity Press, 1975), 69. For helpful discussions on dialogue see Stott, *Christian Mission,* 58–81; and Arthur F. Glasser, "A Paradigm Shift? Evangelicals and Inter-religious Dialogue" in *Contemporary Theologies of Mission,* Arthur F. Glasser and Donald A. McGavran, editors (Grand Rapids, MI: Baker Book House, 1983), 205–19.

11 The issue of getting to know other faiths is discussed in chapter 6.

12 I am grateful to my colleague Ivor Poobalan for alerting me to this point. For more on this type of dialogue, see Stephen Neill, *Salvation Tomorrow* (London: Lutterworth Press, 1976), 22–43; and E. Stanley Jones, *Christ at the Round Table* (London: Hodder and Stoughton, 1928).

13 See Stott, *Christian Mission,* 74–79. Stott cites helpful insights here from Bishop Kenneth Cragg's book, *The Call of the Minaret* (London: Lutterworth Press, 1956).

14 17:4; 18:4; 19:8; 19:26; 26:28; 28:23, 24; cf. 2 Corinthians 5:11. It appeared six times in Acts before chapter 17, but 17:4 is the first time it appears in connection with Paul's evangelism.

15 *Greek-English Lexicon of the New Testament: Based on Semantic Domains, vol. 1,* Johannes P. Louw and Eugene A. Nida, editors (New York: United Bible Societies, 1989), 423.

16 E. M. Blaiklock, "The Acts of the Apostles," *The Tyndale New Testament Commentaries* (Grand Rapids, MI: Wm. B. Eerdmans Publishing Co., 1959), 140.

3

RESPECT AND HUMILITY

Persuading others of the truth of the gospel is an important part of our relationship with people of other faiths. We have established that this is an unpopular aim in today's pluralistic setting. Now we will examine some of the charges brought against evangelism that has persuasion as its goal.

The Charge of Intolerance

One of the most common criticisms brought against Christians is that we are disrespectful and intolerant of other faiths and people in our evangelism efforts. But persuasion is a daily part of many spheres of life. Advertisers seek to persuade us to buy certain products. Politicians seek to persuade us to accept their policies and vote for them.

Yet when it comes to religion this approach to communication is considered inappropriate. Mahatma Gandhi once told his friend, missionary E. Stanley Jones, "Don't attempt to propagate your faith; just live it. Be like the rose, which, without a word, silently exudes its perfume and attracts the attention of the people." Jones responded by reminding Mr. Gandhi that he was the greatest propagandist of all, seeking to propagate his views on independence and freedom to Britain and the whole world.[1]

Bishop Stephen Neill refers to "the awful and necessary intolerance of truth."[2] We are always respectful of people. We never treat them as inferior. But when we know that Jesus is the truth and that other ways will not lead to salvation, we must be intolerant of the untruth that has led them astray—though we will always be respectful of the person who holds this view. Our perception of the truth will cause us to want to persuade them about the truth. But our respect for them will influence the way we present that message.

We will highlight three disrespectful ways of persuasion that we must avoid.

Cultural Imperialism. The first disrespectful method of persuasion is *cultural imperialism.* This occurs when one group thrusts its culture upon another and causes that group to reject many good things in its own culture. The truly Christian way is to seek understanding both of the people and of their culture and to appreciate the good that can be found there.

Sri Lankans traditionally associate Christianity with Western culture, and for good reason. At one time, Sri Lankan converts to Christianity adopted Western culture and gave up many perfectly good cultural practices of their own. This unnecessary transformation has now become a hindrance to evangelism.

Actually, there is much that Western Christians can learn much from their non-Christian neighbors. The cultural history of Asia has preserved some beautiful features of family life that the West has lost in its emphasis on efficiency, productivity, and individual initiative. This is one reason why many postmodern people are looking to the East in their reaction against the unhealthy aspects of Western society.

But while we affirm what is good in other cultures, we always seek to lead their people to repentance of their unbelief. We wish to lead them to put their faith in Christ because we know that unbelief is rebellion against God. (This issue is discussed in detail in chapter 13, the section on "Retaining One's Original Culture.")

Imposition. A second disrespectful method of persuasion is *imposition.* Imposition takes place when authority and power are used to force people to follow the Christian religion. This took place in Europe during the thirteenth century as the Roman Catholic Church sought to combat heresy. Imposition sometimes took place in colonial days when missionaries came along with the European invaders. By making Christianity the official religion of the colonies, the conquering Westerners compelled many to accept it for the sake of survival and progress in society.

Today imposition takes place when employers or parents use their authority to force people to become Christians. Christians should be ashamed of their complicity in these things.

Manipulation. A third disrespectful way of persuasion is *manipulation*. This is the use of things alien to the heart of the gospel in an effort to induce individuals to accept Christianity. Christians may offer material incentives, such as the promise of a job or of aid, which becomes a bribe to "bring" people to Christ.

Manipulation can take place when emotions are roused so that audiences accept Christianity in a way that doesn't involve the proper use of the mind. An emotionally charged evangelistic message that concludes with a highly emotional story can be an example of manipulation. Some may respond to invitations to discipleship more out of their emotional state than because they have considered the implications of the message.

At our Youth for Christ evangelistic camps we discovered we needed to reduce the busyness of the camp schedules. When people are tired they can make crucial decisions without full control of their faculties.

Manipulation takes place in cultic groups that use brainwashing techniques to deceive hearers into making choices they otherwise would not make. Political groups use manipulation as well. Adolf Hitler, through his emotionally charged speeches, forced many Germans to accept his fascist line and usher in the evil Third Reich.

Biblical persuasion, in contrast, is a natural expression of our respect for people. The supreme Lord of Creation does not forcefully thrust His truth upon people but invites them to reason together with Him (Isaiah 1:18). Similarly we, as His servants, must respect each individual's freedom of choice and provide the opportunity to make an informed response to the message of Jesus.

Today many people accuse Christians of unethical conversions, or what they call *proselytization*. What these people are actually attacking is not persuasion but the disrespectful methods we have just described.

Recently my brother, who is a Christian minister, went to meet the editor of a newspaper that had published several articles attacking Christian evangelism. During the conversation the editor said that he could not believe that any Buddhist would become a Christian except for monetary and social gain. They see our social concern as bribery to win converts.

In this environment it is important for us to counter the misconceptions people have about Christian evangelism and conversion. We may need to do what Paul said: "We have renounced secret and shameful ways; we do not use deception, nor do we distort the word of God. On the contrary, by setting forth the truth plainly we commend ourselves to every man's conscience in the sight of God" (2 Corinthians 4:2).

Is Christianity an Extension of the Imperialist Mentality?

Today the practice of persuasion in evangelism is often associated with the imperialist mentality of the colonial era. In a book, *The Revolt in the Temple,* written to commemorate 2,500 years of Buddhism in Sri Lanka, the author claims, "In their imperialistic march, the Western powers had found the missionaries to be their best allies." He quotes an African who said, "The Christian preacher comes and says, 'Look up,' and when we look down again the land is gone."[3] This criticism is certainly unfair, but it demonstrates what happens when colonialism is linked with Christianity.

The pluralist scholar John Hick said, "The . . . doctrine of a unique divine incarnation has long poisoned relationships between Christians and Jews and between Christians and Muslims, as well as affecting the history of Christian imperialism in the Far East, India, Africa, and elsewhere."[4] In Sri Lanka, opponents of evangelism are saying that the current evangelistic impetus of Christians is a "new colonialism" or "new imperialism" by which the West is trying to dominate and control people through religion. They say that the earlier Western imperialists came with the Bible in one hand and a gun in the other. Now they charge that we come with the Bible in one hand and material aid in the other.

The doctrine of the uniqueness of Christ is said to have thrived in the monolithic Western culture dominated by Christianity. But, we are told, we can no longer hold such views in this pluralistic society.

Let us not forget that the doctrine of Christian exclusivism developed in a strongly pluralistic society in the first-century Roman Empire.[5] The Christians there did not belong to the side of the colonial masters but were oppressed by them. Yet they believed in a unique Savior and proclaimed this message. Many had to sacrifice their lives because they did so.

The gospel, then, did not need imperialism to thrive. The phenomenal growth of the church in the non-Western world in the postcolonial era is evidence of this. Dana L. Robert reports, "At the beginning of the twentieth century, Europeans [including those in North America] dominated the world church with approximately 70.6 percent of the world's Christian population." Robert says, "By 1938, on the eve of World War II, the apparent European domination of Protestantism and Catholicism remained strong." The situation had changed markedly by the end of the twentieth century when "the European percentage of world Christianity had shrunk to 28 percent of the total."[6]

In Sri Lanka the Protestant Church made minimal progress under the British. Many joined the church for economic gain. Naturally the membership dropped after we received independence, with some even reverting to Buddhism. Many thinkers in the established churches adopted a pluralistic attitude to the uniqueness of Christ. There was a mood of embarrassment over the past imperialistic connections of the church. But about 15 years ago, more than three decades after independence and after Buddhism had been firmly established as the national religion in a new constitution, the church has started a remarkable period of growth. Those doing evangelism as well as converts from Buddhism have had to face much persecution. But the proclamation of the unique Savior goes on unabated.

The church in India is experiencing a similar period of numerical growth. There the opposition to Christianity is even more intense than in Sri Lanka. Perhaps the three countries where the church has grown fastest in Asia in recent years are Nepal, China, and South Korea. The churches in these countries did not have "Christian" colonial rulers to help them. Rather, the belief in a unique Savior has motivated Christians to be active in bold and costly evangelism. In fact in Korea the Christians stood firmly against the Japanese imperialists and suffered much because of their refusal to adopt Shinto worship.

Past Wrongdoings of the Church

Our newspaper recently carried a lengthy article listing the atrocities of the church in its history. Some non-Christians are enraged over the conversion of people to Christianity, and they are making a connection between our present practice of evangelism and the atrocities of the colonial era. I believe the church should accept its errors and take responsibility for this.

Recently the pope publicly apologized for some of the wrong actions of the Roman Catholic Church in its history. This is a positive step that evangelicals can learn from. True Christians are experienced at accepting their faults. It is a basic requirement for entrance into the kingdom of God. If we find that our forefathers have done wrong, then we would do well to apologize for that. After all, we belong to the same body of Christ and are in solidarity with them. Such admission of the church's wrongdoing by Christians could certainly take away some of the dishonor to God caused by these wrong actions. It could also open the way to a more positive attitude toward Christians by those who have been hostile to them.

Koreans are asking for more than an apology from Japan and from the USA for alleged atrocities committed by them in wars conducted decades ago. Their actions demonstrate that human nature, with its sense of justice, wants an expression of regret and reparation for wrongdoing.

In this environment, white Christians may need to apologize for giving the impression that they believed they are superior to blacks. Having lived abroad for a time, I know how much hurt that impression can cause, even though I experienced it only mildly. Likewise, rich Christians may need to apologize to the poor for exploiting them or for treating them as inferior.

Dana Robert has pointed out, "While courageous individual missionaries mitigated the effects on indigenous peoples, by and large the missions benefited materially from European control." He mentions that the colonial rulers gave prime land to the missions. In Sri Lanka some lands owned by Buddhist temples were given to the Christian church. Recently there has been agitation to get back land on which a large church building stands. Robert also says that, during the era of the independence struggle, "Most missionaries saw themselves as apolitical and preferred the status quo of colonialism to the uncertainties of nationalist revolution."[7] So there *are* things that Christians in postcolonial nations ought to be ashamed of.

While we must apologize for the past wrongdoings of the church, it is also true that there is much anti-missionary rhetoric that grossly misrepresents the ties between the missionaries and the imperialist rulers.[8] In Sri Lanka the Methodist missionaries ran their schools in the vernacular languages, Sinhala and Tamil, thus making education available to the poor. It was the official policy of the British rulers to offer education only in English. Dana Robert points out, "The Christian contribution to Asian nationalism was extremely significant, especially through the impact of mission schools." Robert says, "Mission education, which combined vernacular literacy with Western learning, clearly played a key role in equipping nationalist leadership." Many of those who were active in the struggle for independence, including many of the first leaders of independent nations, were educated in mission schools.

While many missionaries did not support the independence movements, some, such as C. F. Andrews and E. Stanley Jones in India, did. And the dramatic difference between the frugal lifestyle of William Carey and his colonial contemporaries who lived in luxury is a study in contrast. Carey's legacy in terms of the societal welfare of India cannot be overestimated.[9]

One of the things that motivated the great missionary David Livingstone to go into the interior of Africa was the desire to open trade routes so that the horrific slave trade would stop. He consistently attacked the exploitation of black Africans[10] and sought to replace slavery with legitimate trade that would benefit all Africans.

A recent biographer of Livingstone, Rob Mackenzie, says that one of the things that prodded him to write Livingstone's story was his surprising discovery that the people of Africa still have a high regard for Livingstone.[11]

Similarly, in late nineteenth century China "no one but missionaries attacked the opium traffic."[12] One of those who fought against the trade was Hudson Taylor. Taylor's China Inland Mission refused to take compensation for the damage caused to missionary property during the Boxer rebellion.[13] This prompted a declaration of praise from the Chinese governor, with high honor given to Jesus by him.[14]

There is an urgent need to correct the wrong view of mission history that has been propagated by films like *Hawaii*. We need films and books like *The Mission,* which presents the heroic and costly commitment of missionaries to the welfare of the people they serve.

Christians as Patriots

Having said all of this, the church's embarrassing historical association with the colonial rulers remains with us. One of the best ways to overcome this stigma is for Christians to be true patriots. Our people should know us as those who truly love the country. We should work for the welfare of the nation that we belong to. Those belonging to the majority religion may despise us and treat us as foreigners, but our nation is where God has planted us. We will love it and serve it faithfully.

We are reminded of Jeremiah's letter to the exiles in Babylon: "Seek the peace and prosperity of the city to which I have carried you into exile. Pray to the Lord for it, because if it prospers, you too will prosper" (Jeremiah 29:7).

We must let the people in our workplaces know that we are the most reliable workers to be found. Let them see us caring for those of other faiths, even for those of the majority community that may have treated us badly.

Daniel was familiar with the letter of Jeremiah (Daniel 9:2). Though he was an exile in Babylon, he cared for his master, the wicked king Nebuchadnezzar, so that, when the king told him of a bad dream he had, Daniel got so upset that the king had to comfort *him* (Daniel 4:19). The servant girl in exile cared for her master, Naaman, who was the Commander of the Army of Aram that had threatened her people. He had leprosy, and she told her mistress that the prophet Elisha could heal him. The way she shared this news indicates her concern for him: "If only my master would see the prophet who is in Samaria! He would cure him of his leprosy" (2 Kings 5:3).

This may be easier said than done. Nationalism may take the form of ethnic prejudice. In Sri Lanka, where there is an ethnic conflict, a Sinhala Christian should speak up for the rights of those of the other side in the conflict, the Tamil people, as well as for the rights of the Sinhala people. Their own people may consider them traitors for doing this. A true patriot is concerned for everyone in the nation. According to the Old Testament ethic the concern should extend to the aliens in our midst too (Exodus 22:21; 23:9; Leviticus 19:33–34; Leviticus 23:22).

Sometimes nationalism takes a form that is represented by the motto: "My country, right or wrong." This often happens in the sports arena. People support their nation when its team may have done something that is clearly wrong. Hitler drummed up support by appealing to the love for the fatherland, and many Christians were swayed by his powerful appeal.

But a few Christians knew that such nationalism must be opposed. Some Christian leaders, like Martin Neimoeller and Dietrich Bonhoeffer, were vocal in their opposition and suffered for it.

True patriots love their country so much that they oppose the wrong things the nation does. They may have to take a stand that the majority of the people despise. Jeremiah was considered a traitor for his position against the relations his nation should have with Egypt and with Babylon (Jeremiah 37–38).

So we will need to grapple to find out the meaning of true patriotism and see how it can be applied in our particular situations. Certainly we wish that in our history there were more Christians who were involved in the struggle for freedom from Western powers. But that is history, and it is too late to change that. This is a new day in which we have the challenge of demonstrating to our people that we truly love our nation.

Religious Freedom for Those of Other Faiths

The previous discussion concerned Christians who are a minority in their nations. Now we address those Christians who may be part of a majority.

Our belief in the truth of the gospel does not mean that we should deny people of other faiths the freedom to worship and share their faith. The New Testament Christians, especially Paul and Luke, believed that Christians had a right to practice their faith in the multi-faith context of the Roman Empire. Luke tried to show that the Roman Empire generally gave them the right to do so. Would it not be right for us to do to others this thing that we wish for them to do to us? (Matthew 7:12).

In fact, Christians should defend the rights of those of other faiths. If we find that Muslims in our neighborhood do not have an adequate site for burying their dead, we should give them active support in their quest.

Sri Lanka is a predominantly Buddhist nation, and, according to the constitution, Buddhism is the national religion. But we are grateful for the freedom we have to practice and propagate our faith. Some Buddhist, Hindu, and Muslim fundamentalists are trying to restrict this freedom in several Asian countries. They have succeeded in doing this in many Muslim countries.

But sometimes when I hear Christians in the West speak, I must confess they sound very much like these Buddhist, Hindu, and Muslim fundamentalists. We don't need to be so afraid of other faiths that we restrict the freedom of devotees to practice their faith. It is in a multi-faith context that the early church grew and flourished. This can happen today too. And it is happening in several countries where, even though Christians are a small minority and are being persecuted, they are proclaiming the gospel of a unique Savior fearlessly.

The Charge of Arrogance

Humility and Truth. Another common charge made when we affirm the uniqueness of Christ and seek to persuade others is that we are arrogant. Almost a century ago the British journalist G. K. Chesterton observed that the focus of humility was getting misplaced. He observed that humility no longer concerned self-opinion. Rather it now pertained to truth.[15] Whereas humility had been judged on the basis of one's opinion of oneself, now it is being judged on the basis of one's understanding of truth. Those who claim to have the truth are regarded as arrogant. So we are accused of arrogance for claiming that Christ is absolutely unique.

But the uniqueness and supremacy of Christ are not merely claims that the church has created about Christ, they are facts that Christ confronts us with. He presents Himself as the unique Lord of the universe. It is up to us to accept or reject it. If you join a company, you have no option but to accept the president and chief executive officer. It is something you must do if you hope to stay on in the company. Similarly our belief in the uniqueness of Christ is not simply an opinion we hold. We have come to recognize that He is Lord of the universe. It is a fact we submit to.

The real arrogance is rejecting what the Lord of the universe says about Himself. Who are we to take issue with Jesus and reject what He says when it does not match our understanding? Is it not arrogance for fallible humans to say that our understanding of Jesus must replace His understanding of Himself? When non-Christians accuse us of arrogance that is understandable. But it is difficult to understand how Christians can accuse those who believe in the uniqueness and supremacy of Christianity of being arrogant.

The Nature of the Gospel Precludes Arrogance. The very nature of the gospel makes it impossible for a true Christian to be arrogant. Paul specifically says that our means of salvation leaves us with no grounds for boasting (Ephesians 2:8–9; Titus 3:5–6). Christians have accepted their utter inability to save themselves and are amazed by the fact that God has had mercy on them. Such amazement causes us to turn our attention away from ourselves and to be filled with gratitude to God for His grace. Those with such a focus cannot be arrogant. But they are so filled with excitement that they are urgent in their desire to share the gospel with others.

My teacher Dr. J. T. Seamands loved to tell about a clubfooted boy in England. He lived in a small town with his widowed mother. A businessman, who was a friend of the family, visited them one day and told them of a doctor in London who had great success in operating on young people with club feet. "I will take your son to London and see what this doctor can do for him," said the friend. "I will take care of all the expenses." The mother gratefully accepted the offer.

The boy went to London, and the operation was successful. The businessman kept the mother informed of her son's progress. Finally she got a telegram saying that the businessman and her son would be returning by train. The mother could hardly believe her eyes as she saw her son walking up to her. He leaped into her arms and started to say, "Mother, I will . . ." but his mother stopped him and said, "Son, don't say a word. Just run up and down the platform and let Mother see how you can do it."

He ran up and down once or twice and then went to his mother and began to say something. But again she cut him short and had him run up and down the platform. Finally she was satisfied and the son was able to say what he wanted to say. "Mother, I will never be satisfied until you meet the doctor in London. He's the most wonderful man in the world."[16]

Joyous Enthusiasm, Not Arrogance
And it is the same with us. After we know what we know and have experienced what we have experienced, we must share the message of the gospel.

When Peter and John were commanded not to speak or teach in the name of Jesus, they replied, "For we cannot help speaking about what we have seen and heard" (Acts 4:20). After stating that he was eager to preach the gospel in Rome (Romans 1:15), Paul went on to give his reason for such urgency: "For I am not ashamed of the gospel, for it is the power of God for salvation to everyone who believes" (Romans 1:16 NASB).

We have a boldness to proclaim the message because we know that Christ is the only way to salvation. Yet we do this with great humility because we know that we do not deserve salvation at all.

Humble Servanthood

Our critics will find servanthood difficult to understand when we try to explain it to them. But many more will be impressed by a holy and humble life.

The Bible is clear that those who proclaim the lordship of Jesus are servants of the people to whom they proclaim this message. Paul told the Corinthians, "We do not preach ourselves, but Jesus Christ as Lord, and ourselves as your servants for Jesus' sake" (2 Corinthians 4:5). He also said, "Though I am free and belong to no man, I make myself a slave to everyone, to win as many as possible" (1 Corinthians 9:19). Our model is Jesus, who "made himself nothing, taking the very nature of a servant" (Philippians 2:7). This principle of servanthood has numerous applications to evangelistic ministry today.

There has been a welcome rediscovery of the truth that we are engaging in spiritual warfare as we preach the gospel. But when Christians are faced with opposition by human forces, they often act with the same attitude they would use if they were fighting demonic forces. They are attacking people when they should be loving them.

The great Indian evangelist Sadhu Sundar Singh was once proclaiming the gospel on the banks of the Ganges. Several Hindu Sadhus and other devotees were in his audience. One of them lifted up a handful of sand and threw it in his eyes. Others in the audience were enraged by the act and handed the man to a policeman while Sundar Singh was washing the sand from his eyes. When he returned and found that the culprit had been taken into custody, Sundar Singh begged for his release and did not begin preaching again until the man had been freed. The man, Vijayanada, was so surprised that he fell at Sundar Singh's feet, begging his forgiveness and declaring his desire to know more about what he was saying. Later this man joined Sundar Singh on his travels.[17]

Such responses to our enemies will challenge those who consider us arrogant because we preach a unique gospel.

When we are insensitive to the feelings and wishes of non-Christians we can give them the idea that we are arrogant and intolerant. It may even occur in something seemingly innocent. Sometimes Christians, convinced that the sovereign Lord of the universe has given them authority to worship him freely, may shout so loudly while praying that they disturb their neighbors. This has become a problem in many poorer parts of the world where church buildings are not air-conditioned and the sound goes out into the neighborhood. Unnecessary opposition to the gospel has resulted.

The belief in the absolute uniqueness of Christ and the priority of His program on earth should not cause us to be insensitive to others. Jesus said, "So in everything, do to others what you would have them do to you" (Matthew 7:12).

In this age when both pluralists and non-Christian fundamentalists are attacking our belief that Christ is unique, there is a great need for us to live as servants of the people. If people see us as true servants of both enemies and friends, they will find it difficult to attack us. They may even be challenged to think positively about the truth of the gospel.

The Australian missionary Graham Staines and his two sons were murdered in India in 1999 when a mob of Hindu militants set fire to the vehicle in which they were sleeping. Most Hindus in India were greatly embarrassed by these murders and decried them. This outrage was surely aided by the fact that the Staines were working sacrificially among the lepers. And the Hindus witnessed the amazing expression of Christ-like forgiveness by Mrs. Staines.

What if large numbers of Christians adopted a lifestyle of loving servanthood? Initially we might be laughed at or exploited. But soon the world would be forced to take note of the power of our testimony, and the door may be opened to accepting the message of a unique Christ, whom they now resent. Jesus said, "Let your light shine before men, that they may see your good deeds and praise your Father in heaven" (Matthew 5:16).

Chapter 3 endnotes

[1] Cited in J. T. Seamands, *The Supreme Task of the Church* (Grand Rapids, MI: Wm. B. Eerdmans Publishing Co., 1964), 77.

[2] Stephen Neill, *Creative Tension* (London: Edinburgh House Press, 1950), 12.

[3] D. C. Vijayavardhana, *Dharma-Vijaya or The Revolt in the Temple* (Colombo: Sinha Publications, 1953), 499.

[4] John Hick, *God Has Many Names* (Philadelphia: Westminster Press, 1980), 8. Cited in Gary Phillips, "Religious Pluralism in a Postmodern World," *The Challenge of Postmodernism: An Evangelical Engagement,* David S. Dockery, editor (Grand Rapids, MI: Baker Book House, 1997), 261–262.

[5] See D. A. Carson, *The Gagging of God: Christianity Confronts Pluralism* (Grand Rapids, MI: Zondervan Publishing House and Leicester: Apollos, InterVarsity Press, 1996), 270–272.

[6] Dana L. Robert, "Shifting Southward: Global Christianity Since 1945," *International Bulletin of Missionary Research, vol. 24, no. 2* (April 2000), 50.

[7] Robert, "Shifting Southward," 51.

[8] On the topic of the relationship between Protestant missions and British imperialism see Brian Stanley, *The Bible and the Flag* (Leicester: Apollos, InterVarsity Press, 1990). This book provides a much-needed corrective to the anti-missionary rhetoric that is in vogue today. See also Vinoth Ramachandra, *Faiths in Conflict: Christian Integrity in a Multicultural World* (Leicester: InterVarsity Press, 1999), 75–81.

[9] Ramachandra, *Faiths in Conflict,* 77–78.

[10] J. D. Douglas, "David Livingstone," *Who's Who in Christian History,* J. D. Douglas and Philip W. Comfort, editors (Wheaton, IL: Tyndale House Publishers, 1992), 427.

[11] Rob Mackenzie, *David Livingstone: The Truth Behind the Legend* (Eastborne: Kingsway Publications, 1993), 16.

[12] A. J. Broomhall, *Hudson Taylor and China's Open Century/Book Five: Refiner's Fire* (London: Hodder and Stoughton, and Overseas Missionary Fellowship, 1985), 32.

[13] A. J. Broomhall, *Hudson Taylor and China's Open Century/Book Seven: It Is Not Death to Die* (London: Hodder and Stoughton, and Overseas Missionary Fellowship, l989), 32.

[14] Broomhall, *It Is Not Death to Die,* 480–81.

[15] Cited in Phillips, "Religious Pluralism," 261.

[16] Seamands, *The Supreme Task of the Church,* 78–80.

[17] Mrs. Arthur Parker, *Sadhu Sundar Singh: Called of God* (Madras: The Christian Literature Society, 1918), 25–26.

4

SENSITIVITY TO OTHERS

We have examined principles that enable us to witness for Christ without compromising the faith. Yet we have also highlighted the fact that we must treat those of other faiths with respect. In this chapter we will see how Paul acted in ways appropriate to the particular people he was among. He demonstrated *cultural sensitivity*.

When in Athens, Do as the Athenians

Paul "reasoned in the synagogue with the Jews and the God-fearing Greeks, as well as in the marketplace day by day with those who happened to be there" (Acts 17:17). The Jews and God-fearing Greeks were people who were already interested in the religion of the Bible, the Old Testament. Paul went to their place of worship and religious instruction, the synagogue.

The "marketplace" he spoke at was the *agora,* the main public place in the city, populated with public buildings and colonnades. It was the economic, political, and cultural heart of the city. An ancient account of Socrates reads, "He was to be seen in the marketplace when it was most crowded." There he would enter into conversation with those he would meet.[1] So when Paul evangelized the city of Socrates, he used the method of Socrates. His message was different, but his method was similar.

Paul had not always used the style he used in Athens. But when he came to Athens he adapted his method to fit the Athenian culture. This is called *contextualization*. Contextualization takes place when the presentation and outworking of the gospel are done in a way that fits the context. That context may be Athens or New York or Mexico City or a remote village in Uganda.

But context refers to more than one's geographical location. It also incorporates cultural factors like language, customs, and values. A Christian may find that his culture is very different from his Muslim neighbor's, even though they live in the same town and speak the same language.

Contextualization becomes necessary whenever we work with a person of a different culture. It is needed when an affluent person from a New York suburb tries to witness to one from a poorer inner-city neighborhood of New York. It is needed when a highly educated urban Indian tries to witness to a rural Indian who has little formal education, or when a Christian mother tries to witness to the Hindu mother of her daughter's classmate.

Let's bring contextualization right down to the daily life of Christians today. If a Christian family invites their Muslim neighbors home for Christmas dinner, they would be wise not to serve pork, even though they traditionally have ham on Christmas. Similarly, we are careful not to have beef when we invite a devout Hindu for a meal.

There are other cultural traditions we must be aware of. I was passing through a Buddhist village where several youth had come from for Youth for Christ programs. When one of our staff workers learned this he asked me to give a message to someone in the village. I was rushing for a meeting in Colombo and did not have time to sit and have a cup of tea when invited to do so. In the Sri Lankan rural culture that is a necessary part of paying a visit to a place. The word went round that the YFC director had visited the village but was too proud to have a cup of tea with the poor villagers. Since I was so rushed, it would have been better for me not to have gone to the village than to visit for just a brief time.

I could have argued that I had a right to plan my time for maximum efficiency. But by asserting that right I would lose my ministerial effectiveness, though I may increase my efficiency in terms of the volume of work accomplished.

Paul said, "Though I am free and belong to no man, I make myself a slave to everyone, to win as many as possible" (1 Corinthians 9:19). He told how he became like a Jew, as one under the law, when working with Jewish people. Yet he also became as one not having the law when he worked with a secular or pagan audience. He became "all things to all men," and said, "To the weak I became weak, to win the weak" (1 Corinthians 9:22). This statement vividly shows the challenge before us. We don't like to be perceived as weak—that is viewed as failure in today's society. But contextualization may require us to "become weak."

The weakness that many Christians encounter today is that of frustration. While the modern emphasis on efficiency has produced quick ways to do many things, there is no shortcut to effective evangelism. This may be the single biggest challenge that Western missionaries will face in the twenty-first century. They are not skilled at facing frustration, but if they are to be effective missionaries they will have to master that skill.

This skill is necessary not only for missionaries. All Christians need it! We must persevere in loving a roommate whose salvation we desire but who scoffs at all things Christian. We need patience to keep an unbelieving spouse open to the possibility of responding to the gospel. We must face frustration in our workplace when our Christian principles are scorned and we are constantly humiliated because of them.

Contextualization, however, must be distinguished from *syncretism*. Syncretism takes place when, in an effort to identify with non-Christians, elements essential to the gospel are dropped or elements incompatible with the gospel are taken on in the practice and presentation of Christianity.

Syncretism occurred when much of the church adopted the pagan idea of white supremacy so that it supported segregation. It takes place when a Christian, trying to maintain his friendship with a non-Christian, refuses to insist that following Christ is the only way to salvation. It happens when a Christian participating in a peace march worships with the other marchers when they pass a Hindu shrine. It takes place each time a Christian turns to an astrological guide for direction in his or her life. More practically, it takes place when Christians condone things like abortion on demand, euthanasia, and homosexual practice because these things have become accepted by the society in which they live.

The core of the gospel transcends all cultures. And even if some features of this core clash with the culture, Christians cannot dilute or compromise the message. Paul's speech in Athens clashed with the thinking of the Athenians. He refused to be a syncretist. But he was a contextualizer. When he communicated the gospel in Athens, he used the communication style of the Athenians even though his content clashed with their beliefs. Missiologist Paul Hiebert calls this *critical contextualization*.[2]

We must study the people and their culture and also study the biblical teachings that relate to their ideas and practices. Then we come up with a lifestyle and methods of presenting the unchanging message of the gospel that are relevant to their situation. This will make the gospel understandable, relevant, and more attractive to the hearers. This message will challenge the culture through God's principles.

When we do this, some people will be provoked, and they will oppose the Word. Acts records this opposition often. It happened in Athens too (17:32). But others will accept what we say and be transformed by Christ. That too happened in Athens. And though the number of converts was not large, there were some influential people converted, including a member of the Areopagus (Acts 17:34). Those working with non-Christians know how hard it is for such leaders to change their religion.

We see Paul's style of contextualization clearly as we look at his speech in Athens (Acts 17:22–31). We note that here, as in Lystra (Acts 14:15–17), he did not make any direct quotations from the Old Testament. This was very different from his speeches before Jewish audiences. The Jews accepted the authority of the Scriptures, so Paul quoted them. The Athenians did not accept this authority, so he did not make any direct quotes.

Interestingly, Paul quotes from the writers the Athenians looked up to. Of the two statements in verse 28 there is a question about whether the first is actually a quotation, but the second certainly is.[3] Paul would not agree with the philosophical system out of which the statement arose, but he could agree with this individual statement and use it to buttress his argument. Yet his message was what it had always been—the centrality of Jesus as proved by the resurrection and the need to repent and make Christ Lord.

In fact, Paul's message in Athens was thoroughly scriptural. F. F. Bruce says, "His argument is firmly based on biblical revelation; it echoes throughout the thought, and at times the very language, of the Old Testament."[4]

John Wesley called this speech "a divinely philosophical discourse."[5] While Paul's language and ideas were scriptural, the form of his Athenian address was most appropriate for his philosophically-oriented audience. He commented on their own religious practices, quoted from their own philosophers, and used their own logical style of argumentation in his attempt to persuade them to make Christ their Lord.

There are important lessons here for anyone trying to present Christ to non-Christians. We must discover the methods our audience uses to pursue truth. In different cultures different methods become important. In the Tamil culture in Sri Lanka and India, with its rich heritage of rhetoric, oratory could be an effective means to proclaim the gospel. The Buddhists of Sri Lanka love drama and music. Their religious festivals give a high place to those two art forms. Christians could use drama and music effectively in preaching the gospel to them. This is also seen in the West where many churches are using drama and music to attract unchurched people to their services and communicate the gospel effectively to them.

Some key leaders in our ministry who were working among Buddhists needed to get training in music and drama. But we had as teachers those who have distinguished themselves in the "secular" arts orbit. We could not find committed Christians who knew the secular art forms well enough. Our desire in all this is to present the gospel to the Buddhists in a form with which they are familiar. We find that the highly Westernized youth of Sri Lanka also like drama and music. But the type of drama and music that appeals to them is very different from what we use with the Buddhists.

Non-Christians may use the methods we use in ways that dishonor God. But that does not disqualify the method. The method is not evil. When George Frideric Handel first performed his Christian oratorio *The Messiah* in a concert hall, many were displeased. They did not associate the form he used and the place he held it with Christian music.[6] So William Booth, the founder of the Salvation Army, exclaimed, "Why should the Devil have all the good music?" and encouraged the setting of

Christian words to popular music. And Christians in Africa and Asia have taken the drum and used it effectively in Christian worship and expression even though animists have been using it for demonic rituals for centuries. There is nothing evil about the drum, and no scriptural warning against it. It was the way that it was used that made it evil.

In some people's minds terms like contextualization and cultural sensitivity are associated with compromise and syncretism. That is because some who give attention to this area dilute the gospel in the process. In the book of Acts the two best models of contextualization are Stephen and Paul. The former contextualized the gospel to his Jewish audience and the latter to a Gentile audience. The success of their contextualization can be measured by the fact that people understood what they said so well that they realized that they were faced with making a radical choice concerning the gospel. Some made this choice while others not only rejected it but also opposed these two contextualizers.

Scratch Where It Itches

Paul's discussions in Athens attracted sufficient attention to gain him an invitation to address the Areopagus (Acts 17:19). This distinguished body "was a council that had oversight of the educational, moral, and religious welfare of the community."[7] The delegates asked him, "May we know what this new teaching is that you are presenting? You are bringing some strange ideas to our ears, and we want to know what they mean" (17:19–20). Paul's response to the Athenians provides many important principles for our study.[8]

Points of Contact. Paul began with an observation about the religiousness of the Athenians. "Men of Athens! I see that in every way you are very religious" (17:22). Some have taken this statement to be a criticism and so have used the word *superstitious* instead of "religious" (see KJV). But this interpretation does not fit with the rest of the speech. Most modern translations prefer the word *religious*.

While it is not a criticism, neither is it a compliment. Paul was not resorting to flattery to win his audience. According to an ancient writer, Lucian, "complimentary exordia [beginnings] to secure the goodwill of the Areopagus court were discouraged."[9] If Paul had resorted to flattery, he would have disqualified himself from further participation.

Paul was simply making an observation about the life of the Athenians. They were a religious people. The word *religious* essentially means "respect for or fear of the supernatural."[10] The form this religiousness took was idolatry, which provoked Paul to anger (17:16). Paul knew that idolatry would not save the Athenians, so he argued against it (vv. 24–29) and called the Athenians to repent (v. 30). But Paul also knew that behind this idolatry was an appropriate respect for the supernatural.

This sense of the supernatural provided Paul with a stepping-stone to move into an exposition of the truth about God. Paul had found a "point of contact" with the Athenians. They were in agreement about the reality of the supernatural world. Paul mentioned their religiousness to get the Athenians on the same wavelength as he so that he could lead them into the new truths he wanted to present. In the same way, Christian witnesses today must look for an "airstrip" on which they can land—a suitable opening into the lives of their target audience to present the gospel.

The Unknown God. Through his comment about religiousness Paul won the attention of the Athenians. But he went deeper to identify their yearnings. He told them how he arrived at the idea that they were "very religious." He "walked around and observed [their] objects of worship" (17:23a). Then Paul singled out one of these objects obecause it helped him in his task of introducing God. He said, "I even found an altar with this inscription: TO AN UNKNOWN GOD" (17:23b). Paul saw the evidence of a deep, unsatisfied yearning in the Athenians.

The Greeks attributed the various natural phenomena to the gods. Different gods were said to be responsible for their tribulations and their good fortunes, so they wanted to be on the good side of all the gods. But they were not certain that they knew all the gods, so they dedicated an altar to the unknown god "to ensure that no god was overlooked to the possible harm of the city."[11] This altar was an admission that their knowledge of the supernatural was incomplete. Paul used this admission as a launching pad for his description of the God of the Bible. They set up their altar in an attempt to complete everything, but they did not know which god was able to do this. Paul knew the God who completed everything without the assistance of any other gods. He introduced this God to the Athenians: "Now what you worship as something unknown I am going to proclaim to you" (17:23c).

Did God Accept Their Worship? Paul said that the Athenians worshiped God as something unknown (17:23). Does this mean that this worship was acceptable to God? Some say that such a conclusion is implied by this statement, that this kind of worship can bring salvation to a person. The worshipers may not know who God is, but they are saved because they worship God.

Raymond Panikkar in his influential book, *The Unknown Christ of Hinduism,* applied this verse to Hindu worship. He claimed that God would save the Hindus through Christ while they continued with their Hindu worship.[12]

Other scholars say that, though God accepts this non-Christian worship, we still need to present the gospel because that is not the ideal way to worship God.

Yet this text does not leave room for us to imply that the worship of the Athenians was acceptable to God. N. B. Stonehouse has pointed out that the emphasis here is on the ignorance rather than the worship.[13] Paul was focusing on the confessed ignorance of the Athenians because that gave him a foothold for his proclamation of the gospel. He was not making any value judgments about the worship connected with this ignorance. Later in his speech he stated that the ignorance was no longer excusable and that therefore God "commands all men everywhere to repent" (17:30). Such a statement shows that this worship by the Athenians was not acceptable to God. We will show later that this is God's attitude to all worship apart from his revelation in Jesus Christ.

Christ Fulfills Their Aspirations. Paul's handling of the worship of the unknown god tells us how he regarded other faiths. He saw these faiths as the expression of a thirst for God, but he knew that only Christ could satisfy that thirst. So he approached non-Christians with the belief that they were thirsting for God.

Blaise Pascal described this thirst in terms of a God-shaped vacuum in the human soul. The thirst expresses itself in various forms. In Athens it expressed itself in the form of an altar to an unknown god.

We too approach non-Christians with the belief that the gospel fulfills their aspirations. Their search to fulfill these aspirations may take forms that we do not approve. But we must look beyond the form to the emptiness without God that causes it. Then we must show how Christ fills this void.

The present interest in spirituality in the East and the West can become such a stepping-stone for launching Christian witness. This is a feature of the postmodern reaction to the rationalism of the modern era. The expressions it takes may be revolting to us, such as interest in the occult and in spirits and the spiritual disciplines of New Age groups and Eastern religions. But the idols in Athens were revolting to Paul; yet he used them as a stepping-stone to show the people that only God could give them what they were looking for.

Fear of unknown forces is a powerful factor in the lives of people all over the world. Overcoming this fear is one of their most important aspirations. They go to astrologers, shrines, medicine men, exorcists, or others who claim to have power to control or direct supernatural forces. When people are faced with trouble they ask, "Is this because of a charm or an evil spirit?" They use whatever means may be available to counteract the evil forces. Traditionally, this has been a feature of the so-called Third World, but the popularity of astrology, witches, psychic readers, and the like in the West shows that this is a worldwide phenomenon.

Some rationalists, and even some evangelicals, scoff at these practices and say that what happens is really in one's imagination. But this attitude is both unwise and incorrect. It is unwise because we cannot so easily dismiss such deeply ingrained feelings. If we do, our target audience will also dismiss us as having nothing relevant to say to them. And this attitude is incorrect because the Bible clearly tells us there are supernatural powers at work in the world. Even Christians battle with these forces (Ephesians 6:12).

The biblical approach to fear of the supernatural and its manifestations is to show that our God is more powerful. The Bible teaches that because God is maker of heaven and earth, all forces are subject to Him.

So the method of the Christian witness is to recognize the questions and aspirations these people have and show that Christ is the answer.

Some object to this method of witnessing. They say we must emphasize the basic human question, which is the need for a relationship with God, and that this is a relationship humans do not experience because of sin. We agree. But many people do not recognize this basic need. We may tell a non-Christian the moment we meet him that he needs a relationship with God and that he must repent of his sin. But he may tell us that he does not have such a need.

There are other needs, however, which he has and recognizes, such as the need to be free from the influence of evil forces. We can start with this question and from it direct him to the most basic question, that of his relationship with God, which is hindered owing to sin. We must at some stage arrive at this basic question. But we may not start with it, because if we do, he will dismiss us as having nothing to say that is of relevance to his life.

An effective Christian always tries to identify the aspirations of non-Christians and explore how to demonstrate that Christ fulfills those aspirations. In chapter 11 we will examine how to present Christ as fulfilling the thirst for authentic spirituality.

Christ is the answer. But we must discover the specific questions of our audience. Those questions may not be what we think they are or what we think they should be.

Does this approach apply also to self-sufficient Westerners? Do they ask such questions? Many, especially in Europe, feel they don't need religion. They feel quite adequate to face the challenges of life without God's help. So we might conclude that they are not asking any questions of religious significance.

The problem may be that we are looking in the wrong place. Our lifestyle is so different from theirs that we don't know the deep yearnings of their hearts. They *do* have religious aspirations. But those aspirations take forms that we may not recognize as being religious.

From Felt Needs to the Gospel

It is heartening to see many Christians trying to identify with the questions and yearnings of the world. Two types of evangelical groups have seen much fruit recently. One of those groups emphasizes the power of God to perform miracles ("power evangelism"). The other uses what we call a "seeker-sensitive" approach.

In *power evangelism* the focus has been on the power of God to meet felt needs, such as bringing healing from sickness. In the *seeker-sensitive* groups, the emphasis has been on other needs, like loneliness and lack of purpose. A special emphasis has been given to excellence in programming and being relevant to the contemporary scene.

But identifying with people's questions and meeting felt needs is only a first step in the process of proclaiming the gospel. We must be sure that the whole gospel is well presented.

Meeting Needs through Power Evangelism. Today we hear of remarkable miracles performed in the name of Jesus, especially within the charismatic branches of the Church. In places like Sri Lanka, where the Buddhists are so resistant and hostile to Christianity, it often takes the miraculous to gain their attention so they will consider the message of Christ.

All Christians should be alert to the needs of non-Christians that may become items for prayer. I have yet to meet a person who has refused to be prayed over. Most of the members of our church are converts from Buddhism, and most of them first came to church because a friend knew of a need they had and brought them to church to have them prayed over.

With some groups that emphasize God's power, however, other vital features of the gospel are neglected. The primary message is that God will meet our needs, and other essential aspects of the gospel, such as the sovereignty of God and the person and work of Christ, are touched on only briefly.

This trend has become a serious problem. Thousands of Christians do not properly understand Christianity, and their lives could betray the faith they profess. They may know the gospel, but the primary reason they are Christians is that God meets their needs.

The apostles in the book of Acts give us the best answer to this dangerous trend. The great miracle workers in the book of Acts were also great apologists who argued eloquently for the truth of the gospel. Peter, Stephen, and Paul are examples of this. Rarely do we see this combination today. Rather, we have churches and groups that concentrate on apologetics and others that concentrate on ministering in the miraculous. Very few exhibit both these aspects of ministry. Sadly, the programs of some churches show neither the use of apologetics nor the power of God.

Recently a Buddhist lady in Sri Lanka visited a church because of some serious problems she was facing. She was prayed over and miraculously delivered from her difficulties. But after a few years, she went to another church, as there was very little teaching and discipline in that first church. In the new church there was a wonderful ministry of the Word, and her soul was nourished. But this church had few evidences of Christian belief in the supernatural world. She commented to a friend, "I left this church because there was so much power and so little of the Word. But in this new church there is so much of the Word but no power."

Meeting Needs in Seeker-Sensitive Groups. Some of the music, drama, film, and preaching coming out of seeker-sensitive groups today has been eminently successful in analyzing the way people feel and live in today's society. But there has been a weakness in expounding the solutions to the problems. It is not enough to use our creativity in analyzing the human predicament. We must expound the gospel in such a way that our hearers know that the gospel is the answer to their questions. Often our methods of expounding the gospel are so stereotyped and plain that we lose our hearers in the process. They warm up to our analysis of the problem, but the solution we present leaves them cold. They identify with the problem but have no desire to identify with the solution.

Sometimes there is a lack in presenting the hard truths of the gospel like repentance and judgment, both of which themes appear in Paul's speech in Athens (17:30–31). If these truths are not presented early in the gospel presentation people will not incorporate them into their basic understanding of Christianity, and the result again will be Christians who know only half the gospel. This is not always so. My exposure to perhaps the most famous seeker-sensitive church, the Willow Creek Church in USA, convinces me that they make an honest effort to share the whole gospel. In fact one of the best sermons I have heard on hell was by the senior pastor of this church, Bill Hybels.

Here again, Paul is a model for us. His exposition of the gospel

(17:24–31) was as relevant to the Athenians as was his analysis of their aspirations. His exposition was thoroughly biblical. It was a comprehensive message, starting with God, and moving to Jesus and His resurrection, and repentance and the judgment. But the way he presented this unchanging gospel was very appropriate to his audience in that it was philosophical in style. He constantly interacted with the beliefs and practices of the Athenians. He even quoted from the writings of their philosophers.

From Paul's example, then, we see some important keys to effective witness among non-Christians. We must know the gospel thoroughly and communicate it faithfully and clearly. We must also know the world thoroughly. This knowledge of the world becomes the context in which we present the gospel. So when we proclaim the gospel, we constantly interact with the aspirations, beliefs, and practices of our audience. A good witness, then, is a student of both the Word and the world. Karl Barth is reported to have said that the preacher should have the Bible in one hand and the newspaper in the other.

Chapter 4 endnotes

[1] Cited in R. J. Knowling, "The Acts of the Apostles," *The Expositor's Greek Testament* (Grand Rapids, MI: Wm. B. Eerdmans Publishing Co., 1974 reprint), 365.
[2] Paul G. Hiebert, "Critical Contextualization," *Missiology 12* (July 1987), 287–96; reprinted in T*he Best in Theology, vol. 2,* J. I. Packer, editor (Carol Stream, IL: Christianity Today, n.d.).
[3] From the fourth century BC writer Aratus of Soli in Cicilia. Cited in *Hellenistic Commentary to the New Testament,* M. Eugene Boring and others, editors (Nashville: Abingdon Press, 1995), 328.
[4] F. F. Bruce, "The Book of Acts," *The New International Commentary on the New Testament* (Grand Rapids, MI: Wm. B. Eerdmans Publishing Co., 1988), 335.
[5] John Wesley, *Explanatory Notes Upon the New Testament* (London: The Epworth Press, 1966), 464.

6 See Christopher Hogwood, "Introduction," George Frideric Handel, *Messiah: The Workbook for the Oratorio* (New York: HarperCollins, 1992).

7 Everett F. Harrison, *Interpreting Acts: The Expanding Church* (Zondervan Publishing House, 1986), 284.

8 E. M. Blaiklock, "The Acts of the Apostles," The Tyndale New Testament Commentaries (Grand Rapids, MI: Wm. B. Eerdmans Publishing Co., 1959), 140.

9 Cited in F. F. Bruce, *The Acts of the Apostles: Greek Text with Introduction and Commentary,* third edition (Grand Rapids, MI: Wm. B. Eerdmans Publishing Co., and Leicester: InterVarsity Press, 1990), 380.

10 Alan Richardson, "Superstition," *A Theological Wordbook of the Bible,* Alan Richardson, editor (London: SCM Press, Ltd., 1950), 253.

11 Blaiklock, "Acts," 140.

12 Raymond Panikkar, *The Unknown Christ of Hinduism,* revised edition (Maryknoll, NY: Orbis Books, 1981), 88–89, 168.

13 N. B. Stonehouse, *Paul before the Areopagus and other New Testament Studies* (London: The Tyndale Press, 1957), 19.

5

TRUTH IN OTHER RELIGIONS

The West today is highly enamored of Eastern religions. Thousands of Westerners are coming to the East in search of spiritual realities that they feel the West has forsaken in its quest for technological advancement. This is the culmination of a process that started about 150 years ago with a new interest in studying the religions and cultures of what we now call the Third World. Earlier Christians had viewed these cultures as primitive and backward. But as Westerners began to study these cultures they saw a richness they had not realized was there.

Bishop Stephen Neill, British missionary to India, described it like this: "As these 'treasures of darkness' penetrated the consciousness of educated men and women, something like a gasp of astonishment arose. Surprise was followed by appreciation, and even admiration."[1] Neill observed how Hindu writings began to be compared with the Christian Scriptures. When Pope John XXIII instituted the famous Vatican II Council of the Roman Catholic Church, one of the official documents resulting from that council was entitled *Lumen Gentium*—the light of the Gentiles. While emphasizing mission work, *Lumen Gentium* also affirmed the richness of other religious traditions.[2]

Today, as Christians meet people of other faiths and see admirable qualities in their religious practices, they sometimes wonder how they can square what they see with their belief in the uniqueness of Christianity.

Meeting Them at Their Highest

In his speech to the Athenians, Paul quoted approvingly from one or possibly two non-Christian poets (Acts 17:28). This tells us something about his attitude to these faiths. Even though Paul quoted from these unbelievers, he did not accept the whole religious system of their philosophies. Yet he saw glimmerings of the truth in these systems that could be used to buttress his case for Christianity.[3] His audience was familiar with these writers and accepted them as their own teachers. Paul used their literature to develop his case for the Christian gospel. As F. F. Bruce points out, we "may quote appropriate words from a well-known writer or speaker without committing ourselves to their total context or background of thought."[4]

By affirming what was good in Greek philosophy, Paul gave us another important principle about the Christian's attitude toward other faiths. In Stephen Neill's words, "We must endeavor to meet them at their highest."[5]

Neill contrasts this with the approach of the would-be witness who cheaply scores points against other faiths "by comparing the best he knows in his own faith with their weaknesses." People who use this method present Christianity as the answer to the bad behavior of non-Christians. But this ill-advised approach can work against Christians as well.

In 1983 there was an outbreak of violence in Sri Lanka. Many from the Buddhist majority had a hand in the unrest. Some Christians were quick to use this as evidence for the moral bankruptcy of Buddhism.

But as the public began to gain a clearer picture of what had happened, news emerged that Christians too had been involved in the violence. Their involvement was not nearly as prominent as that of the Buddhists, partly because the Christians are a small minority in Sri Lanka. But Christians nonetheless were involved!

If we attack Buddhism by highlighting the moral failures of some of its adherents, all the Buddhist has to do is to point to situations such as Nazi Germany. We do not identify the Nazis as Christians. But since many Nazis were church members, non-Christians often label them as

Christians. And unquestionably these purported "Christians" were instruments of wickedness.

In the past, the "savagery" of the non-Christian world was used to motivate Christians to missionary involvement. Today non-Christians use the same argument to appeal for missionary involvement in the so-called Christian West. The Buddhists believe that the moral restraint of Buddhism is the answer to the immorality found in the West. The Hindus believe the devotion of Hinduism is the answer to the materialism found in the West. The Muslims believe that the brotherhood of Islam is the answer to the racial prejudice found in the West.

We do not argue for the validity of Christianity by pointing to the wickedness that adherents of other religions have caused. We argue for Christianity by pointing to the ravages of sin. It is *sin* that has caused the miserable state of the human race.

Sin is found in Christian and non-Christian environments. Those born into a Christian background need to be saved from sin as much as those born into a non-Christian background.

We must guard against attacking other religions and instead show people how their faith is ineffective and will not save them. We must show them the ineffectiveness of the ways people pursue salvation, such as materialism, idolatry, false gods, and self-effort. Paul did this regarding idolatry in Athens. But Paul did not consider his preaching to be a competitive debate that he must win by denigrating his opposition. Rather, Paul's desire was to proclaim the truth. If there was truth to be found in these other faiths, he was not afraid to affirm it.

But Paul showed, as he did in Athens, that the highest truths in these religions did not go far enough. Paul knew that the truth residing in other faiths would not bring eternal salvation. For that, Christ is the only way.

Because we believe in the supremacy of Christ, we are not afraid to affirm what is good in other faiths. Christ is in a class by Himself. The founders of the other religions explored the meaning of the divine and of truth. In contrast, Christ was divinity incarnate. He said, "Anyone who has seen me has seen the Father" (John 14:9), and, "I am the way and the truth and the life. No one comes to the Father except through me" (John 14:6).

We have come to the Father through Christ and tasted life and truth. We know that nothing in this world can compare with that. Our security in Him takes away our defensiveness so that we are not afraid to affirm what is good in the followers of other ways.

Because we know that Christ is the only way to salvation, we do all we can to bring those following other ways to Christ. Paul presented a different gospel from that of the Greek philosophers he quoted. When he explained the resurrection of Christ he lost most of his audience. But Paul would not compromise the truth to get his hearers to agree with him.

Sources of Truth in Other Religions

This brings us to the question of the source of these truths in other religions. The Scriptures teach that there are three sources of truth available to us apart from the Scriptures.

God's Original Revelation. The first source is God's original revelation to Adam and Eve, the first humans. Paul said that from "one man he made every nation of men" (Acts 17:26; see also Romans 5:12–21). Adam was the father of the whole human race. The Scriptures teach that God had a warm personal relationship with Adam and Eve. This could have been possible only if God had revealed key truths about His nature to them.

Yet with the Fall of the human race, human nature was corrupted and untruths entered our minds. Paul wrote, "They exchanged the truth of God for a lie, and worshiped and served created things rather than the Creator" (Romans 1:25). So human expressions of religion deteriorated.

Yet that original revelation given to Adam and Eve was not entirely lost by the human race. There remained what is called *reminiscent knowledge.*[6] This reminiscent knowledge contains truth about God. In our discussion on the origins of religion in chapter 7 we will see how vestiges of this original knowledge of God are found in the form of a memory of a supreme God in many of the "primitive" tribes all over the world.

Here then is the first source of truth in non-Christian systems— God's original revelation. Though this revelation has been corrupted because of sin, some truth still remains, and that truth may be affirmed and used as a stepping-stone in communicating the gospel.

The Image of God in Humanity. The second source of truth available, apart from the Scriptures, is in the very nature of the human being. We are religious beings. The Dutch theologian, J. H. Bavinck, points out, "This is not to say that every man has this religious trait to the same extent." Some are more religious than others. But if we look at the human race as a whole, we must agree with Bavinck. "It cannot be denied that religiousness is proper to man." Bavinck adds, "Even when a man turns his back upon the religious traditions in which he has been brought up and calls himself an atheist, he still remains in the grasp of his religious predisposition. He can never wholly rid himself of it."[7] In chapter 9 we will see how nontheistic systems like Buddhism, communism, and secular humanism cannot remain nontheistic for very long because of the incurably religious nature of the human being.

The inevitable religiosity of the human race is a vestige of the image of God in humanity (see Genesis 1:26–27). This image was tarnished as a result of the Fall, so no part of us has escaped the taint and pollution of sin. But all humans still have some of the God-implanted characteristics and abilities that were originally created in us. One of the manifestations of these traits is our thirst after God, which is part of the human make-up. Ecclesiastes 3:11 says that God has "set eternity in the hearts of men." That refers to the vestige of the image of God. But it goes on to say that men "cannot fathom what God has done from beginning to end." That is a result of the Fall. Theologians describe as *intuitional knowledge* this awareness of God that comes through our natural inclination toward the religious.[8]

So we find that humans can think reasonably. We have a sense of the reality of the divine that expresses itself in religiousness. We have a sense of truth, of beauty, and of goodness. We have the potential for creativity. We have a sense of the eternal, which makes us want to transcend the limits of time and space. These are qualities that have the potential of being used in the service of truth for the benefit of humanity.

But because of our fallenness they may also be used in ways that are dangerous. So we find accomplished art, literature, and music that are good, and we also find art, literature, and music that are evil. We have beautiful ancient buildings regarded as wonders of the ancient world that were built using slaves in a most inhumane way.

A Christian, therefore, may enjoy the music of the Hindu musician Ravi Shankar or be challenged by the heroism of another great Hindu, Mahatma Gandhi.[9] We may learn from the great classical literature of Greece. We could say that, because these are expressions of the image of God in humanity, their good features are derived in some sense from God. But we also know that those who created them do not know God, and this makes us unwilling to endorse the system of life to which they subscribe. As a youth I used to follow Hindu processions for hours, thrilled by the music I heard but deeply troubled by what caused the musicians to play what they played.

The Plan of the Universe. A third source of knowledge that is outside the revelation of God in the Scriptures is the plan of the universe. By looking at the universe, we are able to make inferences about the One who created it. We may call this the *inferential knowledge* of God. The psalmist said, "The heavens declare the glory of God, the skies proclaim the work of his hands" (Psalm 19:1). Paul explained this knowledge of God more clearly: "What may be known about God is plain to them, because God has made it plain to them. For since the creation of the world God's invisible qualities—his eternal power and divine nature—have been clearly seen, being understood from what has been made" (Romans 1:19–20).

In his speeches in Lystra and Athens, Paul said that the plan of creation is a testimony to God, creating in humans a desire to know more about Him (Acts 14:17; 17:26, 27). By observing the grandeur of creation, people may be led to acknowledge the greatness of the Creator. By observing the laws of nature, people may arrive at a conviction about the importance of order for a secure life. This in turn will become a base for formulating the laws of a given society.

General Revelation and Special Revelation

The three sources of truth outside the Bible are reminiscent knowledge, based on the original revelation of God; intuitional knowledge, which comes by the use of our natural instincts; and inferential knowledge, which comes by observing creation. In theology, this type of knowledge is described under the heading of *general revelation*. It is truth, derived from God and available to all people. It is distinguished from *special revelation,* which is truth communicated by God infallibly in the person and work of Jesus and the words of Scripture. Whereas general revelation gives hints about the nature of reality, special revelation is a clear guide to all that is needed for salvation and for authentic living.

Psalm 19 describes these two sources of truth. Verses 1–6 describe general revelation. This revelation is not made through "speech or language" (v. 3), but "their voice goes out into all the earth" (v. 4). Verses 7–11 describe special revelation. This description begins with the words, "The law of the Lord is perfect" (v. 7). It goes on to describe this revelation as "trustworthy" (v. 7), "right," "radiant" (v. 8), "pure," and "altogether righteous" (v. 9). This passage also describes the amazingly complete influence it exerts on believers. We affirm that only the Bible can exert such infallible authority upon us. No other writing, Christian or non-Christian, is revelation in the sense that the Bible is.

Some recent works on the Christian attitude toward other faiths have disputed the Christian claim to a unique revelation. Sri Lankan writer Wesley Ariarajah says, "What we have in the Bible are not attempts to project objective truths, but a struggle to understand, to celebrate, to witness, and to relate."[10]

To Ariarajah the Bible is an expression of the faith and experiences of its writers. This is the typical approach to truth of religious pluralists, and we will encounter it more frequently in the days to come. Ariarajah says that we must not claim that the Bible presents "absolute and objective" truth based on our belief that it is a unique revelation given by God. Besides, he says, "Most religions, like Islam and Hinduism, are also based on the concept of revelation, and throughout history different persons have claimed to have various revelations from God."[11]

It is not within the scope of this book to defend our belief that the Scriptures are a unique revelation from God, containing objective and absolute truth. This has been accomplished in other fine books on revelation.[12]

Learning from Other Faiths?

If glimpses of truth are found in other faiths, then there may be times when Christians can learn from those religions. This can be explained in two ways.

First, even though the revelation of God is complete in that it gives all that is needed for salvation and authentic living, God has given us the privilege and responsibility of applying this revelation to our own specific situations. In some areas, we have specific instructions that are absolutes, such as the prohibition of adultery. But in other areas, we have general principles. It is our task to apply these principles to our specific cultural situations.

An example of this is seen in the principle of *reverential worship*. Music has been called the language of the heart. We learn much about a culture from the music of the non-Christians in that culture. By listening to their music, we learn what type of music is suitable for the culture we are seeking to reach.

Other ways to learn from other faiths are more complex. Take the issue of God's general revelation to us.

Even though God's revelation is complete, our perception of it is not. The Scriptures contain all that is necessary to live a complete life, but because of our cultural conditioning we are hindered from learning some of the things clearly taught in the Scriptures. Other cultures may not have these cultural hindrances. So even without the light of the gospel, people of other cultures may achieve heights in certain areas simply by availing themselves of general revelation.

In many Third World countries the culture has contributed to healthy family living. The West has lost some of this because of its extreme individualism and its time-consciousness. Consider things such as respect for elders, care of those elders when they are unable to care for themselves, increased interdependence between family members, and assisting the extended family with needs such as looking after a baby. Western Christians can learn much about these aspects of family life from some of their non-Christian neighbors.

Unacceptable Systems

Though we may accept and learn from certain practices in non-Christian systems, we must reject the systems themselves. The faithfulness of Muslims to their spiritual disciplines is indeed admirable and a challenge to us. But Muslim devotion does not lead to salvation. Only faith in Christ does that.

Therefore we disagree with the pluralist who says, "Let us learn from each other and live harmoniously. After all, we are headed in the same direction, even though some of our practices may differ." The biblical Christian says, "We are *not* headed in the same direction. Some of our practices may be similar. We may learn from each other, but there is a sense in which we cannot live harmoniously with each other. We seek to bring all who are outside of a relationship with Christ into such a relationship, and that necessitates the forsaking of their former religions."

The pluralist says that we are one in the center, though we may differ on some peripheral details. The biblical Christian says that, though we may have some peripheral similarities, we are different in the center. Christianity revolves on a different axis from other religions. The way of Christ leads to life. The Bible teaches that other ways lead to death (1 John 5:12).

We approach the issue of truth and goodness in other faiths from the basis of our belief in the uniqueness of Christ. If one aspect of a certain religion conforms to the complete revelation in Christ, we affirm that particular aspect. But if it does not conform to this revelation, we reject it. As Lesslie Newbigin puts it: "Jesus is for the believer the source from whom his understanding of the totality of experience is drawn and therefore the criterion by which other ways of understanding are judged."[13] These are implications of Christ's proclamation that He is "the truth" (John 14:6).

The good points in a religion that have their base in general revelation may be used by the Christian as points of contact and stepping-stones in preaching the gospel. But these same good features in a religion can also lead people astray.

The noble ethic of Buddhism gives many people the encouragement to try to save themselves, especially in the Theravada forms of Buddhism. They are satisfied in their own efforts to win salvation. But self-effort is the opposite of God's way of salvation, which is by faith. Before we exercise such faith we must first despair of our ability to save ourselves. The ethic of Buddhism may cause people to trust in their ability to save themselves and so blind them from the way of salvation.

So, in his work of blinding unbelievers so that they cannot see the glory of the gospel (2 Corinthians 4:4), Satan can use the best in other faiths to lead people away from the truth. In this sense there is a demonic element to other faiths, for they serve the purpose of Satan in keeping people from the truth.

Some may find this statement very offensive because there is so much that is admirable in these faiths. Yet we know that the Bible says, "Satan himself masquerades as an angel of light" (2 Corinthians 11:14). He can use the very things we admire in another faith to keep people from the truth.

Cooperating in Common Causes

Another implication of our belief in general revelation relates to our cooperation with non-Christians in moral, social, or political causes of mutual concern. Theologian John Jefferson Davis has given a rationale for such activity. He says that even unbelievers have a God-created conscience. Because of general revelation, believers and unbelievers can overlap in their moral concerns.[14] So we may cooperate with non-Christians in causes such as peace, ecological responsibility, social development, and opposition to abortion on demand.

We must, however, be warned that such cooperation is fraught with numerous pitfalls. Davis says that one of the keys to avoiding these problems is to define the basis of cooperation narrowly and specifically.[15] We cooperate on certain agreed-upon causes and no more. Davis also says that we must ensure that the coalition has a clear written statement of goals that does not conflict with Scripture.

We must remember that our supreme task, evangelism with conversion in view, is repulsive to most non-Christians. Cooperation with non-Christians must not result in a blunting of that evangelistic emphasis. Sometimes evangelistic organizations downplay their evangelistic emphasis to get assistance from the government or a non-Christian foundation for some social venture. This practice is dangerous. Along with our social concern is an evangelistic concern that we cannot compromise for financial reasons.

Following the recent racial riots in Sri Lanka, I happily participated in a neighborhood peace committee chaired by a Buddhist and of which most of the members were Buddhists. I found that what I did in that committee did not conflict with my Christian principles. There have been many public processions for peace that our politicians have been involved in. Usually if the procession passes by a Buddhist or Hindu temple they stop there and pay homage to the idols or gods. Sometimes Christian politicians join in this. Other times I have seen Christians respectfully refrain from entering the premises without drawing much attention to themselves. The people usually respect them for keeping to their Christian principles.

Murray Harris described the principle Paul laid down in his famous passage about being unequally yoked with unbelievers (2 Corinthians 6:14–16):

> Do not form any relationship, whether temporary or permanent, with unbelievers that would lead to a compromise of Christian standards or jeopardize your Christian witness.[16]

And why such separation? Because the unbeliever does not share the Christian's standards, sympathies, or goals.

Traditional Arts and Alternative Medicine

All that is good about the knowledge and culture of a people can be included under general revelation, but there are some systems and practices that have religious connotations we must discuss. Included here are the various types of alternative medicine ("indigenous medicine"), martial arts, meditation and relaxation techniques, and forms of arts and crafts that are also used for religious or occultic practices.

These practices pose a problem in the West similar to what we face with the gospel in the East. The gospel was often introduced in the East with a connection to colonial rulers; therefore people here reject it in the belief that it is anti-national. People with New Age connections introduced things like acupuncture and Eastern herbal remedies to the West; therefore many Western Christians have rejected them as being New Age practices. To many of us in the East, however, these are the traditional practices of our people that were the only forms of medicine available to us before the influence of Western scientific methods.

As an example, we could take the indigenous system of medicine, sometimes called the *Ayurvedic system*. The etymology of the word suggests connection with the Hindu vedic tradition. But in the East this is simply the word for the indigenous system of medicine. In Sri Lanka this system operates parallel to the Western system. There are government hospitals and even a cabinet Minister of Indigenous Medicine. What we find here are primarily herbal remedies that have developed over the centuries, often through trial and error. Generally they are effective in treating the ailments they are prescribed for. Sometimes doctors trained in Western medicine also prescribe these drugs.

Dr. Benny Tan, Associate Professor[17] of Pharmacology at the National University of Singapore, is a committed Christian. He has been researching how the commonly used herbal remedies work. He has found several cases where the action can be explained in Western scientific terms. In fact, this has become a battleground in the field of international trade, with multinational drug companies trying to patent some of the traditional medicines of the East and market them in the West.

In indigenous medicine the way in which a malady and its remedy are explained is different from the way it is explained in the Western scientific system. For example, we have the system that classifies some foods as "heaty" and others as "cooling." When we eat heaty foods we sometimes have reactions like throat irritation. This can be remedied by eating cooling foods. Often those who are familiar only with Western systems laugh at these explanations. But now Western scientific evidence is emerging to show that there are scientific reasons for these symptoms and for the effectiveness of the remedies (e.g., the presence of excessive amounts of histamines in some of the "heaty" foods).

Acupuncture is part of traditional Chinese medicine. It is explained by the idea that disease occurs when there are imbalances in *ch'i* or the life force in a person. The Chinese believed that "opposing forces within the body, designated *yin* and *yang,*[18] must be in balance or harmony before ch'i can get our vital functions ... to work normally." The life force or ch'i is said to flow along fourteen invisible interconnected main channels ('meridians') on each side of the body." These meridians are found deep within the tissues. But they "surface at various locations on the body called 'acupuncture points' ('acupoints')." Estimates as to how many such points are found in the human body vary from 360 to the thousands. "Each meridian 'services' one or more specific organs such as kidney, liver, gallbladder, colon, or heart, which can be influenced by stimulating the appropriate acupoints."[19] These are the places were the needles are pricked. While research on acupuncture using Western scientific methodology has not been conclusive, there is evidence to show that endorphins are released when the needle is inserted. These compounds are like opiates and are part of the body's natural way to relieve pain.[20]

In Asia it is not uncommon to find Christians who are registered practitioners of indigenous medicine. Because in most cultures the religion of a people enters into their daily life, religion has entered into the practice of indigenous medicine by many practitioners. Christians considering whether to go to a practitioner of alternative medicine should find out if the practitioner incorporates a religious element to his or her practice. If a religious aspect is evident, then Christians should not consult that person. We have found that certain herbal oils are often effective when treating those who are recovering from a stroke or from an orthopedic complaint. But if it is known that the oil has been blessed or subjected to a religious ritual then we do not use it.

This principle applies to many other areas too. The beautiful Indian dances are often used to communicate Hindu ideas, just as the music of Bach and Handel was used to communicate Christian concepts. This does not mean that we cannot use Indian dance forms to communicate Christian ideas. But when young people go to learn these Indian dances they often have to participate in a Hindu ceremony at the start of the class. They need to get prior permission from the teacher not to participate in this, just as Hindus may need to get permission not to participate in a Christian prayer at the start of a school event.

Some practices like transcendental meditation and yoga are overtly religious in their orientation. Such practices are taboo for Christians. In uncertain cases, it is best to avoid participation until one can make a careful study. Paul's guidelines about how to regard food that may have been offered to idols are helpful here (Romans 14–15; 1 Corinthians 8–10).[21]

Many Christian martial arts groups have attempted to respond biblically to this practice, and some have produced literature on the topic.[22] An article appearing in the *Christian Research Journal* has some helpful guidelines for Christians interested in the martial arts. Here is an excerpt:

"We believe the discerning Christian can participate in martial arts so long as he or she (1) studies under an instructor who completely divorces the physical art from faith-destroying Eastern[23] influences; (2) maintains a proper Christian perspective regarding the use of force; (3) is careful not to cause a weaker brother or sister to stumble; and (4) confines the purpose of the practice to self-defense and/or physical conditioning."[24]

On all issues in life it is advisable to develop Christian principles so that we can ensure that we are biblical in what we do. This applies not only to things originating in cultures where other religions are the majority but should also include practices that have developed in supposedly Christian cultures yet incorporate aspects that are inimical to Christian values. For example, Christians must ask how they should biblically apply the principles of competition and of freedom of expression and choice that are prized by many people today, for we see these principles used in many ways that contradict Christianity.

Chapter 5 endnotes

[1] Stephen Neill, *Crises of Belief: The Christian Dialogue with Faith and No Faith* (London: Hodder and Stoughton, 1984), 10.

[2] For an evangelical assessment of *Lumen Gentium,* see Donald McGavran, "Official Roman Catholic Theology of Mission: *Lumen Gentium,*" in Arthur F. Glasser and Donald A. McGavran, *Contemporary Theologies of Mission* (Grand Rapids, MI: Baker Book House, 1983), 195–204. See also David Wright, "The Watershed of Vatican II: Catholic Approaches to Religious Pluralism" in *One God, One Lord: Christianity in a World of Religious Pluralism,* Andrew D. Clarke and Bruce W. Winter, editors (Grand Rapids: Baker Book House, 1992), 207–226.

[3] I. Howard Marshall, "The Acts of the Apostles," *The Tyndale New Testament Commentaries* (Grand Rapids, MI: Wm. B. Eerdmans Publishing Co., 1980), 289.

[4] F. F. Bruce, *First-Century Faith* (Leicester: InterVarsity Press, 1977), 45.

[5] Neill, *Crises of Belief,* 32.

[6] Bruce A. Demarest, *General Revelation* (Grand Rapids, MI: Zondervan Publishing House, 1982), 227–28.

[7] J. H. Bavinck, *The Church Between Temple and Mosque* (Grand Rapids, MI: Wm. B. Eerdmans Publishing Co., 1981 reprint), 15–16.

[8] Demarest, *General Revelation,* 228.

[9] I know a former Hindu who finds it difficult to listen to Shankar because of the associations that Shankar's music has with Hinduism. Perhaps this falls in the same category as meat offered to idols in the Epistles.

[10] S. Wesley Ariarajah, *The Bible and People of Other Faiths* (Geneva: World Council of Churches, and Maryknoll, NY: Orbis Books, 1985), 27.

[11] Ariarajah, *The Bible and People of Other Faiths,* 28.

[12] Leon Morris, *I Believe in Revelation* (Grand Rapids, MI: Wm. B. Eerdmans Publishing Co., 1976) is an excellent non-technical study. Carl F. H. Henry's monumental series, *God, Revelation, and Authority, vols. I–IV: God Who Speaks and Shows* (Waco: Word Books, 1976, reprinted by Wheaton, IL: Crossway Books), deals with almost every conceivable issue related to the doctrine of revelation. See also James Montgomery Boice, *Standing on the Rock: Biblical Authority in a Secular Age* (Grand Rapids, MI: Baker Book House, 1994); *The Foundation of Biblical Authority,* James M. Boice, editor (Grand Rapids, MI: Zondervan Publishing House, 1978); *Scripture and Truth,* D. A. Carson and John D. Woodbridge, editors (Grand Rapids, MI: Zondervan Publishing House, 1983); *Hermeneutics, Authority, and Canon,* Carson and Woodbridge, editors (Grand Rapids, MI: Zondervan Publishing House, 1986); J. I. Packer, *"Fundamentalism" and the Word of God* (Grand Rapids, MI: Wm. B. Eerdmans Publishing Co., 1958); John Wenham, *Christ and the Bible* (Downers Grove, IL: InterVarsity Press, 1972).

[13] Lesslie Newbigin, *The Open Secret* (Grand Rapids, MI: Wm. B. Eerdmans Publishing Co., 1978), 191.

[14] Cited by Randy Frame in *Eternity,* January 1985, 19, 20.

[15] Frame, *Eternity,* 21.

[16] Murray J. Harris, "2 Corinthians," *The Expositor's Bible Commentary,* vol. 10 (Grand Rapids: Zondervan Publishing House, 1976), 359.

[17] An associate professor in a Singaporean university would be equivalent to a full professor in an American University.

[18] For a description of *yin* and *yang* see the description of East Asian Religion in the Appendix.

[19] Isadore Rosenfield, *Dr. Rosenfield's Guide to Alternative Medicine* (New York: Random House, 1996), 32–33.

[20] Rosenfield, *Guide to Alternative Medicine,* 33.

[21] Gary P. Stewart and others, *Basic Questions about Alternative Medicine: What Is Good and What Is Not?* (Grand Rapids, MI: Kregel Publications, 1998) is a helpful little guide. It is produced by the Center for Bioethics and Human Dignity in Bannockburn, IL (E-mail: cbhd@banninst.edu).

[22] Black Belts of the Faith International, a Christian fellowship of martial artists, publishes the *Acts of Faith Quarterly* (P.O. Box 649, Oakley, CA 94561–0649). Bob Orlando has written an article, "Martial Arts and Christian Beliefs: Are They Compatible?" that can be obtained from the following Internet address: http://www.orlandokuntao.com/turning_the_other_cheek.html. I am grateful to my friends, Christian martial artists Donald and Charlaine Engelhardt of the Faith Fighters for Christ Ministry in Ohio, who introduced me to some of this material.

[23] I presume by "Eastern influences" is meant Eastern religious influences, otherwise I too would be excluded! The East cannot be considered any less Christian than the West in today's world. Westerners need to be careful about some of the terminology they use!

[24] Erwin de Castro, B. J. Oropeza and Ron Rhodes, "Enter the Dragon," *Christian Research Journal,* Winter 1994, 24. See their Web site: http: / /www.integrityonline.com/ shockeme/ koinonia/ essays_and_apologetics/christianmartial_arts. htm.

6

GETTING TO KNOW OTHER FAITHS

Paul's speech to the Athenians shows that he had a good understanding of their religion.[1] In his letter to Titus he quoted from one of the prophets of the Cretans (Titus 1:12). Stephen's speech to the Jews exhibited a solid grasp of their history and holy book, which in that case was also the Bible of the Christians.

The early apologists who wrote works that helped shape Christian doctrine and theological method for the rest of Christian history also knew the religious literature of their time well. They expounded Christianity with that context in mind.

It is clear that Paul and these apologists had studied the other religions whose teachings they did not agree with. This was not new for the people of God. The Old Testament hero Daniel and his friends had to master the language and literature of the Babylonians (Daniel 1:4). This was "a polytheistic literature in which magic, sorcery, charms and astrology played a prominent part."[2] Their study was, of course, related to their job and not primarily done with witness in mind. But there is a biblical precedent for studying the literature of the faiths that we will encounter. This will help us present the gospel in a relevant and understandable way.

Means of Learning

There are many ways in which we can get to know other religions. Often it is helpful to read books written by adherents of those religions themselves. The second-best method would be what most Christians will have time for: reading shorter descriptions written by Christians or by other experts.[3] But reading is not the only way to learn.

Getting to know people of other faiths is a good way to go beyond what the books say about these religions and get a sense for the way adherents of these religions think and act. This has been one of the most helpful witnessing tools to me. Even more helpful is trying to share the gospel with them. We do not need to wait until we know these religions well to share the gospel. We can learn while witnessing to them. Listening forms an important ingredient of witness. As they share their convictions and we listen to their objections to what we say, we will begin to learn much about their beliefs.

Another thing we can do is to visit a place of worship. As I was getting ready to write this book I visited Singapore and asked my hosts to arrange for me to see a Chinese Buddhist temple. When I got there I couldn't believe what I was seeing. I knew that Chinese Buddhism was different from the Buddhism in Sri Lanka, but this was so different that it seemed impossible to me that a Buddhist temple could be like this. Later I learned that I had gone to a Taoist and not a Buddhist temple! A few days later I visited a Buddhist temple and saw things I had expected to see. But these two visits were very educational to me as I gained a better understanding of these religions.

Some Christians are reluctant to go to the places of worship of other religions. But this need not be a problem. We are going there not to worship but to observe. Surely the protection of God is with us! It is when we dabble with the practices of these religions that we move into hazardous areas (see chapter 10).

Another way to get a feel for other religions is through the media. Newspapers give us information about what is happening in the world and what people are thinking. John Stott reports that he reads a newspaper that is hostile to Christian values.[4] This is so that he can get a feel, a sense of the way those who need to hear the gospel think.

In Sri Lanka there is a daily newspaper that carries an attack on Christianity almost every day. This is the paper I read, for it gives me an understanding of non-Christian thinking. I know that many Christians prefer to read the paper or the magazine that is closest to their thinking. That is not wrong, and in this world hostile to our values that may be necessary for our survival. But a missionary heart of compassion for the lost may cause us to read what we don't like so that we can effectively share the gospel with those who need to hear it most.

While watching cricket on TV, I suddenly realized that the advertisements were good examples of what I had been reading about postmodern thinking. As a youth worker and a father of teenage children, I decided that I needed to study this further because even in Asia this thinking is having a big influence through the media. My reading on the topic was supplemented by observing what my children were seeing on TV. I began to tell them about postmodernism and the New Age movement and discuss with them some of the ideas that were being presented so attractively and subtly. I also began to read up about some of the popular musicians and to take note of the lyrics of some of the songs they sang. I watched the entertainment news and read reviews of popular movies.

It is extremely important for parents and youth leaders to know what children are hearing over the radio and seeing on TV and in the movies. Pluralism, relativism, and New Age thinking are being presented in a very attractive form. Children need to be made aware of the dangers of these things, not in a harsh, condemnatory manner but through reasoned and informed arguments. Otherwise we may find that our children have imbibed a worldview completely contrary to the Christian one. They may have committed their lives to Christ and may be involved in the youth program in church, but their worldviews are heavily influenced by the popular culture depicted in the media. We may be surprised to find them having attitudes and doing things that we didn't dream possible from committed Christians.[5] We must remember that it is through the media that other ideologies are presented most powerfully to people.

So we have our homework to do, not only so that we can be effective witnesses to those of other faiths but also so that we can protect our own from the insidious influences of the media.

Some Pitfalls

In recent times we have found that some Christians have strayed from biblical Christianity while studying other religions. This happened to some of the early Christian apologists too. They followed Paul's example of quoting from non-Christian writings and studied these faiths. But they made two big errors in the process. First, when trying to accommodate themselves to their audience, they downplayed some of the "offensive" features of Christianity. Second, they accepted some features of the non-Christian religions that were incompatible with Christianity. They set out to contextualize[6] the gospel but ended up diluting it and became syncretists.[7] This still happens today too.

Some believers begin to study non-Christian religions without understanding the supremacy of Christ. During their studies they come to appreciate the good points in these religions, which in itself is not bad. But after prolonged interaction with them, they come to feel that the non-Christian religions may be on a par with Christianity. They end up surrendering the uniqueness of Christ.

Others, who have not fully appreciated the supremacy of Christ, become timid in their witness. They try to be faithful to the revealed Word of God, but they are hesitant to proclaim Christ as the only way to salvation. They may perhaps agree that the way of Christ is the best way. But they don't have the confidence to boldly call non-Christians to make the costly step of forsaking their faiths to follow Christ. So their witness is timid—too timid to encourage the radical step of conversion.

Because of these deviations from the truth by Christians who have delved into other religions, the noble biblical practice of contextualization has fallen into disrepute. Some Christians have gone to the other extreme of advocating that we stay clear of even inquiring about the teachings of other religions. We are advised simply to preach the gospel "the way it has always been done." We are told that to adapt our presentation of the gospel to our audiences is to compromise. If we preach the "plain and simple" gospel, people will come to Christ because of the power of the gospel and the sovereignty of God.

These critics of contextualization cite examples of people from a completely non-Christian background who were instantly transformed through a "simple" gospel presentation. I can attest to such conversions too, and I praise God for them. But we would do wrong to take these isolated instances and make a rule out of them.

It is clear that the witnesses of the Bible, including Jesus, the Supreme Witness, practiced the art of contextualization. What an exciting study of creative communication the evangelistic encounters of Jesus make![8] This is the case with the early apostles too. The record of their evangelistic activity in the book of Acts bears ample evidence of the fact that they knew their audience and their beliefs. They tailored their message in such a way that the unchanging gospel made a powerful impact upon them.[9]

Actually, these evangelistic messages by Jesus and the apostles were also "plain and simple," but they were also relevant and penetrative. We have a motto in Youth for Christ that epitomizes this approach: "Geared to the Times; Anchored to the Rock."

Avoiding the Pitfalls

The mistake made by those who went astray as a result of the study of other faiths was not that they studied these faiths and interacted with their adherents. Their mistake was that while doing so they neglected some of the necessary disciplines of the Christian life.

When a soldier is at the battlefront, he must maintain certain disciplines or he may get himself killed. These disciplines, such as alertness and sticking to the rules of personal safety, are useful in ordinary life too. But they become critical in warfare. In the same way, those who dare to get out of the protection of the "Christian ghetto"—their "comfort zone"—and identify with non-Christians need to be especially alert to the kinds of disciplines all Christians should observe. Three of these disciplines are the Scriptures, the Christian community, and the Great Commission.

The Scriptures. The most important influence in any Christian's life should be God's Word. The effective Christian witness *must* maintain a constant, dynamic contact with the Word of God, the Bible. The Word becomes particularly important when we interact with the heights of non-Christian reasoning. Prolonged contact with such reasoning could cause us to imbibe features that contradict God's Word. There is a great gulf between the highest human thoughts and God's thoughts (Isaiah 55:8–9). Because we are human, we may be influenced in the direction of human thoughts rather than God's thoughts. Human thoughts sometimes seem to fit more naturally with the human mind than God's thoughts. So our thinking needs to be constantly challenged by God's way of thinking, by His principles and values.

One biblical viewpoint under fire today is the uniqueness of Christ. Pluralism seeks to move us in a completely different direction. If we are not in touch with the whole counsel of God it is easy to be swayed by the pluralistic thinking that surrounds us. But if we live close to God's Word, we include the holiness of God into our worldview. This will show us that unbelief is a serious sin. We will realize that the people of other faiths need the Savior. But if we do not spend sufficient time in the Old Testament, it is possible for us to be inadequately influenced by the holiness of God. We will then find it difficult to understand why God should punish unbelief. Then we may buckle under the pressure from the pluralistic thinking that has bombarded us and jettison our belief in the uniqueness of Christ.

So regular and prolonged exposure to the Bible—the Old and the New Testaments—is vitally essential. The Scriptures need to be the atmosphere we live in. The only way I know that one can be influenced in this way is through a daily diet of the Scriptures. This is why Paul, when he was instructing Timothy on how to respond to false teaching, implored him to nourish himself in the truths of the faith and of good teaching (1 Timothy 4:6).

John Stott was asked what are the key requirements for one who wanted to contextualize the gospel. The first thing he said was that this person should know the Word. If we are to study other religions, we must first of all be students of the Bible. It is from the background and the foundation of prolonged exposure to the Scriptures that we expose ourselves to the teachings of other faiths.

Our contact with the Word should also be dynamic. Because the Word is living and active (Hebrews 4:12), its impact upon us should also be living and active. We don't approach the Scriptures only as students to acquire more facts. We go to the Scriptures to hear from God. We go as hungry infants yearning for milk and as obedient servants seeking instructions on how to think and what to do. If this is the type of contact we have with the Scriptures, it will transform us and our thoughts will come into line with God's thoughts.

If our thoughts were God's thoughts, we would see the uniqueness of Christ because God's Word clearly proclaims it. We would also be faithful to the revelation of God in the process of our contextualizing. Our message may be presented in words and methods familiar to non-Christians, but our message itself must spring entirely from the Scriptures. One of the clearest examples of this is Paul's Athenian address, which was clearly biblical even though Paul used the quotes and methods of non-Christian philosophers.[10]

Are we surrendering our intellectual freedom by confining our thinking to the boundaries set by the Scriptures? No! The decision to limit ourselves to the Scriptures is a free choice we have made. We came to accept the fact that the Scriptures contain the truth, and anything that contradicts its affirmations is an untruth. Such a choice was not a blind, unreasonable decision but one based on convincing evidence for the trustworthiness of Scripture. Our decision to live within the confines of Scripture is a free choice we have made, a choice that we believe is the wisest thing we could have done.

The logic of this choice can be explained from nature. I have all the freedom to jump off a high cliff. But I respect the force of gravity and have decided that when it comes to jumping, I confine myself to the boundaries of wisdom suggested by the law of gravity. I know that jumping from a certain height would be harmful to me. I do not feel under bondage because of these facts. Similarly, biblical Christians have chosen to confine their thinking to the boundaries allowed by the Scriptures. But in the Scriptures are contained inexhaustible riches. The opportunities to think creatively within the boundaries set by Scripture are so vast that creative persons have more than enough to explore as long as they live.

Christian Community. The second discipline necessary for effective contextualizing has to do with the need for the contextualizer to be accountable to a body of believers. The community acts as a check to the excesses of creative contextualizers. They may be so eager to identify with non-Christians that they adopt ideas that go beyond the boundaries set by the Scriptures. They may be so excited about an idea that they become blinded to its dangers. Others in the community, who are not so emotionally attached to this idea, serve as the necessary check on the excesses of creative innovators.

The church needs people of a radical disposition who propose bold, new ventures. But it also needs those of a more conservative disposition to give attention to the dangers of deviating from the unchanging, foundational truths of Scripture. Both these types are needed for a community to be healthy. One is a corrective to the excesses of the other. Often the more creative spirits have no patience with the cautious ones, so they become independent. But by doing so they miss out on the enrichment that comes from community life and so minimize the chances of a lastingly effective ministry. Sometimes conservatives are so cautious that they oppose *any* bold venture proposed by prophetic visionaries.

I am not, of course, talking about theological radicals and conservatives. Rather, by "radical" I mean people who, within the foundation of loyalty to Scripture, are willing to try out bold new ways of thought and action. Radicals and conservatives can work together effectively if both are consciously aware that they are subject to the authority of God's Word and if both share a passionate mission orientation. Then, out of the combined input of both groups, a community will emerge that will move forward into bold and exciting ventures for Christ while being faithful to God's eternal principles.

The Great Commission. Implied in what we have just said is the third discipline necessary for contextualization—a continuing commitment to the Great Commission. All Christians who delve into other faiths must bear in mind that their supreme task is to seek to bring people to Christ.

Witnessing is an essential ingredient of a Christian life. For this reason Christ, after His resurrection, kept emphasizing the call to go into all the world. Bishop Vedanayakam Azariah of India used to invite people who had just been baptized to place their hand on their own head and say after him: "I am a baptized Christian: woe unto me if I preach not the gospel."[11] People who are not actively involved in fulfilling the Great Commission are being disobedient to Christ. That is, they are in a backslidden state. It is dangerous for backsliders to be formulating the theology and methodology of the church.

The desire to write about this topic came to me in the mid-1970s when I was a graduate student in a theological seminary. At that time I pushed this desire aside for two reasons. First, I felt I did not have enough experience with other faiths to write such a book. Second, I knew people who had tackled this topic and gave up some of the basic beliefs of Christianity. I feared that I too would stray from faithfulness to God's revealed Word and mission. But some years later, when I felt I needed to work on this project, I had no such fear.[12] I believe one reason for this was that I was actively involved in the work of the Great Commission.

For 25 years now I have been active in ministry that relates evangelistically with non-Christians. I have experienced the power of God at work in the evangelistic outreach of the two Christian communities to which I belong (Youth for Christ and our local church). We have experienced the thrill of being bearers of the gospel of Christ. There is a sense in which the power of the gospel is activated when we launch out into bold ventures of Christian witness. The experience of this power takes away our shame about the "scandal" of the gospel (Romans 1:16) and further fans the flames of passion for evangelism (Romans 1:14–16).

We have seen the joy of those who have come to Christ from other faiths. We know enough of the lives of non-Christians, through personal contact, to be convinced that their greatest need is the salvation that Jesus brings. Involvement in the work of evangelism has increased our love for non-Christians and also deepened our conviction about the uniqueness of Christ. So we do not need to fear interaction with other faiths if we approach it from a background of vital contact with God's Word, of open fellowship and accountability within a Christian community, and of active commitment to the Great Commission.

Chapter 6 endnotes

[1] See the section, "Meeting Them at Their Highest," in chapter 5.
[2] Joyce G. Baldwin, "Daniel, An Introduction and Commentary," The Tyndale Old Testament Commentaries, (Downers Grove, IL: InterVarsity Press, 1978), 80.

[3] I have given examples of such books in the Appendix.

[4] Stott has a helpful discussion on how preachers should get to know what is happening in the world around them, in *I Believe in Preaching* (London: Hodder and Stoughton, 1982), 190–201. The US edition of this book is called *Between Two Worlds* (Grand Rapids, MI: Wm. B. Eerdmans Publishing Co., 1982).

[5] See Charles Colson and Nancy Pearcey, *How Now Shall We Live?* (Wheaton, IL: Tyndale House Publishers, 1999).

[6] I have discussed contextualization in the first section of chapter 4.

[7] I have discussed syncretism in the first section of chapter 4.

[8] For studies of Jesus' method with individuals see Robert E. Coleman, *The Master's Way of Personal Evangelism* (Wheaton, IL: Crossway Books, 1997); and G. Campbell Morgan, *The Great Physician: The Method of Jesus with Individuals* (Old Tappan, NJ: Fleming H. Revell, 1937, 1972).

[9] For a discussion of different evangelistic methods in Acts see F. F. Bruce, *First-Century Faith* (Leicester: InterVarsity Press, 1977). I have a chart describing the different evangelistic situations in Acts with the methods used in my *NIV Application Commentary: Acts* (Grand Rapids, MI: Zondervan Publishing House, 1998), 32–38.

[10] See "When in Athens, Do as the Athenians," in chapter 4.

[11] Cited in John R. W. Stott, *Our Guilty Silence* (Downers Grove, IL: InterVarsity Press, 1967), 59.

[12] Ajith Fernando, *The Christian's Attitude Toward World Religions* (Wheaton, IL: Tyndale House Publishers, and Bombay, GLS, 1987).

7

THE GOD OF THE BIBLE AND OTHER GODS

About 25 years ago the bumper sticker, "Smile, God loves you!" was very popular in the West. Christians assumed that people knew what they meant when the word *God* was used. When we began to concentrate on ministering among non-Christian youth in Sri Lanka we realized that this is an assumption we could not make. It was an assumption that should not have been made in the West either. But today it is much more evident that when we speak of God in the West our hearers may understand something very different from what we understand. In this chapter and the next three we will deal with the Christian and other understandings of God.

The Christian View of God

When Paul described the Christian gospel in the Areopagus in Athens he took a lot of time in his talk to describe what God was like and to respond to his audience's understanding about the divine (Acts 17:23–30). It occupies eight of the ten verses given to the record of this message. The doctrine of God covers all three verses of the short talk that Paul gave in Lystra (Acts 14:15–17). These are the only two evangelistic addresses given to predominantly Gentile audiences that Luke records. The fact that so much space was given to talking about God in both speeches shows how important it is for us to give attention to this topic when ministering to those of other faiths.

When Paul preached to the Jews and God-fearers at the synagogue in Antioch of Pisidia, he did not need to explain such basic things as the fact that God is Creator and that He cannot be represented by idols. There too he began his message by appealing to the activity of God. But he also focused on God's activity in the history of Israel (Acts 13:16–22). All this shows how very important it is to establish a foundation of facts about God before we present God's way of salvation through Christ.

In his Areopagus address Paul makes several affirmations about God, which give us some hints about how to explain the God of the Bible to non-Christians.

1. God is Creator and Lord of the universe: "The God who made the world and everything in it is the Lord of heaven and earth" (17:24a). When speaking to Buddhists and Hindus in Sri Lanka we usually describe God as Creator of the universe. That description demonstrates that God is the One who is supreme over all that is. If this is the case then it would be wise to align oneself with this God. The fact of God's supremacy appears in several of the points mentioned in this listing.

2. God is self-sufficient: "and does not live in temples built by hands. And he is not served by human hands, as if he needed anything, because he himself gives all men life and breath and everything else" (17:24b–25).

3. God made the whole human race out of a common stock: "From one man he made every nation of men, that they should inhabit the whole earth" (17:26a).

4. God is sovereign over the nations: "and he determined the times set for them and the exact places where they should live" (17:26b).

5. God implanted a thirst for the divine in human beings: "God did this so that men would seek him and perhaps reach out for him and find him" (17:27a).

6. God is accessible to humans: "though he is not far from each one of us" (17:27b).

7. Humans depend on God for their existence: "For in him we live and move and have our being" (17:28a).

8. Humans derive their life from God: "As some of your own poets have said, 'We are his offspring'" (17:28b).

9. God cannot be represented by an idol: "Therefore since we are God's offspring, we should not think that the divine being is like gold or silver or stone—an image made by man's design and skill" (17:29).

10. Though God may have overlooked the ignorance of idolatry in the past He now expects repentance from everyone: "In the past God overlooked such ignorance, but now he commands all people everywhere to repent" (17:30).

11. God will one day judge the world through Christ: "For he has set a day when he will judge the world with justice by the man he has appointed" (17:31).

12. God has demonstrated the validity of His gospel through the resurrection of Christ: "He has given proof of this to all men by raising him from the dead" (17:32).

When Paul was describing God in his speech he was likely responding to the two groups he had earlier been debating in Athens, the "Epicurean and Stoic philosophers" (17:18). The Epicureans were like the deists of the modern era who believe that even if there is a God, He is uninvolved in the universe and irrelevant.[1] Though the Stoics believed in a supreme God it was in a pantheistic way, that is, God is in everything, so everything is divine.

The nearness of God and His involvement in the affairs of humans and of the world is presented in points 4, 5, 6, 7, 8, 10, and 11 above. Most of these features could be classified under the immanence of God.

This contradicts the beliefs of the Epicureans. But Paul does not go to the extent of total immanence like the pantheistic Stoics who said that God and the world have the same essence. Though points 7 and 8, taken out of their context, could be interpreted in a pantheistic way, Paul's statements about the transcendence of God and His separateness from creation eliminate that interpretation. Transcendence and/or separateness are proclaimed in points 1, 2, 3, 4, 5, 9, 10, 11, and 12. It is interesting that points 4, 5, 10, and 11 imply both the transcendence and the immanence of God.

Parallels to the Epicureans and the Stoics are represented in several of the major alternate views about God discussed in this book. The parallels to the Epicureans are the atheists and the non-theists like orthodox Buddhists and secular humanists. Hindus and the followers of New Age movements represent the pantheistic view of God.[2] But first we need to reflect on the nature and identity of the gods of other religions.

The Origins of Religion

As we try to understand the phenomenon of the gods of other religions, we must look for the way these religions developed. There are two common approaches to this issue. They both challenge the biblical claim that religion began with a revelation from God. These are the *subjective* and the *evolutionary* approaches to the origins of religion.

The Subjective Approach. This approach emphasizes the idea that religion is essentially a human phenomenon and not the result of divine revelation. We have an instinctive interest in religion. Religious impulses are found in our subconscious (that is, "below the level of conscious awareness") and are more basic to us than what we believe about religion. When these subconscious religious instincts "are brought to consciousness, they are expressed in terms of religious beliefs."[3] So what we believe is an expression of this more basic subconscious religious sense in us.

In his helpful description of this approach, evangelical scholar Winfried Corduan says, "Religious practices function to appease the unrelenting drives of our subconscious, not the demands of the supernatural. In short, all talk about God is really talk about what lies within us as human beings."[4] This approach has been buttressed by the psychological studies of people like Sigmund Freud (1856–1939) and Carl Jung (1875–1961). Essentially then, "Religion is rooted in subjectivity."[5]

Corduan has pointed out that while this approach "can help us understand human nature and the human side of religion, it does not help explain the origin of religion." The question is, did religion originate with God or with humans?[6] The next approach attempts to answer that question.

The Evolutionary Approach. The evolutionary approach claims that religion is the human attempt to answer certain basic questions and challenges. From the earliest times human beings needed to explain how the world, with all its complexity, came into being. People felt insecure because of their inability to control nature, so they began to look for someone bigger than themselves to whom they could go for protection and blessing. They needed to attribute their misfortunes to some source. Gradually humanity developed a belief in ghosts, spirits, demons, and gods to answer its questions. There were gods for different functions and for the protection of different localities. So *animism* (the worship of spirits) and *polytheism* (the worship of many gods) developed.

As societies advanced, the evolutionary theory holds, humans realized that having a supreme ruler for a large area was politically more effective than having many local chiefs. So monarchies emerged. This idea of the supreme ruler was extended to the religious sphere, yielding the belief in a supreme god. The climax of this process was *monotheism*— the belief in one supreme god. The Creator God of the Hebrew prophets and the philosophical monotheism of Plato are said to have paved the way to the "higher forms" of religion.

Carl F. H. Henry regards the evolutionary explanation of religious history as typical of the mood of this age. He says, "In every age philosophers have sought [one] explanatory principle by which to encompass and explain all things." He points out, "In modern times that principle has been the category of evolution."[7] So the development of religion is also explained in terms of evolution.

The Bible affirms the very opposite of the evolutionary view. Scripture describes the first humans, Adam and Eve, as having a warm personal relationship with the one supreme God (Genesis 1–3). The Bible also teaches that the whole human race derives from Adam, as Paul said in his Areopagus address in Athens: "From one man he made every nation of men" (Acts 17:26; see also Romans 5:12–21).

Yet with the Fall, human nature was corrupted and untruths entered the mind. Paul wrote, "They exchanged the truth of God for a lie, and worshiped and served created things rather than the Creator" (Romans 1:25). So human religion deteriorated. The result was polytheism and animism, as well as the other more sophisticated religions. So the biblical view holds to the deterioration of religion rather than to its evolution.

Christians at the turn of the twentieth century had the dilemma of encountering this evolutionary view held by many top scholars. Liberal scholars solved this problem through the documentary hypothesis put forward by Julius Wellhausen, which rearranged the Old Testament to fit the evolution of religion theory. But Wellhausen's reconstruction has now been discredited. Besides, "We also have examples of monotheism and elaborate priestly religion [which Wellhausen considered a later development] long before the time of Abraham."[8]

Anthropological studies carried out in the last century are also giving evidence for the biblical view, which sees the present religious diversity in terms of the deterioration of an original revelation.[9] In the early years of the last century young anthropological students went to so-called primitive cultures and found that most of these cultures held to the idea of a supreme, good God.

Don Richardson relates how these discoveries were embarrassing to many anthropologists because they went against current opinions about the history of religions. They had expected "unadvanced" thoughts about the divine. The so-called advanced concept of a supreme God was a most unexpected discovery because these primitive cultures were not considered to have evolved to the point of developing such an idea. Austrian Wilhelm Schmidt painstakingly recorded these findings and published them in the 1920s as a six-volume work totaling about 4,500 pages. Richardson reports, "Probably 90 percent or more of the folk religions of this planet contain clear acknowledgment of the existence of one Supreme God."[10]

Robert Brow explains what seems to have happened in the following way. "The tribes have a memory of a 'high god,' a benign creator-father-god, who is no longer worshiped because that God is not feared. Instead of offering sacrifice, they concern themselves with the pressing problems of how to appease the vicious spirits of the jungle." Brow then says something that may be true today also: "The threats of the medicine man are more strident than the still small voice of the father-god."[11] Brow says that the evolutionary view cannot be assumed as axiomatic any more. Therefore, "Some anthropologists now suggest that monotheism may be more naturally primitive as a worldview than animism."

African theologian and evangelical leader Tokunboh Adeyemo describes African traditional religion in the following words: "To the African mind, the visible world of nature is not alone; it is enveloped in the invisible spirit world."[12] He says that in African religion "the earth with all of its hosts and the luminaries are believed to have been created and sustained by the Supreme Being."[13] Adeyemo includes four types of entities in his description of the world of spirits: spirit-charged entities, the ancestors, the divinities, and the Supreme Deity who is "at the peak of the cosmic pantheon." This Supreme Deity "is believed to be the owner of the world of humans as well as the spirit world."[14] Yet this God is unapproachable and distant. Elsewhere Adeyemo has shown how Christ brings this distant God near to the people. "Africa's broken rope between heaven and earth has been once and for all re-established in Christ. Africa's God, who, as they say, withdrew from men to the heavens, has now come down to man so as to bring man back to God."[15]

Brow also reminds us that in the Vedic religion of the Aryans, which was the precursor of Hinduism, there was the worship of a supreme God and a regular sacrificial system.[16] This is true of most of the primitive religions of the world. Stephen Neill, who was an English missionary to India and a great scholar, refers to "the immense part that the idea and practice of sacrifice have played in the thoughts and the worship of the human race as far back as we can trace clearly human consciousness."[17] We note that in the first chapters of Genesis this is the heart of the religion of the first humans. They worshiped the supreme God and offered sacrifices to Him when they sinned.

How then did sacrifices for sin disappear from most of the major religions? Brow says, "There came a time when Buddha in India, Confucius in China, and the Greek philosophers reacted against the animal sacrifices of a corrupt priesthood." The result was that "the main non-Christian world religions were built on other premises."[18] But the fact remains that there was a time when there was a universal recognition of a supreme God and of the need for sacrifices for sin.

Often when missionaries have gone out and proclaimed the gospel to primitive animistic tribes, their hearers automatically identify the Christian God with their supreme God, a fact that has simplified the Bible translator's task. Lesslie Newbigin says, "In almost all cases where the Bible has been translated into languages of the non-Christian peoples of the world, the New Testament word *Theos* [Greek for 'God'] has been rendered by the name given by the non-Christian peoples to the One whom they worship as Supreme Being."[19] Bible translations consultant Eugene Nida has said that where translators tried to evade the issue by simply transliterating the

Greek or Hebrew word, the converts would explain this foreign word in the text of their Bibles by using the indigenous name for God.[20]

Giving a name for the God of the Bible has not been as simple as may be inferred by what was just said. All ideas of the supreme God in pre-Christian cultures are inadequate. Taiwanese-born Chinese-American pastor Tsu-Kung Chuang explains the process that took place in the Chinese language.[21] Traditional Chinese religion had two words for the Supreme Deity, each of which gained prominence at different times in its history. They are *Shang-di* (meaning "Lord on high") and *Tian* (meaning "heaven"). The early Roman Catholic missionaries gave the name *Tian Zhu* (meaning "Lord in heaven") to God. But some were not happy with this and simply used *Deusu* from the Latin for God, *deus*.

"Protestant translators of the Bible, on the other hand, also struggled between the two terms [for God], with *Shang-di* being used predominantly in early (late nineteenth century) translations." Later another word, *Shen*, became popular. "Shen in Chinese ancient pictography means the heavenly being who is the source and origin of all things. But in later Chinese literature *Shen* might also represent the good heavenly spirit."[22] Yet even here, though there was controversy about what name to use, we see that the idea of a supreme God was there in the ancient Chinese traditions.

So we have said that the belief in many gods by many of the peoples of the world is the result of the deterioration of religion as it revolted from God's original revelation to the human race. But who are the gods that people worship today?

Who Are the Gods of the Other Faiths?

All Manifestations of the Same God? The major affirmation of pluralists within and without the Christian church is that the same God is worshiped in all religions. They speak of "the Hindu conception of God," "the Muslim conception of God," and "the Christian conception of God." They say that God is so vast that no one tradition can fully understand Him. The Qur'an has what the Muslims have discovered about God out of their unique cultural experience. The Bhagavad Gita has what the Hindus have discovered and the Bible has what the Jews and the Christians have discovered. So they prefer to speak of "the Muslim understanding of God," "the Hindu understanding of God."

In all of these understandings the object is the same God. World Council of Churches leader and Sri Lankan Methodist minister Wesley Ariarajah, who advocates this pluralistic approach, says that Christians are guilty of polytheism when they talk of "the Christian God" and "the Hindu God."[23] This is an important issue today and we need to look at it from the biblical perspective.

The God of Islam. Islam arose after the Bible was written, so the Bible does not have anything to say about it. One of the present controversies among evangelical Christians is on whether Allah, the God of Islam, is the same as the Christian God, and whether it is appropriate to call God Allah when working with Muslims. Some say Allah is an unbiblical spirit and not the God of the Bible.[24] Others—and I fall into this category—say that this is the same God we worship, though the worship of God in Islam is not acceptable in terms of the biblical teaching on how God should be worshiped.[25] This is reminiscent of Paul's words to the Athenians that he was introducing to them the "Unknown God" whom they worshiped in ignorance (Acts 17:22–23). In chapter 3 we showed that Paul did not say here that God accepted this worship because he later called the people to repent of their old ways and turn to God.

The Qur'an explicitly states that the God described there is the same as the God of the Christians: "We believe in what has been sent down to us and what has been sent down to you. Our God and your God are one, and to him we are submissive" (Sura 29:45).[26] Christians in countries like Egypt call God "Allah."

In some Muslim countries like Malaysia, Christians would like to use the name Allah, but they are legally prohibited from doing so. The people of Mecca worshiped many deities at the time that Islam originated. But the people also knew and worshiped Allah, to whom they gave a tithe and prayed for safety.[27] William Miller explains, "In the Arabic language 'Allah' means 'The God,' and it seems that the Arabs recognized Him as the Supreme God. Whether they learned of Him from the Jews or inherited this knowledge from their ancestor Abraham is not evident."[28]

If we believe that the God whom Muslims seek to worship is the God of the Bible, then our evangelistic strategy will be influenced by it. We will need to focus on how we can introduce Muslims to the salvation that God has provided for the human race. We must seek to show them how they can establish a personal relationship with God and worship Him aright.

The God of the Jews. While there are Christians who may dispute the claim that Christians and Muslims worship the same God, hardly anyone would dispute the claim that Christians worship the same God as the Jews. But here we not only seek to worship the same God; we also look for guidance to the same revelation: the Old Testament. In evangelizing Jews much emphasis will need to be given to the Old Testament anticipation of Christ, and how Christ is the fulfillment of what the Old Testament looks forward to. More stress should be placed on the practice of religion as prescribed in the Old Testament, incorporating practices that the Gentile churches discarded because they were specific to the Jews. This is seen in many of the messianic Jewish congregations which are patterned much more according to the Old Testament than the typical Gentile churches.

Many Christians today claim that, because of the common roots in the Old Testament and the fact that we worship the same God, we do not need to engage in evangelism of the Jews. This is clearly contradicted by the teaching of the New Testament. Paul was vivid in his description in Romans 9–11 of the lostness of the Jews apart from faith in Christ. They can come to God only through Jesus Christ. Just a few verses from this section of Scripture are sufficient to give us a sense of Paul's strong feelings about this. In Romans 9 he reflected on the unbelief of the Jews and how that can be explained in terms of the sovereign call of God. Then in 10:1–4 he describes his desire to see them saved and explains why they are not:

> Brothers, my heart's desire and prayer to God for the Israelites is that they may be saved. For I can testify about them that they are zealous for God, but their zeal is not based on knowledge. Since they did not know the righteousness that comes from God and sought to establish their own, they did not submit to God's righteousness. Christ is the end of the law so that there may be righteousness for everyone who believes.

Romans 10:12–15 points out that both Jews and Gentiles find salvation in the same way—through the preaching of Christ which leads people to believe in Christ:

> For there is no difference between Jew and Gentile—the same Lord is Lord of all and richly blesses all who call on him, for, "Everyone who calls on the name of the Lord will be saved." How, then, can they call on the one they have not believed in? And how can they believe in the one of whom they have not heard? And how can they hear without someone preaching to them? And how can they preach unless they are sent?

In 10:16–17 Paul summarizes by saying that the Jews can come to salvation only through exercising faith for which it is necessary for the word of Christ to be proclaimed. Second, not all Jews have accepted God's offer of salvation.

> But not all the Israelites accepted the good news. For Isaiah says, "Lord, who has believed our message?" Consequently, faith comes from hearing the message, and the message is heard through the word of Christ.

Only One God for All People. Roman Catholic scholar Raymond Panikkar, in his influential book *The Unknown Christ of Hinduism,* applies Paul's statement about the Athenians worshiping the unknown God (Acts 17:23) to the gods of Hinduism. He argues that Hindus worship the same God as Christians and that God mediates salvation to them through Christ, though he is unknown to them. Panikkar says that God accepts the religious practices of these people as the means through which salvation is mediated.[29] In chapter 4 we argued that this passage implies that God did *not* accept the worship of the Unknown God by the Athenians. That is why Paul said that they must repent (17:30). But this approach to other gods is a growing one in today's world.

In the Bible there is a strong and unequivocal rejection of all other gods with severe punishment being meted out to the Jews for worshiping these gods. The first two of the Ten Commandments show this:

> 1. You shall have no other gods before me.
> 2. You shall not make for yourself an idol in the form of anything in heaven above or on the earth beneath or in the waters below. You shall not bow down to them or worship them; for I, the Lord your God, am a jealous God, punishing the children for the sin of the fathers to the third

and fourth generation of those who hate me, but showing love to a thousand [generations] of those who love me and keep my commandments (Exodus 20:3–6).

The strong words, "jealous God," are used to describe God's reaction to the worship of other gods. Whether these gods are real or imaginary beings is not always mentioned. But they are clearly not the same as the God of the Bible. They are presented as rivals to the God of the Bible. Indeed Paul equated the anonymous god of the Athenians with the God of the Bible, but he did not do so with their other gods. We are told that he was "greatly distressed" by the idols he saw there (Acts 17:16). The altar to the Unknown God was a confession by the Athenians that the many gods they had were not enough. They needed something or someone more. Paul was saying that this someone is the God who created the world (17:24).

It may be argued that the strong words about other gods were addressed to the Jews and that this does not apply to the other nations, for whom salvation could be received through their gods. But whenever the Old Testament speaks of the salvation of the Gentiles it is through their turning to the God of the Jews. This lies at the heart of the message of the book of Jonah. Isaiah has much to say about this. For example, he says of the Egyptians:

> In that day five cities in Egypt will speak the language of Canaan and swear allegiance to the Lord Almighty. One of them will be called the City of Destruction. In that day there will be an altar to the Lord in the heart of Egypt, and a monument to the Lord at its border. It will be a sign and witness to the Lord Almighty in the land of Egypt. When they cry out to the Lord because of their oppressors, he will send them a savior and defender, and he will rescue them. So the Lord will make himself known to the Egyptians, and in that day they will acknowledge the Lord. They will worship with sacrifices and grain offerings; they will make vows to the Lord and keep them. The Lord will strike Egypt with a plague; he will strike them and heal them. They will turn to the Lord, and he will respond to their pleas and heal them (Isaiah 19:18–22).

Isaiah 56:6–7 speaks of people from all nations.

> And foreigners who bind themselves to the Lord to serve him, to love the name of the Lord, and to worship him, all who keep the Sabbath without desecrating it and who hold fast to my covenant—these I will bring to my holy mountain and give them joy in my house of prayer. Their burnt offerings and sacrifices will be accepted on my altar; for my house will be called a house of prayer for all nations (see also Isaiah 24:14–16).

The Messianic servant of Yahweh is going to be "a light for the Gentiles" (Isaiah 42:6; 47:6).

Who or What Are the Other Gods? If the Bible accepts only one God as legitimate but mentions many gods in its pages, how do we explain the existence of these gods? The Bible often says that these gods are not gods. Deuteronomy 32:21 says, "They made me jealous by what is no god and angered me with their worthless idols" (see also Jeremiah 2:11; 5:7; 16:20). The parallelism in this verse suggests that what is called "no god" here are actually idols. This is clearer in Jeremiah 2:11: "Has a nation ever changed its gods? (Yet they are not gods at all.) But my people have exchanged their Glory for worthless idols" (see also Isaiah 37:19; Jeremiah 16:20). So the Bible is clear about the impotence of idols in comparison with God.

The declaration of the impotence of other gods does not imply that there are no other beings who are worshiped as gods. William Dyrness points out, "The highest statement of pure monotheism [in the Old Testament] comes with the Major Prophets." Yet about other gods he says, "Even here [the Major Prophets] the stress is on their worthlessness rather than on their non-existence: they cannot hear or answer prayer; therefore, they are no gods at all."[30]

In Galatians, Paul stated that these "no gods" had enslaved the Galatians prior to their conversion, even though in comparison to what they have in Christ these "principles" are "weak and miserable." Paul says, "Formerly, when you did not know God, you were slaves to those who by nature are not gods. But now that you know God—or rather are known by God—how is it that you are turning back to those weak and miserable principles? Do you wish to be enslaved by them all over again?" (Galatians 4:8–9).

The word translated "principles" (*stoicheia*) in Galatians 4:9 could refer to supernatural forces. So here he may be implying that these gods are demons. But there is no unanimity among scholars about this interpretation. Other passages present even more clearly the truth that gods of other peoples are demons. Deuteronomy 32:16–17 says, "They made him jealous with their foreign gods and angered him with their detestable idols. They sacrificed to demons, which are not God—gods they had not known, gods that recently appeared, gods your fathers did not fear." Psalm 106:36–37 says, "They worshiped their idols, which became a snare to them. They sacrificed their sons and their daughters to demons." Paul says in 1 Corinthians 10:19–20, "Do I mean then that a sacrifice offered to an idol is anything, or that an idol is anything? No, but the sacrifices of pagans are offered to demons, not to God, and I do not want you to be participants with demons."[31]

Demons are beings belonging to the spiritual world who are opposed to the work of God and have some powers. This may account for the power that we see displayed in other religions. *Newsweek* magazine contained an article on miracles, which showed how many religious traditions had instances of miraculous powers being unleashed through their religious practices.[32]

This should not surprise us, for the Bible also accepts the existence of this phenomenon. The Egyptian magicians were able to perform some of the miracles that Moses performed though Moses' snake swallowed up the snakes of the Egyptian magicians (Exodus 7). Demons sometimes publicly expressed their recognition of who Jesus was (Matthew 8:29; Luke 4:41; Acts 19:15), demonstrating that they had cognitive powers beyond those of humans.

Are we then to attribute to demons the good deeds that are done by modern-day miracle workers who do not acknowledge Christ? This seems rather harsh, as they seem to be doing some very wholesome things like healing people of diseases. Take the example of Satya Sai Baba, whose disciples consider him to be an incarnation of the god Shiva (that is, an avatar).[33] He is possibly the most influential Indian guru in the world today, with disciples all over the world. Not only do his devotees claim that he has performed many miracles and done much good for suffering people, some also say that by his miraculous insight they have been able to stop living immoral lives. Do demons do "good things" like this?

Some Christians have felt that they should not attribute the powers of people like Sai Baba to demons because of the great good that they seem to be doing. In fact Sai Baba has many followers among churchgoing "Christians" today.

When Youth for Christ in Sri Lanka had an article exposing Sai Baba, one of his "Christian" devotees said that on matters like this it would be wise to be safe rather than sorry. That is, it would be best not to take a public stand against Sai Baba, even if we did not believe in him. The implication is that, if he were indeed a legitimate god, we would be doing something for which we would ultimately be sorry.

Yet the Bible is clear that powerful forces that take people away from Christ are to be denounced. Many people are closed to the gospel because they are devotees of people like Sai Baba. When we say, "Jesus is great," they would say, "Sai Baba is also great. You follow Jesus, and we will follow Sai Baba." This shows us that though Sai Baba may do many "good things," he is guilty of the very serious sin of keeping people from seeing the light of the gospel of Christ.

Paul says that this is the work of Satan: "The god of this age has blinded the minds of unbelievers, so that they cannot see the light of the gospel of the glory of Christ, who is the image of God" (2 Corinthians 4:4). Some interpreters say that Paul is talking about God here.[34] But Paul also said, "Satan himself masquerades as an angel of light. It is not surprising, then, if his servants masquerade as servants of righteousness" (2 Corinthians 11:14–15). So we can understand how the Bible gives warrant for us to view some things which seem to be very good and wholesome as actually being demonic.

In this age when inter-religious tolerance is deemed a high virtue, it is difficult for us to uphold the view that some features of other religions are demonically inspired. Many understand tolerance to mean that one must not reject anything in another religion as wrong. We are supposed to "be nice" when it comes to inter-religious relations.

But when we realize that Christ is the only way to salvation and that other ways can keep people from coming to Christ, we see the damage these other ways inflict—even though they seem to be wholesome and helpful.

Pluralism has bred an understanding of "niceness" that is very dangerous. Pluralism keeps people from the truth that sets them free (John 8:32).

Chapter 7 endnotes

1 Craig S. Keener, *The IVP Bible Background Commentary: New Testament* (Downers Grove, IL: InterVarsity Press, 1993), 824, 372.

2 This connection is made in David K. Clark and Norman L. Geisler, *Apologetics in the New Age: A Christian Critique of Pantheism* (Grand Rapids, MI: Baker Book House, 1990), 7.

3 Winfried Corduan, *Neighboring Faiths: A Christian Introduction to World Religions* (Downers Grove, IL: InterVarsity Press, 1998), 24. I am indebted to Corduan's description of the subjective approach for many of the points given here. The reader is directed to his book for a concise description.

4 Corduan, *Neighboring Faiths,* 22.

5 Corduan, *Neighboring Faiths,* 24.

6 Corduan, *Neighboring Faiths,* 24.

7 Carl F. H. Henry, God, *Revelation, and Authority/ vol. I: God Who Speaks and Shows* (Waco: Word Books, 1976, reprinted by Wheaton, IL: Crossway Books), 40.

8 Robert Brow, "Origins of Religion," *Eerdmans' Handbook to the World's Religions* (Grand Rapids, MI: Wm. B. Eerdmans Publishing Co., 1994), 31.

9 Don Richardson has made these insights from anthropology available from a non-technical viewpoint in his book, *Eternity in Their Hearts* (Ventura, CA: Regal Books, 1981), chapter 1.

10 Richardson, *Eternity in Their Hearts,* 44.

11 Brow, "Origins of Religion," 31.

12 Tokunboh Adeyemo, "Unapproachable God: The High God of African Traditional Religion," in *The Global God: Multicultural Evangelical Views of God,* Aida Besancon Spencer and William David Spencer, editors (Grand Rapids, MI: Baker Book House, 1998), 130.

13 Adeyemo, "Unapproachable God," 131.

[14] Adeyemo, "Unapproachable God," 136.

[15] Tokunboh Adeyemo, *Salvation in African Tradition* (Nairobi: Evangel, 1979), 96. Cited in "The God above Tradition Who Speaks to All Traditions: An African (Ghanaian) Perspective," in *The Global God,* 165.

[16] Brow, "Origins of Religion," 32. Brow refers to their religion as *henotheism,* the worship of the same god but using different names to refer to him. He says it was only later that this developed into polytheism.

[17] Stephen Neill, *The Supremacy of Jesus* (London: Hodder and Stoughton, 1984), 138.

[18] Brow, "Origins of Religion," 30.

[19] Lesslie Newbigin, *The Open Secret* (Grand Rapids, MI: Wm. B. Eerdmans Publishing Co., 1978), 192.

[20] Cited by Newbigin, *The Open Secret,* 192.

[21] Tsu-Kung Chuang, "Shang-di: God from the Chinese Perspective," in *The Global God,* 189–206.

[22] *Tsu-Kung, Shang-di,* 205–06.

[23] Wesley Ariarajah, *The Bible and People of Other Faiths* (Geneva: World Council of Churches, 1985; reprinted by Maryknoll, NY: Orbis Books), 10.

24 Abd-Al-Masih, *Who Is Allah in Islam?* (Villach, Austria: Light of Life, n.d.), 65–68.

[25] See John Gilchrist, *Our Approach to Islam: Charity or Militancy?* (Benoni, South Africa: Jesus to the Muslim, 1990), 14–28.

[26] *The Qur'an: A Modern English Version,* translated by Majid Fakhry (Reading: Garnet Publishing, 1997).

[27] *Ishmael My Brother: A Christian Introduction to Islam,* Anne Cooper, compiler (Tunbridge Wells, UK: MARC, 1993), 63–64.

[28] William M. Miller, *A Christian's Response to Islam* (Phillipsburg, NJ: Presbyterian and Reformed Publishing Co., 1976), 14.

29 Raymond Panikkar, *The Unknown Christ of Hinduism,* revised edition (Maryknoll, NY: Orbis Books, 1981).

[30] William Dyrness, *Themes in Old Testament Theology* (Downers Grove, IL: InterVarsity Press; and Carlisle, UK: Paternoster Press, 1977), 49.

[31] See the forthcoming book on "Food Offerings in Chinese Folk Religion" by Charles Lowe, to which I am indebted for some of what is written here.

[32] "What Miracles Mean," *Newsweek,* May 1, 2000, 45–50.

[33] On avatars, see the section "Incarnation and Avatar" in chapter 12.

34 This was a popular view in the early centuries adopted by Chrysostom and Ambrosiaster. See *Ancient Christian Commentary on Scripture,* New Testament VII, 1–2 Corinthians, Gerald Bray, editor (Downers Grove, IL: InterVarsity Press, 1999), 228.

8

PANTHEISM: ALL IS GOD

Perhaps no view of God grew so rapidly in the twentieth century to rival the Christian view as much as pantheism. This is not to say that this is a new view. Varieties of pantheism have been in existence for millennia in both the East and the West. Much of early Greek philosophy and Stoicism were pantheistic, and so are most forms of Hinduism and some forms of Buddhism.

Today pantheism is found in various different forms,[1] but at the base of most of these forms is what we call *monism,* which is a philosophy that views everything in the universe as being the extension of one reality. It is often described with the words "all is one." When we bring in the concept of the God, then monism extends to pantheism, the idea that "all is God." The term is derived from the Greek *pan* meaning "all" and *theos* meaning "God"; that is literally, "all-god." As David Clark and Norman Geisler explain, in pantheism "there may be forms or levels of reality, but in the final analysis, all reality is unified ontologically, that is, in its being. No qualitative distinctions can differentiate kinds of real things."[2] God is the ultimate reality, and we are all part of God. But so are all things. Plants, animals, and inanimate objects like books and tables are all part of God. We can see how, with an approach like this, "the idea of a personal God is abandoned in favor of an impersonal energy, force or consciousness."[3]

Pantheism is a vast topic, but the discussion here will be confined to only four areas that are important for us in understanding its present popularity.

The Appeal of Divinity

Over 50 years ago when most observers had not detected the growth of pantheism in the West, C. S. Lewis highlighted both its popularity and its appeal in his book *Miracles*.[4]

Lewis's comments are so good and so prophetic that they will be quoted extensively. His point is that humans in their natural state do not like the holy God of the Bible with His plans for us and demands upon us. Instead they prefer an ethereal life force that makes no such demands but gives them the satisfaction of having some sort of religious experience without the demands of a holy and purposeful God. He presents the appeal of pantheism thus: "Speak about beauty, truth and goodness, or about a God who is simply the indwelling principle of these three, speak about a great spiritual force pervading all things, a common mind of which we are all parts, a pool of generalized spirituality to which we can all flow, and you will command friendly interest."

Lewis contrasts this with the response to the biblical idea of God: "But the temperature drops as soon as you mention a God who has purposes and performs particular actions, who does one thing and not another, a concrete, choosing, commanding, prohibiting God with a determinate character. People become embarrassed or angry."[5]

We must remember that the basic sin of the human race is rebellion against the supreme God who makes a claim to be Lord of our lives. In his Areopagus address Paul presented God as Lord of heaven and earth (17:24), as sovereign over the nations (17:26), as impossible to be represented by idols (17:29). Then he said that God calls all people to repent (17:30) in order to be ready for the coming judgment (17:31). All this can be summarized under the designation "the transcendence of God." This is a sharp challenge to rebellious human beings. In their rebellion they would prefer a view of the divine that is not so specific as to its character and demands. Pantheism not only meets these requirements but also proclaims that humans are god.

Swami Muktananda, an Indian guru who is popular in America, says, "Kneel to your own self. Honor and worship your own being. God dwells within you as you!"[6] That certainly sounds better to self-sufficient people rebelling from the lordship of God than a call to repentance from sin and to submission to God. Therefore Lewis says that pantheism "is the attitude into which the human automatically falls when left to itself."[7] So we must not be surprised that pantheism is growing in the West among those who have rejected the biblical idea of God.

Yet the transcendence of God described above must be balanced with what Paul says of the immanence of God. We saw in the last chapter that immanence is the term that is used to represent the nearness or presence or indwelling of God in creation. Here, of course, we are a little closer to the pantheist, and this could become a point of contact for witness. At the Areopagus Paul says that God is accessible to humans ("He is not far from each one of us," 17:27), that we depend on God for our existence ("in him we live and move and have our being," 17:28a), and that we derive our life from God ("We are his offspring," 17:28b).

In biblical religion the combination of the transcendence and immanence of God results in the only relationship which truly satisfies the deep yearning of the soul. This is our main argument in our discussion of spirituality in chapter 11. We enter into a loving relationship with a God who is higher than we are. In this relationship there is freedom from the guilt of sin because our sins are forgiven. There is great peace and security because the God who is committed to us is greater than all the challenges of life. There is joy emerging from the experience of God's love, forgiveness, and acceptance. And there is bright hope for the future because we know that the one who holds the future also holds our hands. And when He seeks to relate to us, He does not force His way into our lives. He honors us by giving us the freedom to choose Him as our Lord and Savior.

We have said that contemporary people are revolting against the idea of submitting to a God to whose lordship they need to yield. Unfortunately many people have been exposed to bad examples of leadership that may affect their decision to reject the idea of the lordship of God over their lives. But the model of God's transcendence and immanence, His holiness, and His love is the perfect model that meets the yearnings of all humans for good leadership. This Leader, this Father, is one we respect because of His greatness and holiness. But He is also one with whom we can be affectionately intimate because of His grace in providing a way of salvation for us that results in an intimate relationship with Him. There is great security in having leaders and fathers who can be trusted and respected and also who can be loved intimately. God meets this need in the human soul perfectly.

Yet the benefits of the transcendence and immanence of God are for those who humble themselves before God. As Isaiah 57:15, "For this is what the high and lofty One says—he who lives forever, whose name is holy: 'I live in a high and holy place, but also with him who is contrite and lowly in spirit, to revive the spirit of the lowly and to revive the heart of the contrite.'" Our task is to show this to the world. Indeed pantheism is attractive to people in their natural state. But as the proverb says, "All that glitters is not gold."

A Reaction to Radical Individualism

Indian Christian apologist and social reformer Vishal Mangalwadi has connected the growth of pantheism with the radical individualism of the West that many are reacting against. In pantheism there is a natural undermining of individuality that comes because individuals are identified with the divine. Mangalwadi shows how Hindu mystics compare the oneness of humans with the divine with the oneness of the wave with the ocean. He explains, "The ocean is real, but the wave's individuality is only a temporary phenomenon of the ocean. It is not really real." Sometimes the individual will have a mystical experience through something like transcendental meditation. Then his or her consciousness merges with the divinity that is at the heart of everything. This is sometimes called *samadhi*. This is like the wave merging back into the ocean.

This understanding of the relationship between the individual and the whole gave rise to the idea "that our individuality was ultimately an illusory, limited experience. The wave seems real while it lasts, but it disappears back into being the ocean."[8] This lies at the base of the Hindu idea of *maya,* which is used to describe the illusory nature of the everyday reality. Geisler and Clark explain, "Maya does not imply . . . non-existence. Rather, maya acknowledges that the world is something, but it is not what it appears; it is really Brahman [or the Absolute God, the Ultimate Reality]."

The biblical understanding of the person is very different from this. We are creations of God but are distinct from God. In Paul's Areopagus speech he agreed with the pantheist that God is Creator (17:24) and that we are totally dependent on Him for our existence (17:28). But the pantheist says that God created the world out of Himself. As C. S. Lewis puts it, the pantheist thinks that we are parts of God or contained in Him, whereas the Christian sees the relationship with God in terms of Maker and made.[9] We know that we are distinct individuals because the Bible says that we retain our identity after death. We recognize others and we know who we are. We are conscious of the fact that the judgment we receive is based on the way we lived our life on earth. No such permanent individuality is found in the pantheist understanding. There when people are reincarnated in another life, they have no memory of their past lives.

In the West, however, individualism seems to have been taken to an extreme. Even in the church there is little understanding of the glorious truth of the body of Christ through which we share solidarity with other Christians that is so deep that the theologians described it as a "mystical union." Unfortunately, many Christians like to guard their individuality so much that they do not know the type of spiritual accountability, interdependence, and unity about which the New Testament speaks.[10] Radical individualism was a feature of the modern era that postmodern people are reacting against. And it seems that along with a new stress upon community some have gone to the extreme of espousing pantheism, which, as we saw, undermines individuality.

The damage caused by the undermining of the individual is seen in the East where the religious environment permitted some people to be treated as "untouchables" resulting in the depriving of basic human rights to millions. Though today much of the West has rejected Christianity, its present emphasis on human rights grew during its Christian era and was certainly influenced by the Christian emphasis on the value of the individual.

Yet the critics of Christianity would point to the slavery and apartheid that co-existed with Christianity in many Western nations. These two scars upon the history of Western civilization are alien to Christian belief and indeed hostile to it. They could only have been tolerated in the church through selfishness, which blinded people's eyes to the truth, or through ignorance or misrepresentation of God's Word, which gave them the license to pursue these unchristian practices. Often it is Christians, like William Wilberforce in England and Desmond Tutu in South Africa, who battled to rid their nations of these terrible practices.

In biblical Christianity we see the beautiful combination of the recognition of the worth of an individual with the recognition of the importance of community for healthy living. Christian community life is the only form that will answer the postmodern quest for community in the West. In the East, where community solidarity was so strong for centuries, we are suddenly faced with social changes that are shaking the existing community structure at its roots. Both Buddhism and Hinduism have little concept of community to help people tide this. I do not think the socio-religious ties that powerfully bind the Muslim community together will be sufficient to enable the next generation of Muslims to find an authentic life in this postmodern world with its complex moral, ethical, and social challenges.

Biblical community is the answer for the groping for authentic community that we are seeing in both East and West in this twenty-first century. During the time of the early church, people would comment on how Christians loved each other, and this was a powerful means of attracting people to Christ. The present worldwide search for community could be a great opportunity to the church. If we practice true biblical community people would realize that this is what they are looking for, and an evangelistic harvest could result. But we must first get our act together. Often our church structures are derived from the corporate world. So we may be exhibiting the very problems that people are trying to find a solution to.[11] If we are to seize this opportunity we will need to restore biblical Christian community life. That will attract the world. Such community life will be characterized by the value placed on each and every individual and also by a solidarity that will enable Christians to be truly helpful to each other.

The Deification of Nature

As nature is also a part of the divine in pantheism, there is a very "high" view of nature in Western pantheism. It is very fashionable now for people to claim that they worship nature. In fact Western New Age analysts like Theodore Roszak are blaming Christians for pronouncing nature dead and removing its sacredness.[12] They blame us for the development of secular humanism because we made God so distant making it possible for people to forget Him entirely. This opened the door, they say, for the present ecological crisis.[13] Besides, they say, the Protestant work ethic was so productivity-oriented that in their quest for productivity people exploited nature to such an extent that the environment was neglected. So New Age people are in the forefront of ecological activism today.

How Do Christians Respond to This Situation? The Bible as God's full revelation to humanity must give the fullest answer that meets the aspirations of people represented in the various approaches to nature found in the world today. However, we as a church may have missed out major portions of this revelation owing to our cultural blinds.

How Should Christians View Nature? We can highlight three important principles in the Scriptures that will help us at this time. First, we are called to care for the earth. God gave Adam a clear mandate about this as two texts from Genesis show: "Be fruitful and increase in number; fill the earth and subdue it. Rule over the fish of the sea and the birds of the air and over every living creature that moves on the ground" (1:28) and "The Lord God took the man and put him in the Garden of Eden to work it and take care of it" (2:15). Though John Calvin and his "Protestant work ethic" are often blamed for the neglect of the environment in the modern era, Calvin's comments on Genesis 2:15 have a clear call to humans to look after the creation with care.[14] Therefore Christians are committed to ecology and to protecting the environment. If some Christians did not do this, that is because they have not obeyed the clear instructions of the Scriptures. So we should support the efforts of Christians and others to protect the environment whenever that is possible within Christian principles.

Second, we have a very high place given to creation because it is a mouthpiece of God. This was discussed the chapter 5. David said, "The heavens declare the glory of God; the skies proclaim the work of his hands" (Psalm 19:1). He follows this affirmation with an impressive description of how creation speaks to us about God (Psalm 19:2–6). Canadian poet Margaret Clarkson in the preface to a book about nature says, "Everything I see around me shouts to me of God, whether at the river or around the ravine at my suburban home in Toronto."[15] She is echoing one of the most important things that the Bible says about nature. Nature is a mouthpiece of God through which He communicates with humans.

In his evangelistic message in Lystra, Paul described the voice of nature as a testimony to God. He said, "Yet he has not left himself without testimony: He has shown kindness by giving you rain from heaven and crops in their seasons; he provides you with plenty of food and fills your hearts with joy" (Acts 14:17). In Romans he said that people have a responsibility to respond to this knowledge communicated through nature: "For since the creation of the world God's invisible qualities—his eternal power and divine nature—have been clearly seen, being understood from what has been made, so that men are without excuse" (Romans 1:20).

Third, the Bible presents nature as a thing of beauty to be delighted in. This feature about nature is beautifully discussed in C. S. Lewis's book, *Reflections on the Psalms*. He points out that because the Psalms emerged from an agricultural society we find the psalmists approaching nature from a gardener's or farmer's interest. So we find references to rams, grass, vine, and oil. But they go beyond this. "Their gusto, or even gratitude, embraces things that are no use to man."[16] So God is praised for things like lions and whales (Psalm 104:21, 26). Lewis says that because Christians view all of nature as God's creation, to us nature is more than a resource for a fruitful life. It is a thing of beauty to delight in.

The Jewish psalmists then had a very high view of nature, higher than that of their neighbors who viewed nature as divine. But this divinity was not as high as the biblical understanding of God, for all nature was part of it. The Jews, on the other hand, saw nature as the creation of and bearer of messages from the supreme and almighty Creator of the universe. So as Lewis says, "The same doctrine which empties Nature of her divinity also makes her an index, a symbol, a manifestation, of the Divine."[17] And because we have such a high view of the Divine we say that our view of nature is higher than that of the pantheists. We have a higher view of nature than that of the naturalists also. By refusing to go beyond the confines of scientific study they reduce nature into a datum to study whereas we view it as an achievement to be delighted in.

The present interest in creation therefore could be a steppingstone to presenting the gospel of Christ.[18] Without scoffing at the interest in nature, but also without affirming the deification of nature, we could seek to turn the attention of people to the exalted approach to nature that is found in the Bible. This common interest in and appreciation of nature could be a point of contact that we have with people today who are deifying nature. Paul used creation in his evangelistic preaching (Acts 14:17), and he also taught that the creation should lead people to seek God (Romans 1:19–20).

A young unbelieving Australian, who had adopted the hippie lifestyle of a few decades ago, went on a holiday to New Zealand. During her long journeys by bus and train she was struck by the beauty of nature, and though she was an irreligious person this made her think about God. It also seemed that wherever she went on this trip, she met Christians. She says that through the witness of nature and through the witness by word of the Christians she became a Christian. She subsequently became a staff worker in Youth for Christ.

Non-Christians in the East often live closer to nature than those in the West. Therefore nature could also be used effectively in evangelism among them too. It is not difficult to impress them with the glory of nature. This is what happened to a high school science teacher in Sri Lanka. She was a Buddhist and she did not believe in God. But as she studied science she came to believe that such a complex universe could not have just happened. This made her look for answers to the meaning of nature. This, in turn, led her and her husband to discussions with some Christians. They started coming to our Youth for Christ programs and then to the church where our family worships. Today they are both active Christians.

Pantheistic Spirituality in a Pluralistic Environment

Religious pluralism has swept the world, and the trend is to unite religious traditions rather than divide them, to look for the "inner unity" of all religions rather than "the external details that divide them."[19] Pluralism has been the basic approach that has influenced inter-religious relations during many eras in many parts of the world. This was the background from which the Christian church did its pioneering evangelism in the first century.

It is enormously significant that the church proclaimed an absolutely unique Christ in that pluralistic society. The West was not religiously pluralistic until recently because it was influenced by Christianity, which believes in an absolutely unique Christ. Pantheistic spirituality harmonizes well with the new ideal of inter-religious unity, and because it fits in so well with the way society is headed, we can expect its popularity to grow.

An experience of one of India's most famous gurus, Sri Ramakrishna (1936–1986), shows how pantheistic spirituality fits in with the pluralistic mood of today. Ramakrishna "recorded that he meditated on a picture of the Madonna with child and was transported into a state of samadhi, a consciousness in which the divine is all that really exists."[20]

Kenneth Woodward comments, "For that kind of spiritual experience, appeal to any god will do." Woodward quotes Deepak Chopra, the Indian medical doctor who has done much to popularize New Age thought in the West, who says, "Christ-consciousness, God-consciousness, Buddha-consciousness—it's all the same thing. Rather than 'love thy neighbor,' this consciousness says, 'You and I are the same beings.'"[21] We can see how this type of thinking will appeal to those seeking a new world order based on pluralistic principles.

What has been said above about pantheism and Christianity and in the chapter on spirituality (chapter 11) will give a Christian answer to pantheistic spirituality. Here we can simply note that the religious milieu in which we live in both the East and the West is very friendly to pantheism, and we can expect to see it grow even more in the years to come.

Chapter 8 endnotes

[1] See David K. Clark and Norman L. Geisler, *Apologetics in the New Age: A Christian Critique of Pantheism* (Grand Rapids, MI: Baker Book House, 1990), 17–114. On pantheism, see also the chapter, "Comparing Gods" in Douglas R. Groothuis' *Confronting the New Age* (Downers Grove, IL: InterVarsity Press, 1986), 37–56. I did not have access to the latter book when writing this chapter.

[2] Clark and Geisler, *Apologetics in the New Age,* 8.

[3] Douglas R. Groothuis, *Unmasking the New Age* (Downers Grove, IL: InterVarsity Press, 1986), 20.

[4] C. S. Lewis, *Miracles: A Preliminary Survey* (New York: The Macmillan Co., 1947). Reprinted in *The Best of C. S. Lewis* (Washington, DC: Christianity Today, Inc., 1969).

[5] C. S. Lewis, *Miracles,* in *The Best of C. S. Lewis,* 279.

[6] Quoted in Groothuis, *Unmasking the New Age,* 21.

[7] C. S. Lewis, *Miracles in The Best of C. S. Lewis,* 281.

[8] Vishal Mangalwadi, *When the New Age Gets Old* (Downers Grove, IL: InterVarsity Press, 1992), 18.

[9] C. S. Lewis, *Miracles,* in *The Best of C. S. Lewis,* 282.

[10] When I was on a six-month sabbatical in the USA in 1988, I was so worried by what I saw of the lack of biblical community that I wrote a book on community called *Reclaiming Friendship* (Leicester: InterVarsity Press, 1991, and Scottsdale, PA: Herald Press, 1994).

[11] For a incisive look at how the church has been influenced by worldly models of leadership, along with some remedial insights, see E. Glenn Wagner with Steve Halliday, *Escape from Church, Inc.: The Return of the Pastor Shepherd* (Grand Rapids, MI: Zondervan Publishing House, 1999).

[12] Theodore Roszak, *Where the Wasteland Ends* (Garden City, NY: Doubleday, 1972). Cited in Groothuis, *Unmasking the New Age,* 42.

[13] See Groothuis, *Unmasking the New Age,* 43.

[14] John Calvin, *Commentary on Genesis* [1554] (Edinburgh: Banner of Truth, reprint of 1847 translation). This point is made by Vinoth Ramachandra in *Gods That Fail: Idolatry and Christian Mission* (Carlisle: Paternoster Press, 1996), 71.

[15] Margaret Clarkson, *All Nature Sings* (Grand Rapids, MI: Wm. B. Eerdmans Publishing Co., 1986), ix.

[16] C. S. Lewis, *Reflections on the Psalms* (New York: Harcourt, Brace, & World, Inc., 1958), 83.

[17] C. S. Lewis, *Reflections on the Psalms,* 81.

[18] On the use of stepping stones, see the section, "Scratch Where it Itches," in chapter 4.

[19] See S. J. Samartha, *One Christ, Many Religions: Toward a Revised Christology* (Maryknoll, N.Y: Orbis Books, 1991); John Hick, *God Has Many Names* (London: Macmillan, 1980).

[20] Cited in Kenneth L. Woodward, "The Other Jesus," *Newsweek,* March 27, 2000, 80.

[21] Woodward, "The Other Jesus," 80.

9

THE DISTANT GOD

Pantheism has God so near to us that everything is said to be a part of the divine, but other views of God have Him quite removed from human life. We will discuss some of these views in this chapter.

The Trandscendent God of Islam

How often we hear people say that Muslims and Christians worship the same God and accept the same book, the Old Testament. Therefore there is no need to try to convert Muslims, because their religion is so similar to ours. Yet a closer look at Islam shows that the differences are marked. It is not correct, for example, to say that Muslims accept the Old Testament. The Qur'an cites incidents and names that appear in the Old Testament, but that is not the same as accepting it as a book of doctrine. In chapter 7 we said that when Muslims speak of Allah they refer to the same God as we do, even though the way they seek to reach God is not acceptable to God.

Like Christianity, Islam emphasizes the transcendence of God, and in this way it stands in sharp contrast to pantheism. In Islam the basic concept of God is His oneness. This means not only that He is a unity but also that He is distinct from all else, wholly other, indescribable, and not to be compared with anything else in creation. The unforgivable sin in Islam is ascribing equals to God; this sin is called *shirk*, which means "associating." This principle is applied to the Christian doctrine of the Trinity. The foundation of Islam is the confession of faith (*shahada*), which emphasizes the oneness of God:

> I bear witness that there is no God but God;
> I bear witness that Muhammad is the Apostle (Prophet) of God.

Muslims speak of the ninety-nine names of God that they call the excellent or beautiful names of God. Though there is no unanimity about the exact names in this list, there is unanimity about the number 99. Muslims are often seen with a rosary that has either ninety-nine or thirty-three beads representing the names. In the case of the latter, the faithful must go around the rosary three times, adding up to ninety-nine, to complete the ritual. Some Muslims recite the names while they move the beads. Abd-Al-Masih has listed the ninety-nine names and includes an indication of the frequency of their occurrence in the Qur'an. The qualities that occur most are those expressing God's greatness and mercy.[1] Mercy also emphasizes His utter greatness, for the sovereign God grants salvation to insignificant humans. The focus on God's greatness is well expressed in the statement *Allahu Akbar* (God is greatest), which is repeated with each set of prayers in the mosque and on numerous other occasions.

The emphasis in Islam on the transcendence of God is taken well beyond the Christian idea to yield a different understanding of God. Ida Glaser has written such a helpful article on this topic that we will use her insights often in this discussion. The main difference in the Christian and Muslim ideas of God, Glaser says, is that whereas the former focuses on relationships, the latter focuses on the otherness of God.[2] At heart the Christian God is one who relates, and this makes the Trinity possible and even necessary. Relationship is so much a part of the Godhead that it was there from eternity.

We often summarize the Christian understanding of God as holy love. Muslims would use the same words to describe God, but they understand something very different; Islam emphasizes the will of the sovereign God. This is why we often hear Muslims add *insha'llah,* meaning "if God wills," after they make a statement about something they want to do. As God is sovereign in this way, "He can therefore be tied down to no law, not even one that He has made."[3] Therefore sin can affect only people, not God. Christians think of sin as breaking a love relationship and of God being grieved because of that (Ephesians 4:30). We view sinners as being enemies of God who are reconciled to Him at salvation (Romans 5:10). By contrast, in Islam there is no such relationship with God, and while humans may be injured by human sin, God is not. The Bible describes many instances of God's pain over human sin, but this is not a characteristic emphasis in Islam.

The Muslim idea of love focuses on God's mercy in granting the possibility of salvation. It is a sovereign act that God, who is bound to no one, grants to humans. Whereas the Christian idea of salvation has at its heart establishing a relationship with God (John 17:3), the Muslim idea of salvation is "an escape from judgment and an entry into paradise."[4] In Christianity God has chosen to act within His laws of justice in forgiving humans; therefore it was necessary for a penalty to be paid and the punishment to be borne by Jesus. Muslims would say that nothing is necessary for God. He is able to forgive without needing to provide an atoning sacrifice. And the idea that God became incarnate in order to be such a sacrifice is particularly revolting to them. Of course, during the Hajj each year, Muslims sacrifice animals to commemorate how Abraham was willing to sacrifice his son and how God provided a substitute. Perhaps this could be a point of contact to help them see the idea of a substitute in their thinking about God.

A relationship between God and us is possible because humans are made in the image of God. Glaser explains, "There is likeness between creature and creator. This likeness includes the quality of personhood: the essential characteristic of God that implies the ability to relate is present in man also."[5] In fact, it is for this relationship that God made us. In Islam the relationship is "more like between potentate and subject than that between father and son, since man is made primarily for worship rather than relationship."[6] It is interesting that the idea that humans are like God and that we can have a relationship with God is found in the mystical, more experiential, branch of Islam, *Sufism*.[7] This is why some people feel that Sufism is a bridge to Islam, for Sufism directly expresses aspirations that Christianity fulfills.[8] The growth of Sufism in the twentieth century suggests that the need for a personal relationship with God is an acknowledged felt need of many Muslims. This could give us some keys to witnessing to Muslims. For example, when we share a testimony about the beautiful relationship we have with God, it could give to Muslims the message that we have what they are searching for.

With the growth of Islamic fundamentalism, Sufism seems to have been on the decline in the past twenty years. The religious life of many Muslims has to do more with the religion of Islam, with its systems and practices and with the solidarity of the Muslim community, than with God. Yet there are people in the Muslim community who want to please and know God and to be close to Him. Perhaps these people will be more receptive to the Christian message of salvation that includes the experience of relating to God in an intimate way.

The Christian view of human nature as bearing the image of God makes it easier for us to understand the mystery of the Incarnation. God can take a human form because humans are made like God. "In Jesus God himself comes among his creatures and relates with them. Not only does he speak to them, guide them and judge them: he also touches them, weeps with them, rejoices with them and eats with them."[9] But Muslims do not emphasize the likeness of humans to God. Therefore, Glaser explains, "If there is no likeness between God and man, this [the Incarnation] cannot be. The very thought of it is blasphemy."[10]

Muslim converts to Christianity have expressed great joy and wonder over their discovery that God can relate to them as a father. Their minds may have to go through radical transformation before they can break through that veil that keeps God so distant from humans. But once they realize this, it becomes a liberating truth to them. This process is vividly described in a book about the conversion of a wealthy Pakistani woman, Bilquis Sheikh, which is appropriately entitled *I Dared to Call Him Father*. Madame Sheikh was in a hospital with her grandson, who had an ear complaint, and she had a Bible beside the bed. A nun, Dr. Santiago, who was in charge of the hospital, expressed surprise about this. In the conversation that ensued, she told the nun of her search for God and of some of the experiences she had had. Then she said, "You seem to make God . . . I don't know . . . personal!"

The doctor told her, "Why don't you pray to the God you are searching for? Ask Him to show you His way. Talk to Him as if He were your
friend." Madame Sheikh describes what happened next:

I smiled. She might as well suggest that I talk to the Taj Mahal. But
then Dr. Santiago said something that shot through my being like elec-
tricity. "Talk to him," she said very quietly, "as if He were your father."

I sat back quickly. A dead silence filled the room. . . . Talk to God as
if He were my father! The truth shook my soul in the peculiar way truth
has of being startling and comforting. . . .

Alone in my room [that evening] I got on my knees and tried to call
Him "Father." But it was a useless effort and I straightened in dismay. It
was ridiculous. Wouldn't it be sinful to bring the Great One down to our
level? I fell asleep that night more confused than ever.

Hours later I awoke. It was after midnight. . . . [She remembered
how she would go near her father as a child and always be greeted with
his welcoming acceptance.] It was always the same with Father. He
didn't mind if I bothered him. Whenever I had a question or a problem,
no matter how busy he was, he would put aside his work to devote his
full attention just to me.

It was well past midnight as I lay in bed savoring this wonderful memory. "Oh thank you . . . ." I murmured to God. Was I really talking to Him?

Suddenly a breakthrough of hope flooded me. Suppose, just suppose
God were like a father. If my earthly father would put aside everything to
listen to me, wouldn't my heavenly Father . . . ?

Shaking with excitement, I got out of bed, sank to my knees on the rug,
looked up to heaven and in rich new understanding called God, "My Father."

I was not prepared for what happened.

"Oh Father, my Father . . . Father God."

Hesitatingly, I spoke His name aloud. I tried different ways of speaking to Him. And then, as if something broke through for me I found
myself trusting that He was indeed hearing me, just as my earthly father
had always done.

"Father, oh my Father God," I cried, with growing confidence. My voice
seemed unusually loud in the large bedroom as I knelt on the rug beside my
bed. But suddenly that room wasn't empty any more. He was there! I could
sense His presence. I could feel His hand gently laid on my head.[11]

Atheism: There is No God

The most distant view of God is one that either denies His existence or declares Him unnecessary. We could regard this approach as being equivalent to the approach of the Epicureans that Paul debated in Athens. The deists in Europe and North America in the eighteenth century did not deny the existence of God, but they had Him so distant from the world that He had no part in its activities. If He did create the world, He was like a watchmaker who set it in motion and then took His hands off it.

Atheism is still alive and well despite the growth of interest in religion in this postmodern society. A recent poll conducted by the Forsa Institute in Germany found that one in three Germans does not believe in God.[12] In Asian countries we commonly encounter young people, especially Buddhist and Hindu students, who claim that science has proved that there is no God. Atheists usually do not come to Christ through arguments like those described below. Instead they often come to Christ when they see Christianity as being relevant to a need they have. But we need to know these arguments in order to answer the questions atheists have and to speak intelligently with them. Sometimes such dialogue opens them to being more receptive to the Christian message.

Typical Apologetic Arguments. It is not within the scope of this book to present a full response to atheistic views, and such a response has been adequately given in several recently published books.[13] Many good, basic books on apologetics also deal with the issue of whether there is a God and of whether God is necessary for an authentic human life.[14]

J. P. Moreland's *Scaling the Secular City* has four chapters about the existence of God. Moreland first presents the *cosmological* argument, which "generally begins with the existence of the world or some part of it and seeks to establish the existence of a necessary Being who causes the existence of the world."[15]

Next Moreland presents the *design* or *teleological* argument, which he considers the most popular argument for God's existence. He has grouped many arguments that all come under the argument for design. Some have argued that the order, pattern, and regularity of the world point to a Creator. Others see "both the unity of the world and its simplicity . . . as evidence that the world is a result of a single, rational, efficient mind."[16]

Along with this is the marvelous complexity of the world, which also gives evidence of an intelligent Creator. Another design argument comes from the beauty of the world (and another from the beauty of the theories that describe the world). Then comes the argument from "our ability to perceive and think about the world accurately," which several philosophers see as "evidence that these abilities were designed by an intelligent being for such purposes."[17] And yet more types of design are discussed.

Moreland's third chapter is about a group of arguments that come from looking at the way the mind operates. Human consciousness could not have evolved from matter. John Calvin, at the beginning of *The Institutes of the Christian Religion*, said, "No man can survey himself without forthwith turning his thoughts towards the God in whom he lives and moves; because it is perfectly obvious, that the endowments which we possess cannot possibly be from ourselves."[18] The various arguments in this category "in one way or another . . . point out that man as a rational agent implies God as the Ground or Cause of his rationality."[19]

In his fourth chapter Moreland argues for the existence of God on the grounds that "Christian theism is the best answer to questions about the meaning of life."[20] An outstanding book on apologetics by William Lane Craig follows a similar line with a chapter entitled "The Absurdity of Life without God."[21] Craig describes this as an "apologetic for Christianity based on the human predicament . . . associated primarily with Francis Schaeffer. Often it is referred to as 'cultural apologetics' because of its analysis of post-Christian culture." What this does is to explore "the disastrous consequences for human existence, society, and culture if Christianity should be false."[22] As precursors of this method of apologetics, Craig mentions the thoughts (*Pensées*) of French mathematician and physicist Blaise Pascal (1623–1662), the novels of Russian writer Fyodor Dostoyevsky (1821–1881) and the theological writings of Søren Kierkegaard, a Danish philosopher (1813–1855).

Scientific Evidence for God. Recent advances in science have taken place because advances in technology have given us more information about the world around us. Telescopes and satellites sent into space have given us new knowledge about the universe. The electron microscope, x-ray crystallography, and nuclear magnetic resonance have given us more information about living cells and about the DNA genetic code.[23] And this new information has given us fresh perspectives on the arguments about God's existence.

Michael Behe, a professor of biochemistry at Lehigh University, has responded to the Darwinian affirmation that complex forms evolved from simpler forms. He points out that the basic unit of life, the cell, contains so many highly complex items and processes that cannot be reduced, or simplified, any further. He says such items and processes could not have emerged gradually through a Darwinian process.[24]

Even more amazing is the functioning of the DNA (deoxyribonucleic acid) molecule, which carries loads of information that enable the cell to function as it should. Science writer Nancy Pearcey and scientist Charles Thaxton observe that "the amount of information contained in a single human cell equals the entire thirty volumes of *Encyclopedia Britannica* several times over."[25] Pearcey and Thaxton have an extended discussion of the significance for science of the revolution caused by the discovery of DNA structure. One result is that it has given fresh evidence for the design argument, something that Francis Crick, one of the researchers who discovered DNA, denied in his autobiography.[26]

This argument states that there are certain regularities in nature, and people who believe in God attribute those regularities to God. These same regularities might be given a purely naturalistic explanation by atheists. Although Christians would say that a Mind created and coordinated the structure of shiny crystals, the hexagonal patterns in oil, and the whirlpools in a bathtub, other people would give naturalistic explanations. But other types of order, such as the letter arrangements in written messages, can be explained only in terms of an intelligent designer. The order in DNA is like this; it has an informational structure.

Thaxton points out that the DNA molecule is characterized not just by order but also by "specified complexity," that is, information. "A structural identity has been discovered between the genetic messages of DNA and the written messages of a human language." He argues, "Because we know by experience that intelligence produces written messages, and no other cause is known, the implication . . . is that intelligent cause produced DNA." He further explains, "We are not dealing with anything like a superficial resemblance between DNA and a written text. We are not saying, DNA is like a message. Rather, DNA is a message." He concludes, "True design thus returns to biology."[27]

Pearcey and Thaxton say of those who reject this line of argument from design: "It's as though a geologist were to gaze on the four presidential faces carved into Mt. Rushmore[28] and then insist, despite obvious marks of workmanship, that the faces are the product of natural forces alone—of wind and water erosion." They conclude, "In DNA the marks of intelligent workmanship are equally evident."[29]

For many years the argument from the second law of thermodynamics has been popular. Thermodynamics is a science that deals with energy, and the second law states that "the amount of energy available to do work [in the universe] is decreasing and becoming uniformly distributed. The universe is moving irreversibly toward a state of maximum disorder and minimum energy."[30] To put it another way, "the whole universe is wearing down irreversibly." We can attempt to explain this by using nontechnical language and by borrowing examples from Moreland's characteristically helpful explanation in *Scaling the Secular City*. A hot cup of coffee, if left to itself, will cool down until the coffee reaches room temperature. "If someone opens a bottle of perfume in a room, the perfume will leave the bottle and disperse in such a way that it will become uniformly distributed throughout the room."

This suggests that if the universe had already undergone an infinite past, it by now would have come to a state of maximum disorder and uniform energy distribution in which the sun would have been burned up. The inference is that, as this is not the case, the universe cannot have existed forever. Moreland concludes, "It would seem, then, that the second law implies a beginning to the universe when the universe was, as it were, wound up and energy and order were put into it."[31]

Along with this we place the scientific community's growing acceptance of the big bang theory of the origin of the universe.[32] A discovery in the late 1920s by astronomer Edwin Hubble indicated that the universe is expanding. "Galaxies are moving away from one another much like dots on the surface of an inflating balloon."[33] This has led some scientists to conclude that the universe as we know it began from a large explosion a few billion years ago and has continued to expand since then. This has lent evidence to the Christian belief that the world began with an act of creation.[34]

In recent times eminent scientists from several fields have written in support of belief in God.[35] Philosophers Craig and Moreland and theologian R. C. Sproul have also written helpful books on the topic,[36] as has mathematician William Dembski.[37] Treatment of this issue here has been sketchy, but it may whet the appetite of readers who want to pursue this matter. Exciting material is being published as scientists and philosophers ponder the universe and its phenomena. Darwin's theory of naturalistic evolution has increasingly come under fire from various quarters,[38] and not all of them are Christian.[39]

Perhaps a personal testimony is appropriate. I did my undergraduate studies at a university that had only recently changed from being a Buddhist seminary. Our vice-chancellor (president) was a Buddhist monk. In keeping with our system of education I studied only three subjects during my final two years: botany, zoology, and chemistry. Most of my teachers were Buddhists, and there were only about five Christian students in the faculty (college) of science where I studied (I was the only Protestant Christian). I loved science, despite my clumsiness with my fingers, which made laboratory work a problem.

I went into the university as a Christian, and I came out with a vastly greater appreciation for God's work in creation. The beauty and complexity of the universe seem to give clear evidence of the existence of a Creator. In my case these studies made me praise God much more than before for His creation. But I had many friends who were not attracted to God by their scientific studies. Some may even have thought that science gave them evidence against belief in God.

Later I did meet Buddhists whose study of science made them ask questions that ultimately led them to faith in the God of the Bible. What they asked had to do with the implications of their scientific studies. Perhaps what made them pursue the issues further was their need to find meaning in life, which they ultimately found was provided by God through the Christian gospel.

Buddhism, Communism, and Secular Humanism: No Need for a God

Many orthodox Buddhists deny that gods have any part in Buddhism. Others, however, say that gods have been so much a part of the practice of most Buddhist people that one cannot separate this belief from Buddhism.[40] Many scholars consider original Buddhism to be a nontheistic system, as the gods were not necessary in its approach to life.

Gunapala Dharmasiri, a Buddhist writer, begins his critique of the Christian concept of God with the words, "The Buddha did not accept the existence of God."[41] The learned Buddhist monk Narada Maha Thera says, "There are no petitionary or intercessory prayers in Buddhism. . . . The Buddha does not and cannot grant earthly favours to those who pray to him. A Buddhist should not pray to be saved, but should rely on himself and strive with diligence to win freedom and gain purity."[42]

Both of these scholars belong to the Theravada branch of Buddhism, and their comments reflect a key theme in the most basic of Buddhist scriptures, the Dhammapada, which consists of sayings that are attributed to the Buddha himself. It says, "Self is the lord of self, who else could be the Lord? With self well subdued, a man finds a lord difficult to find" (verse 160). A little later we find the statement, "By oneself the evil is done, by oneself one is defiled. Purity and impurity belong to oneself, no one can purify another" (verse 165).[43]

A Buddhist tract entitled "The Four Spiritual Laws" has as its fourth law, "You are already saved!" Under this it says, "No one can save us—except our own self! This is the most wonderful message the Buddha gives us."[44] One reason Buddhism is growing so rapidly in the West is that it fits with the Western quest for self-actualization. Westerners have rejected the idea of submitting to the lordship of the God of the Bible, but in this postmodern era they do not want the irreligious approach to life of the secular humanism of the modern era. They feel that the modern era neglected the spiritual nature of the human being. Into this scenario comes Buddhism, with its attractive, pleasing spiritual disciplines and its affirmation that we and not God control our destinies.

In Sri Lanka, Burma, Thailand, and Cambodia, *Theravada* Buddhism is practiced. Theravada means "the doctrine of the elders." This branch of Buddhism prides itself on being close to the teachings of the Buddha and the early Buddhist (*Pali*) scriptures. Yet Buddhists belonging to Theravada Buddhism have also included the divine factor in the practice of their religion. Many Buddhists in Sri Lanka have deified the Buddha, a practice he would have opposed. Despite the downplaying of prayers and of help from the divine, most Theravada Buddhists go regularly to shrines of various deities and to other practitioners of supernatural divine arts in times of need and for help and support in life. Many Buddhist temples in Sri Lanka have shrines to the gods beside the temple or sometimes within the temple premises. The chief officer of the most sacred Buddhist temple in Sri Lanka, which houses the tooth relic of the Buddha, once said that the temple lands "are dedicated to the Buddha and the gods." Some observers say that despite Buddhist claims to being nontheistic, there has never been a time when most Buddhists, at least in Sri Lanka, did not worship the gods.

Mahayana ("greater vehicle") Buddhism is the largest branch of Buddhism, and varieties of it are practiced in Japan, China, Tibet, Korea, and Singapore. Mahayana Buddhists worship and address prayers to the Buddha and to the *bodhisattvas* as they would to a god. A bodhisattva is one who has postponed final enlightenment and attaining the final state of bliss, *nirvana,* to aid other beings in their quest for enlightenment. My missions professor, J. T. Seamands, said he once went to a Buddhist temple in Southeast Asia and heard children singing to the tune of the familiar Christian chorus:

Buddha loves me, this I know,
For the Dhamma [teaching] tells me so.
Little ones to him belong,
They are weak, but he is strong.

When I was a theological student in the early 1970s the Cultural Revolution under Mao Zedong was at its height. It was the time of the cold war, and Westerners often talked about the communist threat. Seamands once told us that communism would not last long, because it is a godless philosophy, and no philosophy that denies God can survive for long. This comment sounded unlikely at the time, but unknown to the Christian church outside, a remarkable religious revival was taking place in the communist world.[45] And although the communist party rules in the People's Republic of China, North Korea, Vietnam, and Cuba, it has lost the ideological appeal that it had a generation ago. A friend of mine recently lectured about Christianity in a university Department of Atheism in the former Soviet Union. He encountered a receptive audience.

The early 1970s was also a time when Christians talked about the threat of secular humanism. Now there is little talk about it. The postmodern era has dawned, and its reaction against the ultrarationalism of the modern era has resulted in religion and spirituality becoming popular again.

The practical theism of most Buddhists and the fact that the non-theism of communism and secular humanism had such a short lifespan points to the necessity of God for human life. What we said about Christian theism being the best answer to questions about the meaning of life is relevant here. This argument for God is expressed in the provocative title of Ravi Zacharias's *Can Man Live without God?*[46]

I know many people who once confidently said that they did not need God because they were strong enough to thrive in life without the help of a god. They said that God is a crutch needed to give confidence to weak people. Then they faced a crisis in their lives, and in their desperation they turned to God for help. They ended up as fervent followers of Christ with a deep faith in God. A Christian worker recently told me that his parents-in-law had discouraged him about being in the ministry. They had told him that God would not to provide money for him and that he needed to be practical and find a better-paying job. Then the father-in-law was diagnosed as having a dangerous disease. This experience led them to seek God earnestly.

Chapter 9 endnotes

[1] Abd-Al-Masih, *Who is Allah in Islam?* 84–87. The most frequently occurring are The Merciful (169); The Omniscient (158); The Compassionate (114); The Ultimately Wise (95); The Most Forgiving One (91); The Unique and Mighty One (89).

[2] Ida Glaser, "The Concept of Relationship as a Key to the Contemporary Understanding of Christianity and Islam," *Solid Ground: 25 Years of Evangelical Theology* (Leicester: Apollos, 2000), 247–255. This is a reprint of an article that appeared in *Themelios,* vol. 11.2 (1986).

[3] Glaser, "The Concept of Relationship," 249.

[4] Glaser, "The Concept of Relationship," 253.

[5] Glaser, "The Concept of Relationship," 249.

[6] Glaser, "The Concept of Relationship," 250.

[7] Glaser, "The Concept of Relationship," 255, n. 7.

[8] See Phil Parshall, *Bridges to Islam: A Christian Perspective on Folk Religion* (Grand Rapids, MI: Baker Book House, 1983).

[9] Glaser, "The Concept of Relationship," 254.

[10] Glaser, "The Concept of Relationship," 254.

[11] Bilquis Sheikh with Richard Schneider, *I Dared to Call Him Father* (Eastbourne: Kingsway Publications, 1979; US edition, Lincoln, VA: Chosen Books, 1978), 38–42.

[12] Reported by Wolfgang Polzer, *Idea,* May 3, 2000.

[13] The notes below present many of these books.

[14] The categories for discussing the case for the existence of God appear in such books as John M. Frame, *Apologetics to the Glory of God* (Phillipsburg, NJ: P & R Publishing, 1994); A. J. Hoover, *The Case for Christian Theism: An Introduction to Apologetics* (Grand Rapids, MI: Baker Book House, 1976); J. P. Moreland, *Scaling the Secular City: A Defense of Christianity* (Grand Rapids, MI: Baker Book House, 1987); and R. C. Sproul, John Gerstner, and Arthur Lindsley, *Classical Apologetics: A Rational Defense of the Christian Faith and a Critique of Presuppositional Apologetics* (Grand Rapids, MI: Zondervan Publishing House, 1984). Peter Kreeft and Ronald Tacelli present "Twenty Arguments for the Existence of God" in *Handbook of Christian Apologetics* (Downers Grove, IL: InterVarsity Press, 1994). C. S. Lewis's brilliant defense in *Mere Christianity* (first published in 1944) is still worth consulting. The debate between theist J. P. Moreland and atheist Kai Nielson is recorded in *Does God Exist? The Great Debate* (Nashville: Thomas Nelson Publishers, 1990).

[15] Moreland, *Scaling the Secular City,* 15.

[16] Moreland, *Scaling the Secular City,* 47.

[17] Moreland, *Scaling the Secular City,* 49.

[18] John Calvin, *Institutes of the Christian Religion* [1536] (Associated Publishers and Authors, n.d.), 1.1.1. Cited in Moreland, *Scaling the Secular City,* 77.

[19] Moreland, *Scaling the Secular City,* 77.

[20] Moreland, *Scaling the Secular City,* 132.

[21] William Lane Craig, *Reasonable Faith: Christian Truth and Apologetics* (Wheaton, IL: Crossway Books, 1994).

[22] Craig, *Reasonable Faith,* 51.

[23] Ronald H. Nash, *Life's Ultimate Questions: An Introduction to Philosophy* (Grand Rapids, MI: Zondervan Publishing House, 1999), 298–304, a brief and understandable summary.

[24] Michael Behe, *Darwin's Black Box: The Biochemical Challenge of Evolution* (New York: Free Press, 1996).

[25] Nancy R. Pearcey and Charles B. Thaxton, *The Soul of Science: Christian Faith and Natural Philosophy* (Wheaton, IL: Crossway Books, 1994). An excellent introduction to science for Christian laypeople.

[26] "Biologists must constantly keep in mind that what they see was not designed, but rather evolved"; in Francis Crick, *What Mad Pursuit* (New York: Basic Books, 1988), 138. Cited in Pearcey and Thaxton, *The Soul of Science,* 245.

[27] Charles B. Thaxton, "DNA: A New Argument from Design," in *Evangelical Apologetics,* Robert Bauman and others, editors (Camp Hill, PA: Christian Publications, 1996), 178. Thaxton describes and defends the abductive method of reasoning that links cause to effect by reasoning from experience.

[28] A mountain in America with carvings of the faces of four presidents in the rock.

[29] Pearcey and Thaxton, *The Soul of Science,* 245.

[30] Moreland, *Scaling the Secular City,* 34.

[31] Moreland, *Scaling the Secular City,* 35.

[32] Moreland's *Scaling the Secular City,* 33–34.

[33] Moreland, *Scaling the Secular City,* 33.

[34] Among those who have explained this connection are Cambridge Professor of Mathematical Physics turned Anglican priest, John Polkinghorne, *The Way the World Is: The Christian Perspective of a Scientist* (Grand Rapids, MI: Wm. B. Eerdmans Publishing Co., 1984), 7–16. See also his *Science and Creation* (London: SPCK, 1988). See also the work of astronomer Hugh Ross, *The Creator and the Cosmos: How the Greatest Scientific Discoveries of the Century Reveal God* (Colorado Springs; NavPress 1995); Ross, *The Fingerprint of God* (Orange, CA.: Promise Publishing, 1991); and Ross, *The Genesis Question: Scientific Advances and the Accuracy of Genesis* (Colorado Springs: NavPress, 1998).

[35] In addition to the scientists mentioned above, we list the following: Physicist (and priest) Stanley Jaki has written *Science and Creation* (Edinburgh: Scottish Academic Press, 1974); Jaki, *The Road of Science and the Ways to God* (Chicago: University of Chicago Press, 1978); Jaki, *God and the Cosmologists* (Washington, DC: Regnery Gateway, 1989). Professor Donald MacKay of Keele University, who headed a department doing research on the brain, wrote *The Clockwork Image: A Christian Perspective on Science* (Leicester: InterVarsity Press, 1974). British scientist Robert E. D. Clark has written *God Beyond Nature* (Exeter: The Paternoster Press, 1982).

[36] William Lane Craig, *The Existence of God and the Beginning of the Universe* (San Bernardino, CA: Here's Life Publishers, 1979); J. P. Moreland, *Christianity and the Nature of Science* (Grand Rapids, MI: Baker Book House, 1989); and R. C. Sproul, *Not a Chance: The Myth of Chance in Modern Science and Cosmology* (Baker Book House, 1994). See also the collection of essays, *The Creation Hypothesis,* J. P. Moreland, editor (Downers Grove, IL: InterVarsity Press, 1994).

[37] William A. Dembski, *The Design Inference* (Cambridge: Cambridge University Press, 1998); Dembski, *Intelligent Design: The Bridge Between Science and Theology* (Downers Grove, IL: InterVarsity Press, 1999); *Mere Creation: Science, Faith, and Intelligent Design,* Dembski, editor; contributors: Hugh Ross and Michael J. Behe (Downers Grove, IL: InterVarsity Press, 1998).

[38] Behe, *Darwin's Black Box;* Phillip Johnson, *Darwin on Trial* (Downers Grove, IL: InterVarsity Press, 1993). Johnson is a professor at the Berkeley University School of Law.

[39] Douglas R. Groothuis provides the following annotated bibliography of books without an overtly Christian viewpoint. Michael Denton, *Evolution: A Theory in Crisis* (London: Adler and Adler, 1985), a pivotal work challenging major assumptions of Darwinism from an empirical and scientific standpoint; Norman Macbeth, *Darwin Retried* (New York: Dell Publishing Company, 1971), written by a lawyer who looks at Darwinism logically and evidentially; Norman Macbeth, *Darwinism: A Time for Funerals:* An Interview with Norman Macbeth (San Francisco: Robert Briggs Associates, 1982), taken from a magazine interview; Richard Melton,

Shattering the Myths of Darwinism (Rochester, VT: Park Street Press, 1997), a scientific writer offers a compelling case against Darwinism.

[40] See L. A. de Silva, *Buddhism: Beliefs and Practices in Sri Lanka* (Colombo: Ecumenical Institute for Study and Dialogue, 1974), 137–142.

[41] Gunapala Dharmasiri, *A Buddhist Critique of the Christian Concept of God* (Colombo: Lake House Investments, 1974), ix.

[42] Dharmasiri, *A Buddhist Critique of the Christian Concept of God,* ix.

[43] *The Dhammapada,* translated by Irving Babbit (New York: New Directions Books, 1965).

[44] *The Four Spiritual Laws* (*Dharma for the Millions, no. 1*).

[45] See David H. Adeney, *China: The Church's Long March* (Ventura: Regal Books, 1985); Tony Lambert, *China's Christian Millions* (England: Monarch Books, 1999); Carl Lawrence, *The Church in China: How It Survives and Prospers under Communism* (Minneapolis: Bethany House Publishers, 1985).

[46] Ravi Zacharias, *Can Man Live Without God?* (Dallas: Word Publishing, 1994). This point is also made in R. C. Sproul's *If There Is a God, Why Are There Atheists? Why Atheists Believe in Unbelief* (Wheaton, IL: Tyndale House Publishers, 1989).

10

PROTECTION, HELP, AND GUIDANCE FROM THE DIVINE

At the conclusion of chapter 9 we mentioned people who allege that God is a crutch to give confidence to weak people. And there is some truth to that: in Christianity it is a virtue to admit that we are weak and need help. But a different approach to the Divine looks at the Divine as a force to go to for help in times of need.

Help from the Gods

It is widely acknowledged that fear is a powerful emotion that markedly influences the behavior of people the world over. When people fear that they cannot control something in their lives, they often go to a divine source for help. Certain requirements are followed to secure the help of the god, but there is no question of handing over the lordship of one's life to these gods. Sometimes, however, these forces will enslave people and keep them in bondage.

This approach to the Divine may be the most popular religious attitude in the world today, and it looks at divine beings as entities to go to for a favor. The deities are believed to have special powers that make it advisable to worship them, pray to them, and appease them. It seems that Paul encountered this view in Athens, for that city was full of idols, and there were many temples, including one to the Unknown God. The Athenians had gods for the various eventualities they faced, but they knew that they might have overlooked some god. That oversight could result in harm to the city, so they had an altar to the Unknown God.[1]

Tribal Religions. Tribal religions usually are found among peoples not too influenced by technological progress. Expressions of this type of religious life are found among jungle peoples in Africa, Indians in the Americas, the so-called Tribals in South and East Asia, the Aboriginal people in Australia, and the Melanesians and the Polynesians in the Pacific islands.

In the description of the origins of religion (chapter 7) we saw how tribal people who follow what we call primal religions discarded worship of the supreme Creator God in favor of appeasing vicious spirits. The term "primal religion" may be a misnomer, because it suggests that this form of religion was primary and thus came prior to monotheism. But if "primal" is used in the sense of basic, then it may be appropriate, because these practices "usually have the main basic features that belong to all religions." Among these features is "a belief in a spiritual world of powers or beings that are stronger than man himself."[2]

Most tribal people also believe that the spirits of the dead live on and have dealings with people who are still living. Much tribal religion has to do with responding to, protecting oneself from, and getting the help of these spiritual powers. Specialists, usually called *medicine men,* are necessary in this religious life; a medicine man "may perform the activities of a priest, medium, diviner, healer and herbalist, and shaman but not a witch, sorcerer, or a mere magician."[3] *Shamans* are people who enter into a trance and believe that they leave the body and visit other worlds. Their "role is to convey sacrifices to the gods, to escort the dead to their destination and to return with divine prophecies."[4]

Vestiges of tribal religions are seen in every culture, and with the growth of the New Age movement, this trend is increasing in the West. Devil dancers, medicine men, spirit guides, and the like have been popular in Third World countries but are now becoming accepted in affluent Western countries too. For example, Buddhism is the religion of the majority of the people in Sri Lanka, but folk religion includes many pre-Buddhist practices. In Korea the popular religion of the people is a mixture of Buddhism, Confucianism, and the primal religion of the people known as *shamanism*.

Buddhism. Although Buddhism claims to be a non-theistic religion (see chapter 9), in practice most Buddhists are essentially theistic. Buddhists in Sri Lanka often use the greeting, "May the gods bless you." They usually have auspicious times for important events. When they start construction of a building, they will bury expensive items with the foundation so that evil will be warded off. While they construct a building, they often display a hideous figure—a devil's face or a scarecrow—to distract observers and thus avoid the evil eye. Evil eye comes when people can look at a thing and wish something evil for it. Sometimes evil eye is the misfortune that comes as a result of a person looking with envy at something he or she desires. In the Sinhala language we call it eye poison. Babies usually have a big, round, black mark painted on their foreheads to avoid evil eye.

At the start of a farming venture such as sowing rice fields, there usually will be a religious ceremony to elicit the help of the gods. For many of these events, Buddhists have their *pirit* ceremony, which is somewhat akin to a service of blessing.[5] A Buddhist monk will recite sacred scriptures to ward off evil and disease and bring blessing to the people. While the chanting goes on, those participating in the ceremony usually hold a long thread that is held on the other side by the monks. After the ceremony the thread is broken up, and the individual pieces are tied around the wrist, and sometimes the neck, of the participants. These pieces of thread are commonly seen on the wrists of athletes, who usually attend a pirit ceremony before an important sporting event.

Sri Lankans have divided the country into separate geographical regions, each of which is under the control of a certain god. On the main roads, at the entrance to the territory of a new god, one will find a shrine to that god. Travelers stop at this shrine and make an offering, usually of money, for protection during the leg of the journey that goes through the territory of this god. Most buses in Sri Lanka have framed pictures above the driver's seat of the Buddha, several Hindu gods, and often Mary and Saint Anthony. Sometimes Jesus also makes it into the gallery!

Painted on the buses are prayers or wishes asking these gods or the triple gem of Buddhism—the Buddha, the monastic order or *sangha,* and the teaching or *dhamma*—for protection.

As a response to the Four Spiritual Laws that Campus Crusade for Christ distributes, a Buddhist tract was circulated recently in a Southeast Asian university. This latter tract is also called "The Four Spiritual Laws," and the laws are

1. The Buddha lives!
2. The Buddha can help you!
3. Buddhist prayer works!
4. You are already saved!

The second law has this comment: "Whenever you are in trouble, all you need to do is to look to the Buddha for help. For he says, 'Fear not, as you look upon me, I will release you, just like a person saving an elephant which has sunk in the mud!' ("The Story of Elder Vakkali," *Dhammapada Commentary* 4:119)."

The third law has this comment: "Just give it a try—Buddhist prayer works! You can communicate with the Buddha directly. The Buddha says, 'When you are in the forest or in empty places, if fear and panic should arise in you, immediately call me to mind. For if you do so, the fear of panic will be overcome!' ("Discourse on the Banner Top," *Kindred Sayings* 1:219—Paraphrased)."[6]

Hinduism. Most of what has been said about Buddhists in Sri Lanka also applies to Hindus. Although most Hindus consider one temple to be their regular temple, there are many Hindu temples. These temples are dedicated to different gods who are said to be effective in answering specific kinds of prayers. In Sri Lanka we have a temple considered effective when one wants to go abroad. Businessmen frequent another temple because it is said to help a person to become prosperous. Another temple is deemed helpful for those who want to take revenge against someone. This is usually a temple of Kali, the goddess of destruction and the giver of life. She is the consort of the god Shiva and is portrayed with fangs dripping blood and a necklace of human skulls.

Taoism. If one were to go to a Taoist temple one would be struck by how much Taoism is influenced by the idea that favors can be granted through the performance of certain rituals. Like Buddhism, the Taoism we see is very different from the original, philosophical Taoism associated with Lao-Tse. Over the centuries "Taoism evolved a pantheon of innumerable spiritual beings, gods, or celestials and immortals, as well as deified heroes and forces of nature."[7] These deities oversee everything imaginable, and they have accompanying priests, sacrifices, and temples.[8] In Hong Kong and Singapore one can see streets that have several Taoist temples in a row. Each temple specializes in some area. When parents want a child to do well in studies, for example, they will go to one temple, and when business people want success in a business venture they will go to another temple.

In Taoist temples there are often cylinders containing sticks on which sayings are written. The cylinders are shaken, and one stick is allowed to fall to the ground. The message in that stick is considered special for the person. This is a form of fortune telling, and a similar idea lies behind the fortune cookies that are given at the end of a meal in a Chinese restaurant. The paper inside the cookie has a message for the person who opens it. In the West, however, this practice does not usually have religious significance.

Islam. Traditional Muslim prayer is ritualistic and is not essentially petitionary. Yet in many places in Asia there are special shrines, usually the tombs of holy people, where people go to make vows and present their personal needs. In a recent article in *Newsweek,* it was reported that in popular devotions many Muslims ask Jesus or Mary or John the Baptist for favors.[9] In the discussion about the God of Islam (chapter 9) we referred to the growth of the Sufi movement, which emphasizes a more personal experience of God than does traditional Islam. It must be noted, however, that according to some observers, Sufism and other practices are less popular with the growth of Islamic fundamentalism.

Christianity. In the Roman Catholic Church many saints are viewed as having power to grant favors. In Sri Lanka, when I have tried to talk to a non-Christian about the gospel, he or she might say, "I also believe in

Christianity." When I pursue the matter I find that the person means he or she believes in the power of Saint Anthony. Saint Anthony's church in my city attracts thousands of people each week who come to have favors granted. Among those attending are Buddhists, Hindus, Muslims, and Protestant Christians. Trucks and buses owned by Catholics have framed pictures of Jesus, Mary, and Saint Anthony and/or another saint, often accompanied by a plea for protection. Many Catholics have a rosary or a statuette of Jesus or a saint near the driver's seat in their cars. On buses or trucks owned by Catholics the words "Jesus save" are often painted on the outside. Protestants would say "Jesus saves" as an affirmation, but "Jesus save" is a plea for protection during the journey. In Sri Lanka, through the influence of a Christian army officer, soldiers of all religions used to take a card with Psalm 91, which talks of divine protection, onto the battlefield.

In most places where the Christian church is growing among non-Christians we see that what attracts people most to the Christian God is the knowledge that He is powerful—more powerful than all other gods—and able to meet their personal needs through His power.[10] The American leader John Wimber popularized the term "power evangelism," which seeks to attract people to Christ through demonstrations of God's power. When I ask converts to Christianity from Buddhism or Hinduism what attracted them to Christ, they often say that it was a miraculous answer to prayer. A friend who works with Muslims told me that the possibility of an answer to prayer is the most common reason for a Muslim to express interest in Christianity.

Toward a Biblical Response

A Felt Need. How should biblical Christians respond to the immense popularity of the idea that divine beings have the power to meet personal needs? The first thing is that this clearly indicates a felt need that expresses itself in people who attempt to get help from divine beings. The immense popularity of this form of religion is sufficient evidence for that.

The book of Acts shows us that the early evangelists ministered to felt needs, and this ministry attracted people to the gospel. In Acts, a miracle often led to a gospel proclamation. When people realize that the God of Christians is able to meet their personal needs, they are open to hearing about this God. Otherwise they would not be interested in

Christ. They belong to another religion, and their first impression is that becoming a Christian involves such a costly, radical change that they would not want to even consider Christianity.

So far I have never encountered a person who has been unwilling to have me pray for him or her. When I know that people are in need, I tell them that our God cares about their need and can help them; then I ask whether I can pray for them. When people know that Christians pray to our God, they often request that we pray for them. A few days ago a Muslim teacher whom I had met when we took a music and drama team to a school called me and asked me to pray about a certain need. I was happy to oblige.

Of course I do not usually promise that people are going to be immediately healed. I do not have the gift of miraculous healing, and so I do not usually have a conviction that such would happen in a miraculous way. I know others who have this gift and who make such claims. Sometimes I have seen these predictions not come to pass, with unfortunate results.

Sometimes, however, even though there is no healing, the prayers for healing open people to becoming receptive to the gospel. I know of a Buddhist family in which one member was sick with cancer. Some Christians came and prayed for him, but he was not healed. However, the concern that the Christians showed and the comfort that came from casting their cares on the almighty God caused the whole family to take the gospel seriously and ultimately led them to becoming Christians. Today two of the children in that family are in full-time Christian ministry.

The custodian of our church was a Buddhist, but through the witness of our members he was led to faith in Christ. Shortly after his baptism he got sick, and we prayed fervently for his healing. But he deteriorated and died. The family did not permit us to conduct a Christian burial service for him, although they let us conduct a service beside his body on the night before the funeral. His wife, however, was impressed by the care the Christians showed, and she started coming to our church. She was converted and started bringing her neighbors to church. Today several members of our church are from that neighborhood.

The Fuller Picture of God. There is more to evangelism than just attracting people through meeting felt needs. In chapter 4 we said that in Acts those performing miracles were also apologists. They argued for the truth of the gospel facts in addition to demonstrating the power of God through healing.

We also see in Acts that the evangelists gave considerable attention to introducing God to their audience. The evangelistic messages show a God who is fuller and greater than one who simply responds to individual needs with a display of power. This fuller picture of God emerges especially in the emphasis on the sovereignty of God. In these speeches attention is given to proclaiming God's sovereignty in the death of Christ and in raising Christ from the dead. Five purely evangelistic speeches in Acts are given to Jews and God-fearers (Gentiles who were attracted to the Jewish religion who had not yet become full Jews or proselytes).[11] Of these five speeches, four contain references to the fact that the death of Christ fulfilled God's purpose or prophecy (2:23; 3:18; 8:32–35; 13:27, 29). Four of these and the only full message to a purely Gentile audience mention that God raised Jesus from the dead (2:24; 3:15; 10:40; 17:31). Three times it is stated that the resurrection or reign of Christ was predicted in prophecy (2:25–31; 3:21–26; 13:32–37).

God's sovereignty in Israel's history is presented twice to Jewish audiences (3:22–25; 13:14–42). In both messages to Gentile audiences, that is, in Lystra and Athens, God is presented as the sovereign Creator and Lord of the universe and of history (14:15–17; 17:24–27). The coming judgment by God or Christ is also proclaimed in five of the seven evangelistic messages in Acts (2:40; 3:23; 10:42; 13:40–41; 17:31).

The sovereignty of God is presented in various other ways: for example, in the election (2:34), the appointing and sending of Jesus (3:20, 26), and the call to audiences to repent, which appears in four speeches (2:38; 3:19, 26; 14:15; 17:30). The last of these is an all-inclusive command to "all people everywhere to repent" (17:30). In his two evangelistic talks to Gentile audiences Paul attempts to give a full introduction to who God is (14:15–17; 17:23–31).

All this shows that although the demonstration of power in a personal and individual way attracted people, when the apostles proclaimed the gospel they gave a much fuller picture of who God is. We have a lot of work to do in presenting Christ to people who are attracted by God's power to meet personal need.

The need to present this fuller picture of God is urgent, especially because converts to Christianity who view God primarily as a protector and helper may simply transpose their previous view of God into their Christian belief system. The result could be that they think of God as one who answers prayer and can be appeased through certain rituals and by keeping certain rules such as tithing. They may miss out on having their lives influenced by the glory and majesty and holiness of God.

Most non-Christians come from what may be called shame cultures, in which sin is often defined as losing face. There isn't the strong sense of holiness that comes from the concept of a holy and supreme God to whom we are accountable. This will be increasingly true in the West, where the belief in a supreme and holy God is being replaced by a pantheistic understanding. If we do not pay special attention to this need we may end up with a church of lukewarm Christians who have been converted to Christianity through seeing God's power but who have not fully grasped the fact that followers of this God are expected to live holy lives.[12]

There are other evangelistic values in presenting this other side of God. If what we say about God is true, if He is indeed sovereign over history, if He is holy and judges sin, then the wisest thing that one could do would be to align himself or herself with this God. The power of God to meet personal needs can arrest someone who is uninterested in the gospel, but this power may not impress some non-Christians. Instead the sovereignty and holiness of God may be what impresses them. Some years ago I wrote a book about the doctrine of hell. I was amazed at the number of people who, when they heard what I was doing, told me that the doctrine of judgment had led them to commit their lives to Christ.[13] Let's then include the full picture of God in our Christian witness.

The Appeal of God's Loving Concern. In the discussion about the origin of religion (chapter 7) we said that tribal people gave up worshiping the Creator-Father-God to concentrate on avoiding the immediate terror they faced from vicious spirits. But those who understand that God is a loving Father find this to be a wonderfully liberating truth. In the discussion on spirituality in the next chapter I will tell the story of a Hindu accountant, Satchi, who was sent to our office by the firm that does our audit. Someone in the office talked to him about Christ, and that started a process that ended with him not only coming to Christ but also joining our staff. What finally convinced him that he needed to yield to Christ was the realization that Jesus had died for him. Satchi realized that there is no God in Hinduism who was so committed to him as to die for him.

Namal Weerasinghe was a young Buddhist boy who would often help his brothers with their illegal liquor business (the Sri Lankan equivalent of moonshine). His father had died when he was very young, and his loving mother was not in good health. He feared that he would be stranded with no one to help him if his mother also died. So he decided to look for someone who would help him. He went to various shrines and temples and participated in their rituals in order to get the help and protection of the Hindu gods. During this time Youth for Christ volunteers came often to his neighborhood to invite the youth there to meetings that were held nearby. He did all he could to avoid them, but they would follow him when he ran away to hide.

Namal attended a few Youth for Christ meetings and even went to a camp. He could not agree with this religion, and he debated with the Christians about their beliefs. One day he heard a speaker quote and explain Isaiah 49:15: "Can a mother forget the baby at her breast and have no compassion on the child she has borne? Though she may forget, I will not forget you!" He realized that this was the God he had been looking for all along. He became a Christian and eventually joined our staff as an evangelist to other young people from a similar background to his.

People go to small gods to get small favors done for them. We need to tell them that the supreme God of the universe cares for them enough to be their loving Father!

Astrology, Palmistry, Psychic Readers

Types of Practices. Most popular magazines and newspapers in the East and the West have a section devoted to astrology. Psychic counselors advertise in major media. Many of the practices that are common today could be classified as *divination*.[14] Divination is the art of foretelling the future, finding the lost, identifying the guilty, or even finding the best place to dig a well, by using a wide range of techniques. Often diviners claim to involve the services of spirit beings.

Astrology is based on the belief that the stars and planets influence people's lives. The idea is that the arrangement of the stars and other celestial bodies at the time of one's birth sets a pattern for the person's life. There are twelve signs of the zodiac, and people are categorized according to the particular sign under which they were born. For example, Taurus (Latin for "bull") falls between April 20 and May 20.

Palmistry is the practice of reading the lines and bumps on the palms and fingers of the hand in order to determine a person's future and interpret his or her character.

I Ching, which is also called *The Book of Changes,* is one of the earliest works of Chinese literature. It forms the basis for an ancient Chinese divinatory system. This technique involves finding the flow of the life forces, *yin* and *yang,* that when read properly can determine the course of future actions. Yin stands for the feminine, passive, negative, or receptive life force. Yang stands for the male, active, or positive life force. According to the Chinese system the flux, balance, or imbalance of the universe is caused by the reaction of the yin and the yang. I Ching computer programs are common among Chinese business people.

Feng shui (literally meaning "wind and water") or *geomancy* is a popular practice among Chinese all over the world. This is a divinatory practice used to locate suitable building sites and for the design and construction of office towers, hotels, restaurants, and shopping centers. A specialist uses a magnetic compass in a disc to divine the appropriate information.[15]

Numerology is a system of divination and occult practice based on the idea that the universe is mathematically constructed and all things can be expressed in numbers. The numbers are given specific values and meanings.

The *tarot* is a deck of playing cards that is used for fortune telling. The cards have various symbols such as king, queen, knight, and page that signify spirit, soul, vitality, and body respectively. The skeleton symbolizes death. Each card and the way in which the cards are arranged are important to this system.

Channeling is the process by which a medium is said to communicate information from nonphysical beings such as spirits, demons, deities, or even aliens. During this process the medium usually enters a trance or some other form of altered consciousness.

Necromancy is closely related to channeling, but a necromancer communicates with the dead.

Psychic reading and *psychic counseling* are terms that can be given to many of the practices mentioned above. These practices involve the use of a psychic, one who is said to be able to find information through a supernatural means, or a medium, one who is said to have the ability to communicate with the dead or spirits.

A *séance* is a meeting of a group of people who attempt to communicate, usually through a medium, with a spirit or a dead person.

A *charm,* from the Latin word *carmen,* which means "song," is a formula intended to be sung or recited to propitiate a spirit or to achieve some other desired effect, for example, cursing an enemy.

Talismans are objects made of stone, metal, wood, or parchment and inscribed with allegedly magical signs, characters, or drawings. Talismans are believed to harness powers that protect and prosper the owner. Often talismans are worn around the neck or the waist.

Exorcism is a word that Christians use to describe driving out of evil spirits, but here we use it to refer to the work of occultic practitioners such as devil dancers, sorcerers, and exorcists. This is a common practice in our part of the world when sickness or other misfortunes are suspected as being caused by evil spirits, and also when people show signs of possession by an evil spirit. The ritual involves dancing, chanting, or sacrifices to appease the demons, and often it lasts a whole night.

Is There Power Here? We will not give a detailed critique of these practices, as many Christian books already do that.[16] Some evangelical writers deny any supernatural power in these things, saying that it is all illusion and deception.[17] They have interpreted the passages of Scripture suggesting that evil forces have power over humans to mean something else.

Perhaps most occultic practitioners can be described as those who use deception and illusionary arts. But to include all such activity under this category is going too far. I know of several instances in which observations about people's backgrounds or predictions made about them are so uncannily accurate that they could not be explained by purely natural causes. The Bible clearly presents many instances in which those who were under the influence of Satan and his forces exhibited supernatural powers.

Many people resort to astrology. It is part of normal life in Sri Lanka. But these practices do not give people the peace and security that they seek. Often an astrologer or palmist predicts a bad period, and all sorts of precautions are taken. National elections are held at inconvenient times to avoid a bad period for the party in power. Important projects are delayed. People are bound by the prediction. I heard about two friends who do not want to marry each other but who will marry because their horoscopes match. Many people do not marry the one they want to marry because their horoscopes do not match. Others have to delay marriage, as they cannot find a person whose horoscope matches theirs.

How much more liberating it is to be able to trust God and say, "My times are in your hands" (Psalm 31:15) and to know that there are no bad periods with God. Even in the things that seem to be disasters we know that "God works for the good of those who love him" so that "in all these things we are more than conquerors" (Romans 8:28, 37). With such a faith we do not need a horoscope. We can trust God to look after us. Paul's instruction is "Do not be anxious about anything, but in everything, by prayer and petition, with thanksgiving, present your requests to God. And the peace of God, which transcends all understanding, will guard your hearts and your minds in Christ Jesus" (Philippians 4:6–7).

The Bible Prohibits Involvement. Whatever one's interpretation about the nature of the alleged powers, we can be certain that the Bible strictly prohibits these practices.

Leviticus 19:26, 31 says, "'Do not practice divination or sorcery. . . . Do not turn to mediums or seek out spiritists, for you will be defiled by them. I am the Lord your God.'" In Deuteronomy 18:10–12, 14, we read, "Let no one be found among you . . . who practices divination or sorcery, interprets omens, engages in witchcraft, or casts spells, or who is a medium or spiritist or who consults the dead. Anyone who does these things is detestable to the Lord, and because of these detestable practices the Lord your God will drive out those nations before you. . . . The nations you will dispossess listen to those who practice sorcery or divination. But as for you, the Lord your God has not permitted you to do so."

Later God, speaking through the prophet Isaiah, warned: "Keep on, then, with your magic spells and with your many sorceries, which you have labored at since childhood. Perhaps you will succeed, perhaps you will cause terror. All the counsel you have received has only worn you out! Let your astrologers come forward, those stargazers who make predictions month by month, let them save you from what is coming upon you. Surely they are like stubble; the fire will burn them up. They cannot even save themselves from the power of the flame" (47:12–14).

In spite of the unequivocal prohibitions in the Scriptures, it is amazing how many Christians resort to these practices in a crisis or out of curiosity. Sometimes these activities take an appearance of innocent fun. There is a lure in the promise of knowing what one's future holds. In desperate times, when nothing else seems to provide a solution for a serious problem, people can be attracted to the power of these forces.

In Sri Lanka, looking at another's palm and commenting on what it has to say about the person and his or her future is a common and normal activity. My friends did it all the time in my youth. But I have never allowed anyone to read my palm. Once, when a friend read my palm without my knowing it, I prohibited him from telling me what it said. Considering the insidious hold that these practices can have upon us, it is best to stay away from them. I am very poor at remembering numbers and such things; therefore I do not remember my astrological sign, and I am not eager to know it. But some people are not blessed with a poor memory like mine, and they know their sign. It would be best for them not to even look at the horoscope in a newspaper or magazine.

Freedom from Occult Power. Being freed from the hold of occult powers may involve some spiritual therapy. There may need to be prayer for deliverance from any foothold that Satan has on a person because of pre-Christian activities. Some years ago a young Youth for Christ volunteer rented a home and went to live there with his bride. He noticed that there were charmed bottles placed on the wall near the ceiling. He asked me and a colleague to come to his home. When we went there we read Scripture and prayed for protection and cleansing and took the bottles with us as we left. We threw them into a trash heap.

My university roommate had an expensive gold talisman, which he had got for a lot of money from a Buddhist monk. Shortly after committing his life to Christ he realized that he should throw this away. I thought this would be an easy decision for him to make. But that was not so. One day, however, when he was coming back to our hostel from the university he threw it into a rice field that he passed on the way.

We must remember that people are attracted to these practices because of the possibility of quick results or of knowledge of the future that they feel they need in a time of crisis. We must show people the danger of playing with these forces. Not only are these forces opposed to the almighty God, but also they will also be crushed by Him one day. We must also help Christians have a firm grasp of the sovereignty of God. If their security lies there, then they will not fear any circumstance, for they know that it will be turned into something good. If God is sovereign, the only thing to fear is disobedience. And dabbling in the occult is disobedience!

Chapter 10 endnotes

[1] See E. M. Blaiklock, "The Acts of the Apostles," *The Tyndale New Testament Commentaries* (Grand Rapids, MI: Wm. B. Eerdmans Publishing Co., 1959), 140.

[2] Harold Turner, "World of the Spirits," in *Eerdmans' Handbook to World Religions* (Grand Rapids, MI: Wm. B. Eerdmans Publishing Co., 1994), 130.

[3] Turner, "World of the Spirits," 131.

[4] *Eerdmans' Handbook to World Religions*, 445.

[5] L. A. de Silva, *Budddism: Beliefs and Practices in Sri Lanka* (Colombo: Ecumenical Institute for Study and Dialogue, 1974), 81.

[6] *The Four Spiritual Laws* (*Dharma for the Millions, no. 1*).

[7] Julia Ching, "East Asian Religions," *World Religions: Eastern Traditions*, Willard G. Oxtoby, editor (Don Mills, ON, Canada: Oxford University Press, 1996), 429.

[8] George A. Mather and Larry A. Nichols, *Dictionary of Cults, Sects, Religions, and the Occult* (Grand Rapids, MI: Zondervan Publishing House, 1993), 271.

[9] Kenneth L. Woodward, "The Other Jesus," *Newsweek,* March 27, 2000, 78–79.

[10] See John Wimber and Kevin Springer, *Power Evangelism* (San Francisco: Harper and Row, 1986); and Charles H. Kraft, *Christianity with*

Power: Your Worldview and Your Experiences of the Supernatural (Ann Arbor, MI: Vine Books, 1989).

[11] Two were given in Jerusalem (Acts 2 and 3), one in Antioch of Pisidia (Acts 13), and one each to the Ethiopian eunuch (Acts 8) and those assembled at Cornelius's house (Acts 10).

[12] For a fuller treatment, see my "God: the Source, the Originator, and the End of Mission," in *Global Missiology for the 21st Century,* William D. Taylor, editor (Grand Rapids, MI: Baker Book House, 2000): chapter 13.

[13] Ajith Fernando, *Crucial Questions about Hell* (Wheaton, IL: Crossway Books, 1994). In this book I have discussed many practical issues relating to proclaiming the message of judgment.

[14] Several dictionaries and books were used for these descriptions, especially Mather and Nichols, *Dictionary of Cults, Sects, Religions, and the Occult;* and *Guide to the Occult and Mysticism* (London: Geddes and Grosset, 1997).

[15] This description has relied on Ching, "East Asian Religions," 367.

[16] John Ankerberg and John Weldon, *Encyclopedia of New Age Beliefs* (Eugene, OR: Harvest House Publishers, 1996); Joseph Bayly, *What about Horoscopes?* (Elgin, IL: David C. Cook Publishing Co., 1970); Doug Groothuis, *Confronting the New Age* (Downers Grove, IL: InterVarsity Press, 1988); André Kole and Terry Holley, *Astrology and Psychic Phenomena* (Grand Rapids, MI: Zondervan Publishing House, 1998); Josh McDowell and Don Stewart, *The Occult: The Authority of the Believer Over the Powers of Darkness* (San Bernardino: Here's Life, 1992); John Warwick Montgomery, *Principalities and Powers: The World of the Occult* (Minneapolis: Bethany House Publishers, 1973); Robert A. Morey, *Horoscopes and the Christian* (Minneapolis: Bethany House Publishers, 1981); Morey, *Satan's Devices* (Eugene, OR: Harvest House, 1993); Charles Strohmer, *What Your Horoscope Doesn't Tell You* (Milton Keynes, England: Word Publishing, 1991; originally published by Wheaton, IL: Tyndale House Publishers); J. Stafford Wright, *Christianity and the Occult* (London: Scripture Union, 1971).

[17] See Kole and Holley, *Astrology and Psychic Phenomena.*

11

SPIRITUALITY: CHRISTIAN AND NON-CHRISTIAN[1]

All over the world we are seeing a resurgence of interest in spirituality. The East has always given a high place to spirituality, and the Eastern religions have spiritual disciplines to give expression to that. In chapter 5 we said that about 150 years ago the study of other cultures and the discovery of riches in them began a new trend of appreciating these cultures. But this appreciation has become a particularly significant feature of postmodern Western society since the last quarter of the twentieth century. Postmodern people are revolting against what they see as the tyranny of the rationalism of the modern era. They claim that owing to the preoccupation with objective facts the individual, with his or her feelings and drives, is neglected. One of the things neglected is the spiritual side of the human being.[2]

Twenty years ago there was a lot of talk about secular humanism, which generally ignored or denied the spiritual aspect of human beings. This view has given way to an attitude toward life that gives a higher place to the spiritual. But the spirituality that has attracted people in the West is closer to New Age or Eastern spirituality than it is to Christian spirituality.[3] We see people taking interest in astrology, in magic and the occult, in psychic and spiritual counselors, and in Eastern meditation.

Meditation and belief in reincarnation have become commonplace even in the West. Many new versions of old films and television serials such as *Star Trek, Robin Hood, Hercules,* and *Sinbad the Sailor* give evidence of such spirituality. I found it amusing to see the Muslim Sinbad, who calls God "Allah," involved in many magical activities that are generally scorned by Muslims.

Defining Spirituality

Though "spirituality" is a word much in vogue, it is difficult to define. In the preface to an important reference work on Christian spirituality the editors say, "'Spirituality,' we confess, is a vague word, often used with no clear meaning, or with a wide and vague significance."[4] The word seems to have originated with French Catholics, but it is now common to evangelical Protestants too.[5] Christians in the Orthodox tradition prefer to refer to this field as mystical theology.

For the purpose of this study, which goes beyond the boundaries of Christianity, the comments of Gordon Wakefield are most helpful. "In all [Christian] traditions, and in many non-Christian faiths and philosophies, the underlying implication is that there is a constituent of human nature which seeks relations with the ground and purpose of existence, however conceived."[6] In his speech to the Areopagus, Paul implies that this thirst for the spiritual comes from God. Regarding the course of God's dealings with the nations (Acts 17:26) he says, "God did this so that men would seek him and perhaps reach out for him" (17:27).

Seeking the divine and reaching out for the divine have taken various forms, and we could classify all of these under the term *spirituality.* Wakefield says that for Christians the basic expression of spirituality is prayer. But in other faiths it can take the form of spiritual disciplines such as meditation, fasting, yogic exercises, almsgiving, and pilgrimage. Some expressions of spirituality are not usually included under religion because they are evil and clearly harmful to humanity. Wakefield points out that "Adolf Hitler was a spiritual being, a man, more than most, 'possessed': yet his spirit was surely evil."[7]

Geoffrey Parrinder, an emeritus professor at London University and one of the world's top authorities in the field of comparative religion, has written a book describing the forms of spirituality in the world's religions.[8] He uses the word *mysticism,* a word that is notoriously difficult to define but that for our purposes is virtually synonymous with what we call spirituality. He classifies the different forms of mysticism into two types. Parrinder calls the first type *monistic mysticism,* and this would include pantheistic forms of spirituality. These forms seek self-identity or union with the All. Here he includes the various Asian religions from Hinduism to Buddhism, with its goal of *nirvana,* from Tao to Shinto. The second type is *theistic mysticism,* which seeks communion but not identity with God. Here Parrinder includes Indian monotheism (as seen in the famous Hindu writing the Bhagavad Gita), Judaism, Islam, and Christianity. In the chapters on the different views of God, we briefly touched on these different forms of religious expression.

Defective Evangelical Spirituality

It could be that many expressions of evangelical Christianity have been defective in the area of spirituality. In many evangelical traditions conversion was defined as intellectual assent to the message of the cross. After conversion the emphasis was on obedience to Christ, so that sanctification was equated with obedience. There was little emphasis on the work of the Spirit in sanctification. The teaching about the assurance of salvation was almost entirely an appeal to the rational—the Bible says those who believe are saved; therefore if you have believed, you are saved. There is little mention of the experience of Christ through the Holy Spirit, the transformed life, and the witness of the Spirit as means of assurance. Any display of emotion in religion, or what Jonathan Edwards called "religious affections," was viewed with suspicion.

The growth of Protestantism in the West coincided with the growth of industrialization or what we would call the modern era. Perhaps some Protestant attitudes that placed a high value on work and productivity (the so-called Protestant work ethic) helped in speeding the technological advancement of the West. In this environment science ruled supreme as a most worthy field of study. And mathematics was the queen of the sciences.[9]

Two side effects of this growth of science and technology were the high place given to the rational side of human experience and to efficiency and productivity. This may have resulted in a lowering of the value and quality of spirituality among many Protestants. In classic spirituality, time must be devoted to cultivate the contemplative life through the spiritual disciplines. But time was considered precious, given the efficiency and productivity orientation of the age. So the contemplative disciplines could have unwittingly been pushed to the background. Emphasis on the rational could also have resulted in downplaying the more mystical sides of Christian experience.

To many postmodern people, Christianity is an expression of the dry rationalism of modernism that they are revolting against. In recent years this situation has changed; in the charismatic and other wings of the evangelical church there is a resurgence of interest in spirituality. But when some people still are rejecting Christianity and looking for spirituality elsewhere, they find non-Christian spirituality attractive. As they look at certain forms of non-Christian spirituality they wonder whether those forms are superior to Christian spirituality.

The Dangers of Identifying Christianity with One Culture

The first point to make is that the discovery of riches in other faiths is coming alongside a discovery of riches in other cultures. Some cultures may have preserved good features in God's original revelation that were obliterated in the West, owing to its pragmatism or to some other cultural features.

I remember one summer in the mid-1970s, when I was a student in the United States. I was struggling with what women wore, or maybe I should say, didn't wear. In an airport I met an American Hare Krishna follower gracefully dressed in a sari. I found it so refreshing! As far as wholesome appearance was concerned, she was much more attractive than were many Christian women I met at that time. We could also mention the strong family ties, the close community life, and the commitment to the contemplative life that are found in Asia.

People made in the image of God are made with the capacity for spiritual experience. And living in a world fashioned by God they could achieve significant heights of moral and spiritual understanding and experience without a Christian influence. Many of these emphases are found in the Bible, but they may have been neglected in some forms of Western Christianity.

Therefore our claim for the uniqueness of Christ is not a claim for the uniqueness of Western culture, as some thought in earlier times. They saw mission as Christianizing the heathen. But to many of them, Christianizing meant Westernizing. The new appreciation of riches in non-Western cultures forces us to stop identifying the gospel with Western culture. It also forces us to ask where the church in the West has been deficient in its understanding of the whole counsel of God.

Biblical Spirituality: Relating to a Holy and Loving God

The Bible has a fully developed and deeply meaningful understanding of spirituality. Much of that spirituality is given in the Old Testament, which was the Bible of the early church, and therefore it did not need to be reemphasized in the New Testament. Because many Christians do not assign sufficient significance to the Old Testament, they may not have fully grasped this emphasis. Biblical spirituality is founded upon a personal relationship with God, who is both loving and holy. Deepening this relationship gives life's most fulfilling experience. David said, "You have made known to me the path of life; you will fill me with joy in your presence, with eternal pleasures at your right hand" (Psalm 16:11). We believe that our relationship with God is most fulfilling because God is the Creator of human spirituality and Jesus is God's answer to human need. Jesus said, "I have come that they may have life, and have it to the full" (John 10:10). We will now look at how the fact that God is both loving and holy influences biblical spirituality.

God Is Loving. The heart of Christian spirituality is a love relationship with a personal God. This is very different from Eastern and New Age spirituality. The God of the Bible is separate from humanity but has reached down to establish an interpersonal relationship with us—a relationship of love. New Age spirituality has a pantheistic understanding of God that understands everything as being God. God is not personal. You are God, and I am God. Our task is to become one with the Divine. The official Hare Krishna magazine is entitled *Back to Godhead*. New Age analyst Theodore Roszak says that our goal is "to awaken the God who sleeps at the root of the human being."[10] Therefore these spiritualities have to do with experiences of the divine through spiritual disciplines. The aim is to be enlightened so that we may experience the oneness with the Divine that forms our essential nature. We are not experiencing this oneness with the Divine owing to the ignorance of our present way of living. Techniques are used to alter ordinary consciousness so that we can see true reality.[11]

These spiritual disciplines are satisfying to some people, because they give some fulfillment to the spiritual nature of humans. But they fall short of complete satisfaction. Humans are made to find fullest satisfaction through personal relationships of love. This is why love songs are so popular in music, which is the language of joy. The heart of Christian spirituality is just this—a love relationship with God.

In marriage, which is often used to describe our relationship with God, a personal relationship takes time to cultivate. Through the practice of spiritual disciplines we cultivate a personal relationship with God. Many Christians are not doing this, and they are missing the beauty of Christian spirituality. The one-minute devotionals that are available in abundance are not helpful, unless they become means by which an appetite for the spiritual life is kindled. One must soon graduate from them to lingering with God through the spiritual disciplines of prayer, praise, adoration, Bible reading, meditation, and corporate worship. Christians who do not know the joys of lingering in the presence of God will be at a loss to know how to respond when people speak of serenity through New Age disciplines such as transcendental meditation. One encouraging sign is that in the past three decades there has been a welcome renewal of interest in the spiritual disciplines within the evangelical movement. Associated with this interest are Richard Foster, James Houston, John Piper, and Dallas Willard in the United States and Peter Toon in Britain.[12]

When those who have practiced non-Christian spiritual disciplines come to Christ, they take to Christian spirituality with relish. Their skills in the art of spiritual disciplines help them to cultivate a deeply satisfying spiritual life. The accounting firm that does the annual audit of Youth for Christ sent a young man, Satchithanandakumar, who was a devout Hindu, to check on our books. Someone in our office spoke to him about Christ, and that led him to becoming a Christian. I had the privilege of meeting him weekly to help him in his spiritual growth. I found that he had cultivated a deep prayer life. Later, when he joined our staff, this prayer life became a key to his phenomenal success in leadership development. He prayed people into leadership. If we were to ask him whether he would go back to Hinduism, he would decisively say, "Never!" The rewards of practicing the Hindu spiritual disciplines could not be compared with the glory of a relationship with a loving God. But this background in the disciplines gave him a head start in his spiritual pilgrimage as a Christian.

Sadhu Sundar Singh was a young Sikh in India who was skilled in Hindu and Sikh disciplines. But he was engaged in a quest for peace that was yet to be satisfied. He "attained a mastery of the Yoga technique and became oblivious of the external world for short spells." Sundar Singh said that during these moments he experienced in some measure the peace and joy that his soul craved. "But when he returned to consciousness, he was again plunged into the turmoil of unrest and discontent."[13] Others have told me of similar experiences. After Sundar Singh became a Christian he became a master of the Christian spiritual life. He also found that God establishes a relationship with him that does not end at the mountaintop, for God comes down to the valley with him. Sundar Singh once said, "Without Christ I was like a fish out of water. With Christ, I am in an ocean of love!"

Biblical Spirituality: God Is Holy. Because God is holy, we must become holy like Him if we have a relationship with Him (1 Peter 1:16). Christian spirituality requires moral and ethical purity. The beauty of it is that just as justification is by grace through faith, so is sanctification, by which we are made holy. On our own we do not have the strength to become holy, but as we repent of our sin and trust in God and obey Him, He makes us holy. Therefore to many in the Protestant tradition the words *spiritual* and *holy* and *saint* are almost synonymous with moral and ethical purity. When we use the word *saint* we generally refer to a righteous and loving person, even though that is not its essential meaning. This is perhaps the great strength of evangelical spirituality. Catholic and Orthodox spirituality has emphasized the sacramental and mystical aspects of spirituality. Charismatic spirituality has emphasized the power aspect of spirituality (the charismatic movement is, of course, a group within the evangelical spectrum). But evangelical spirituality has emphasized the ethical and moral aspects of spirituality. There is truth in all of these emphases.

In pantheistic cultures there is no developed concept of a supreme

God who is holy. Therefore a concerted push for morality is often lacking in pantheistic spirituality. This is why, despite the strong tradition of spirituality in Asia, our countries are plagued by corruption. The gods of Hinduism are morally neutral, and they are often seen to be doing things that we consider quite unholy. The emphasis in those spiritualities is not so much on holiness in the sense of moral purity but on holiness in the sense of spiritual power—of power over the mind, over the body, over anxiety and circumstances. People go to astrologers and psychic readers to have some power over their circumstances. They do yogic exercises to have power over the mind and the body. We have seen that when there is an emphasis on spiritual power, even in Christian circles there sometimes is a tendency to neglect teaching on moral issues.

People from the West go to places like the Himalayan Mountains in search of exotic spiritual experiences. They often have such experiences. But many of them are seen to behave in ways that are morally impure, such as dabbling in drugs and promiscuous sex. Though there are exceptions, pantheistic spiritualities generally have not succeeded in producing just, morally upright, and fair societies. The only country in our region that has succeeded somewhat in doing this is Singapore. But they have done it through a strong emphasis on law and order and government control. Westerners sometimes find it difficult to understand the strictness of that system. But, without the firm foundation of a fear of the sovereign God, perhaps one needs such strong constraints so that the sinful nature of individuals will not destroy a nation.

Presently the societies in many Western countries are fashioned according to a system of trust based on transcendent absolutes and of submission to a supreme God. Structures such as the freedom of expression, democracy, and even the supermarket operate on these assumptions. One shudders to think what will happen as one by one these presuppositions are being jettisoned. The pluralism and pantheism that are sweeping the West and replacing biblical absolutes do not have these constraints that come from the fear of God.

In Christian spirituality we enter into the experience of a personal relationship with the holy God through humble recognition of our sinfulness and inability to help ourselves. We first bow before the supreme God in repentance. Once we enter into a relationship with God, we submit to

His lordship and become subject to His will for our lives. The pantheistic approach is the opposite of this. We can see how this approach fits in with the postmodern mood and its quest for self-actualization. You don't need to bow before a supreme God who is an objective reality outside of yourself. You are God! In the discussion of pantheism (see chapter 8) we referred to the statement of Swami Muktananda, who said, "Kneel to your own self. Honor and worship your own being. God dwells within you as You!"[14] That sounds much better to people seeking to rule their lives than the words, "Kneel in humble submission and repent for your sin before the almighty God."

We shouldn't be surprised by the growth of pantheistic spirituality. It fits with the aspirations of people in both the East and the West. People want something spiritual to answer the cry of the heart that atheism, secular humanism, and communism could not satisfy. Pantheism provides an answer without violating the quest for a life without submission to objective realities like a supreme God, a strict moral code, and an infallible Bible.

Yet no one can find full satisfaction without solving the sin question in his or her life. An American Methodist preacher of an earlier generation, Henry Clay Morrison, is reported to have said, "God did not fix me up so that I couldn't sin. He fixed me up so that I couldn't sin and enjoy it." According to the psalmists, the law of the Lord is not a burden that enslaves us; it is a delight that gives life.[15] The objective truth of the Word is not an obstacle to freedom. Jesus said that the truth will make us free (John 8:32–36). The context of that affirmation shows that the freedom Jesus spoke about had much to do with living a life freed from enslavement to sin.

And what can we say about liberation from our past actions? The law of *karma*, with its belief in repeated incarnations, is being presented as an alternative to the Christian emphasis on sin and judgment, grace and justification. But can people negate all their bad karma by their own efforts accumulated through several lives? Many honest people who are committed to this scheme admit that this is a long and dreary climb along a path that does not carry much hope of liberation at the end. Although the adherents of this path have the satisfaction of doing something to save themselves, they will not experience the freedom of knowing that their wrong actions are behind them eternally and forgotten. The Christian gospel, by contrast, speaks of "having our hearts sprinkled to cleanse us from a guilty conscience" (Hebrews 10:22) through the perfect and sufficient sacrifice of Christ Jesus. Without such freedom from a guilty conscience there can be no permanently fulfilling experience of spirituality.

An Opportunity for the Church

While the new interest in spirituality is a challenge to the church, it is also a great opportunity.[16] Christian spirituality is one of the key aspects of the uniqueness of Christ, and therefore it could figure prominently in evangelism. Sooner or later people will realize that the serenity that New Age or Eastern spirituality provides does not fully satisfy. Although these spiritualities have been described as holistic, only the Creator of human life can give humans a truly holistic spirituality. It is He who created every aspect of the human makeup, and therefore only He can satisfy the yearnings of the whole human soul. This is why Jesus, who was God's answer to the human dilemma, said, "I have come that they may have life, and have it to the full" (John 10:10).

The preceding discussion has shown us that the current interest in spirituality could be a stepping-stone in the evangelization of postmoderns and people of other faiths. Worship, the supreme expression of Christian spirituality, could therefore be an important means to evangelism. Many years ago I paid my first visit to Mannar, a city in northern Sri Lanka, where we had just begun a Youth for Christ ministry. The population there is primarily Roman Catholic and Hindu. On that visit I spoke at an evangelistic program. I was surprised to see that, instead of the usual Youth for Christ crowd breakers that involve a lot of fun, this meeting began with about thirty minutes of worship.

I thought that this was not the best way to start the program, that these people had not understood YFC's strategy of evangelizing youth. But because this was my first visit to Mannar, I did not say anything about it to the people there. We soon began to realize that this worship attracted youth to our programs. They liked the music, and they were impressed with the sense of vibrancy and intimacy with God that was evidenced during the worship. It seemed to strike a chord in their hearts and answer their yearning for contact with the Divine. We learned from this new program in YFC that worship can be an important means of evangelizing youth.

The current interest in spirituality is a challenge to the church. We have the answer that the world is looking for. But have we ourselves experienced it? Do we know the glory of intimacy with the loving and holy God who is supreme above creation? Has this relationship transformed us into morally pure people? If we can answer these questions in the affirmative, we will truly be light to the darkness of the world in this era of so much moral and religious confusion.

Chapter 11 endnotes

[1] Some of the material in this chapter appears in my "The Uniqueness of Jesus Christ," in *Telling the Truth: Evangelizing Postmoderns,* D. A. Carson, editor (Grand Rapids, MI: Zondervan Publishing House, 2000).

[2] For bibliographical details on postmodernism, see notes 9, 10, 17, and 18 in chapter 1.

[3] See Douglas R. Groothuis, *Unmasking the New Age* (Downers Grove, IL: InterVarsity Press, 1986), 37–56.

[4] *The Study of Spirituality,* Cheslyn Jones, Geoffrey Wainright, and Edward Yarnold, editors (Oxford: Oxford University Press, 1986), xxii. For a study of the word see xxiv–xxvi of the book.

[5] Gordon S. Wakefield, "Preface," *The Westminster Dictionary of Christian Spirituality,* Gordon S. Wakefield, editor (Philadelphia: The Westminster Press, 1983), v.

[6] Wakefield, "Preface," v.

[7] Gordon S. Wakefield, "Spirituality," in *The Westminster Dictionary of Christian Spirituality,* 362.

[8] Geoffrey Parrinder, *Mysticism in the World's Religions* (Oneworld Publications, 1995).

[9] For a helpful analysis of the history of science from a Christian perspective see Nancy R. Pearcey and Charles B. Thaxton, *The Soul of Science: Christian Faith and Natural Philosophy* (Wheaton, IL: Crossway Books, 1994).

[10] Theodore Roszak, *Unfinished Animal* (New York: Harper and Row, 1977), 225, quoted in Groothuis, *Unmasking the New Age*, 21.

[11] From a description by Groothuis, *Unmasking the New Age*, 22.

[12] Richard J. Foster, *Celebration of Discipline* (San Francisco: Harper and Row, 1988; UK edition by London: Hodder and Stoughton); Richard J. Foster, *Prayer: Finding the Heart's True Home* (1993); James Houston, *The Transforming Friendship: A Guide to Prayer* (Oxford, Batavia, and Sydney: Lion Publishing, 1989); John Piper, *A Hunger for God: Desiring God through Fasting and Prayer* (Wheaton, IL: Crossway Books, 1997); Dallas Willard, *The Spirit of the Disciplines: Understanding How God Changes Lives* (San Francisco: HarperSanFrancisco, 1991, 1988); Dallas Willard, *The Divine Conspiracy: Rediscovering Our Hidden Life in God* (San Francisco: HarperSanFrancisco, 1998; UK edition, London: HarperCollins Publishers); Peter Toon, *From Mind to Heart: Christian Meditation Today* (Grand Rapids, MI: Baker Book House, 1987); Toon, *Meditating as a Christian* (London: HarperCollins Publishing, 1991).

[13] A. J. Appasamy, *Sundar Singh: A Biography* (Madras: The Christian Literature Society, 1966), 19.

[14] Quoted in Groothuis, *Unmasking the New Age*, 21.

[15] See especially Psalm 19 and Psalm 119.

[16] For some warnings and guidelines to evangelicals as we seek to grapple with the issue of spirituality amidst the present interest in the topic see D. A. Carson, "Appendix: When is Spirituality Spiritual? Reflections on Some Problems of Definition" in *The Gagging of God: Christianity Confronts Pluralism* (Leicester: Apollos, InterVarsity Press; and Grand Rapids, MI: Zondervan Publishing House, 1996), 555–569; and Gordon R. Lewis, "The Church and the New Spirituality," *Journal of the Evangelical Theological Society, 36* (1993): 433–44.

12

THE UNIQUENESS OF CHRIST

In Acts 17:23–30 Paul gives the most amount of space to his introduction to who God is. In comparison with the other evangelistic messages in Acts, here Paul says less about Jesus and His life and death. Perhaps Paul couldn't finish his speech because of the opposition he faced. Or perhaps Paul did not intend to give a comprehensive evangelistic message, as this was one among many messages he gave in Athens and was given before something like a court. Perhaps Luke did not record some of what Paul said about Jesus, because Luke had already given fuller descriptions of that in his records of four other evangelistic messages (2:22–36; 3:13–26; 10:36–43; 13:23–39) and of Philip's conversation with the Ethiopian (8:32–35).

Luke records that Paul talked about the resurrection of Christ in this speech (Acts 17:31). If so, he must have said something about the death that preceded the resurrection. Although not much space is given to Jesus in Luke's record here, as in the earlier speeches Jesus is the crucial point of this message. Jesus will wrap up history as Judge of the world, and His resurrection is the proof of all that Paul has been saying. "For he has set a day when he will judge the world with justice by the man he has appointed. He has given proof of this to all men by raising him from the dead" (17:31). Jesus' resurrection proclaims Him the Lord of the universe who holds the key to the judgment that will end history. This is another way of saying that Jesus is absolutely unique and that His resurrection proves His uniqueness.

In this chapter we will use the phrase "absolutely unique" several times. This seems to say the same thing twice, but the reason for choosing this double designation is that people could say that Jesus is unique, just as Muhammad and the Buddha are unique. According to that idea the pluralists also could describe Jesus as unique. By adding the word *absolute* we include the idea that Jesus is the absolute truth for the whole world, and He is therefore the only way to salvation. The other founders may have taught unique truths, but Jesus was absolute truth. This puts Him in a different class from the founders of the other religions.

The Bible Affirms It

I have already written a book about the supremacy of Christ,[1] and so I will not go into this topic in detail. Instead we will highlight a few important issues here. The uniqueness of Christ is a theme that is implicitly or explicitly stated hundreds of times in the Bible. We will cite three texts from three different sections in the New Testament to show how clear the Bible is in affirming this belief. The first text is from the Gospels: "I am the way and the truth and the life. No one comes to the Father except through me" (John 14:6). The second is from Acts: "Salvation is found in no one else, for there is no other name under heaven given to men by which we must be saved" (Acts 4:12). The third text is from the Epistles: "For there is one God and one mediator between God and men, the man Christ Jesus" (1 Timothy 2:5).

John 14:6 presents a comprehensive case for the uniqueness of Christ. As the Way He is unique, because only through Him and His work can we find salvation. As the Truth He is unique, because He alone is absolute truth. Although other ideologies may have many truths, Jesus is absolute truth. As the Life He opens the way for us to experience life to the full. This is what God made us for, and it is the only completely fulfilling life. Because John 14:6 gives us such a comprehensive picture of the person and work of Christ, I structured my book *The Supremacy of Christ* around the three statements there.

Jesus knew that many people would object to the claim He made in John 14:6, so in that same chapter He gives us evidence to back this claim.[2] He says, "If you really knew me, you would know my Father as well. From now on, you do know him and have seen him" (John 14:7). This is a claim to be equal with God Himself. At the start of his Gospel John says that Jesus is the great God who created the universe (John 1:1–3). If Jesus is the Creator of the universe, then we can understand that He can claim to be the absolute Lord of the universe. And if He were God and the absolute Lord of the universe, He would surely be the source of absolute truth.

But many people would also object to Jesus' claim that He is equal to God. Jesus anticipated this and gave evidence to back this claim too. In John 14:10 He said that His words show that he is equal with God: "Don't you believe that I am in the Father, and that the Father is in me? The words I say to you are not just my own. Rather, it is the Father, living in me, who is doing his work." He says His words are the evidence that He is equal with God. We know that Jesus made many claims that proclaimed His absolute lordship and deity.

But some people would reject the claims of Jesus! Jesus anticipated this too, and He said in John 14:11, "Believe me that I am in the Father and the Father is in me; but if you do not, then believe me because of the works themselves" (NRSV). Here He is saying that if we can't believe His words, then we should look at His actions. What we see is that He was a good man who made some amazing claims and backed those claims with His spotless life and miracles. As has often been said, a person who made such claims is a liar, a lunatic, one who is deluded about himself, or what he claimed to be. When we look at Jesus' great life, we cannot say that He was a liar or a lunatic or a deluded person. His life forces us to regard His words with utmost seriousness, and His words proclaim Him as the absolutely unique Lord of the universe!

Pluralists Reject It

The Bible is clear about the absolute uniqueness of Christ. In chapter 1 we talked about the pluralistic attitude to truth and how it rejects the uniqueness of Christ. Pluralists say that there is no such thing as absolute truth. By absolute truth we mean truth that is so perfect and complete that all people everywhere need to submit to it. Instead pluralists say that truth is personal or subjective. Truth is discovered through experience and is not necessarily disclosed without error by a supreme God. In Buddhism and Hinduism this has been the approach to truth for centuries. But as we said in the first chapter, with the onset of the post-modern era pluralism has become popular in the West too.

In the modern era there was emphasis on having our lives and activities fashioned by objective truth, that is, truth outside of ourselves. Examples of objective things that fashioned people's lives are social rules, scientific laws, the Bible, and God. Today Western people say that this bondage to objective truth made machines out of people, so that their personal freedom and experience were neglected. Now the emphasis is on subjective truth: "You have your truth, and I have my truth. And my truth is as valid as your truth." We can see how people with such an approach to truth would object to the Christian claim that Jesus is the absolute truth for the whole world and that He is therefore the only way to salvation.

But what do pluralists do with the clear words of Jesus in the Gospels that proclaim His uniqueness? Pluralists have responded to this challenge in many ways, and we will mention three of them here.[3]

The Gospels Express the Faith of the Early Christians

The first view is related to the typical pluralistic approach to truth, which sees truth as being subjective. Some people say that what the Gospels record as Jesus' words are not necessarily what He said. Instead they are early Christians' expressions of faith in Christ and love for Him. These Christians had a deeply fulfilling experience of Christ that is reflected in their writings about Him. The uniqueness of Christ was a precious reality to them. But this does not necessarily apply to non-Christians, especially because we do not know whether Jesus Himself said these words.

This is said to be particularly true of the statements in the Gospel of John. John attributes to Jesus theologically loaded statements such as the seven special "I am" statements,[4] most of which show Jesus associating Himself with things we normally associate with God. Statements like "Before Abraham was born, I am!" (John 8:58) and "I and the Father are one" (10:30) must have been startling to the fiercely monotheistic Jews. People who reject John's teaching about Christ's uniqueness say that the fact that it has so much theology shows that the writer is not interested in history. By doing this they dismiss these statements about the uniqueness of Christ, claiming that Jesus did not make these statements.

Many Christians, however, have experienced what the New Testament says about the uniqueness of Christ to be true. What do pluralists do with that? Wesley Ariarajah, who advocates the preceding approach to the Gospel records,[5] answers that problem in this way. "When my daughter says that I am the best daddy in the world, and there can be no father like me, she is speaking the truth. For this comes out of her experience. She is honest about it; she knows no other person in the role of her father." Then he says that the little girl in the next house may also say the same thing about her father, and that is true for her too.[6] So, while we must respect the right of Christians to hold that Christ is unique, we must not convert such ideas into absolute truths that are binding on all people.

In *The Supremacy of Christ*[7] I have made a fuller response to this approach to the Gospels, so I will make only a few observations here. Like John, the Synoptic Gospels have a lot to say about the absolute uniqueness of Christ. If the "I am" statements present Christ's supremacy in John, the "Son of Man" statements present it in the Synoptic Gospels. As George E. Ladd has shown, "Son of Man" in the time of Jesus was "a messianic title for a pre-existent heavenly being who comes to earth with the glorious kingdom of God."[8]

The Synoptic Gospels portray the Son of Man as coming in great glory with clouds and angels (Matthew 16:27; 24:30). He will be sitting at the right hand of power (Mark 14:62), on His glorious throne (Matthew 19:28). When He appears, all the nations of the earth will mourn (Matthew 24:30). He will judge the nations (Matthew 25:32). Those who acknowledge Him before men will be acknowledged before God the Father in heaven (Matthew 10:32). Even though heaven and earth may pass away, Christ's words will not pass away (Matthew 24:35). The Son of Man is Lord of the Sabbath (Matthew 12:8). He has authority on earth to forgive sin (Matthew 9:6). These passages show how the Christ of the Synoptic Gospels regarded Himself, so we are not surprised to find Him asking people to forsake everything and follow Him, a theme repeated often in these Gospels.

We have been told that statements such as "I and the Father are one" (John 10:30) do not appear in the Synoptics. But Matthew 11:27 is very similar to this statement: "All things have been committed to me by my Father. No one knows the Son except the Father, and no one knows the Father except the Son and those to whom the Son chooses to reveal him." In the next verse Jesus went on to say, "Come to me, all you who are weary and burdened, and I will give you rest" (11:28).

In view of these passages, it is surprising that some writers claim that the Synoptic Gospels do not teach the uniqueness of Christ in the way that John's Gospel does. The whole New Testament presents Christ as absolute and unique, as the only way available for salvation. To deny this is to be untrue to the New Testament.

But what of the claim that the Gospels are not interested in history and that what they give are the faith reflections of the early church rather than what Jesus said? When we read the Gospels we see that the writers of the Gospels were eager to write what happened in the life of Jesus, not merely what the church believed about Him. Luke's Gospel starts with these words:

> Since many have undertaken to set down an orderly account of the events that have been fulfilled among us, just as they were handed on to us by those who from the beginning were eyewitnesses and servants of the word, I too decided, after investigating everything carefully from the very first, to write an orderly account for you, most excellent Theophilus, so that you may know the truth concerning the things about which you have been instructed (Luke 1:1–4, NRSV).

Luke took pains to write what Christ said and did. Interestingly, out of the four Gospels, John's is the one that has the most details about geography, time, and social and political conditions. He was interested in historical details, and where possible these details have been verified as being correct. In recent years there has been a reappraisal of the historical value and accuracy of John.[9]

The writers of all four Gospels wrote as if they were writing history. Consider these points:

- They wrote in an era when people's powers of memorization were much better than ours because of the system of education they adopted.
- They wrote a relatively short time after the events, about events and teaching that they considered to be vital. Therefore they would have been careful to record what is accurate.
- At the time the Gospels were written there would have been people who knew what Jesus said. If Jesus did not say the things that the Gospels say that He said, wouldn't we expect them to contest the validity of the statements?
- The early Christians were committed to truthfulness and honesty.
- Jesus ministered in public, and many people heard His statements.

Taking all of this into account, the most reasonable conclusion is that the Gospels have an accurate account of what Jesus said and did. And the Gospels have this perfect man claiming to be absolute Lord and doing miracles to back His claim. We too would be wise to accept the words of this great man.

We will not critique in depth the validity of the practice of looking at the Gospels through the lens of subjectivity and then refecting their historicity.[10] Many pluralists say that the Gospels are subjective reflections based on what the early Christians experienced about Jesus. Therefore they do not reflect what Jesus said and did but what the early Christians believed about Jesus based on their experience.

But the Gospel writers claimed to be writing history! It is unfair to the Gospel writers to impose our ideas of how people wrote in those days and use those ideas to dismiss the historicity of what they claimed to be historical. Here are people, almost two millennia after the events, rejecting the record of what the authors claim happened in their century. And why do they do that? Because of an idea they have about how people should have written in those days. Lesslie Newbigin calls this "cultural chauvinism."[11] There is ample evidence that the Gospels fit into the style of writing history that was prevalent in the first century.[12]

Don't Build Theology from a Few Proof-Texts

A second method used to reject texts about Jesus as the only way to salvation is to claim that we can't build our theology on a few proof-texts. Those who believe in the uniqueness of Christ are accused of developing a full-blown theology of uniqueness from a few isolated texts like John 14:6 and Acts 4:12. Thomas Thangaraj describes this approach: "We choose the texts we like or those we think are central in the Bible and base all our beliefs and values on them." He says that to balance off the two texts quoted above there are texts like the following:

> Then Peter began to speak to them: "I truly understand that God shows no partiality, but in every nation anyone who fears [God] and does what is right is acceptable to [God]." (Acts 10:34–35 NRSV)

> John answered, "Master, we saw someone casting out demons in your name, and we tried to stop him, because he does not follow with us." But Jesus said to him, "Do not stop him; for whoever is not against you is for you." (Luke 9:49–50 NRSV)[13]

Thangaraj says that the Bible is not just a book; it is a library consisting of sixty-six books. "No one goes to a library and asks, 'What does this library say about other religions?'" He says, "We need to look at each author, each book, and each subsection to see what we have there."[14]

But our belief that all of Scripture is inspired by the same Holy Spirit leads us to be suspicious of an approach that permits incompatible truths to be found in different places of the Bible. This is a whole topic in itself, and the numerous books published on the authority of Scripture will provide evidence for the Christian belief in the unity of the Bible. A host of biblical scholars have sought to find harmony where there was apparent contradiction without pronouncing these texts to be contradictory. There is a solid case for harmonizing so many of these supposedly contradictory statements in Scripture; we are now not so quick to pass judgment upon those few texts that we initially seemed unable to harmonize.

As for the texts Thanaraj presents, they do not give convincing evidence for a belief in salvation for those who do not explicitly know Christ.

It is precarious to use Luke 9:49–50 in constructing a theology about the possibility of salvation for those of other religions, because the person in this text was "casting out demons in [Jesus'] name."

But more important is the claim that people who use passages like John 14:6 and Acts 4:12 as absolute statements are constructing their theology of salvation from a few proof-texts. Anyone who reads the Old and New Testaments will realize that all the parts of both segments of Scripture point to the absolute uniqueness of God's way as opposed to other ways. The texts from the Synoptic Gospels in the previous section give evidence of this. This so-called library of books is united in affirming that all people everywhere must come to this God through the way that He has prescribed in His special revelation to humanity. Texts like John 14:6 and Acts 4:12 present this truth in vivid and explicit ways. But all of Scripture witnesses to what those verses say. One could ask readers to go through the New Testament and note where the absolute uniqueness of Christ is implied. You will find it on virtually every page. This was what I found when I was working on *The Supremacy of Christ*.

Jesus Did Not Address the Issue of Other Religions and Salvation

Another way to sidestep the strong claims about the uniqueness of Christ in the Bible is to state that He was not addressing the issue of whether other religions could be ways to salvation when He said that He is the only way to salvation. Those who hold this view say that statements like John 14:6 teach that for Christians Jesus is the only way to salvation. Thangaraj says, "To place John 14:6 in today's multi-religious setting to judge the destiny of people of other religions would be to take it totally out of its context and derive conclusions that are not intended in that verse." He says, "Even today, for Christians, Christ is the only way, the truth, and the life. God's ways—very often, mysterious ways—of dealing with other people cannot and should not be limited to this text alone."[15]

To confine the application of these passages to Christians is to go against the texts' clear meaning within their context. The apostles believed without a doubt that the only way that anyone anywhere can be saved is through faith in Jesus. The popular passage on the way to salvation through Christ, John 3:16, says, "God so loved the world." John has the whole world in view. But John's description of the means by which this salvation goes to people includes the expression "whoever believes in him." People all over the world must believe in Jesus. Therefore His Great Commission includes a call to "make disciples of all nations" (Matthew 28:19). In Acts 1:8 Jesus says that we are to be witnesses "to the ends of the earth." Paul said, "Now he commands all people everywhere to repent" (Acts 17:30). When the apostles thought about salvation through Christ they thought about the whole world.

Besides, as we pointed out in chapter 3, the context in which John and the rest of the New Testament was written was a multi-religious one, as is today's context. The background of the New Testament is a pluralistic society. This is a new phenomenon in the West, but it was not so in the early church. The first Christians forged the doctrine of Christ's absolute uniqueness in a pluralistic, multi-religious society.[16] Societies in Asia are also multi-religious. We have grown up with people of other faiths and had them as our dear friends. Yet we were faced with the unmistakable teaching in the Bible that Jesus is the only way to salvation. So we accepted it because we believed the words of Jesus.

Jesus: Lord of the Universe

We must bear in mind that two major factors make the doctrine of Christ's absolute uniqueness difficult for people in this era to accept. First is the pluralistic mood, which goes against any attempt to affirm the uniqueness of one faith at the expense of another. Second is the revolt against the supposed tyranny of objective facts. This makes it difficult for us to uphold the idea that an objective fact, the Christ event, is the basis for the salvation of all people everywhere. In what theologians call the Christ event is included the incarnation, life, death, resurrection, ascension, and exaltation of Jesus.

We saw that Jesus answered this issue by saying that His words confirm His uniqueness and that His works authenticate His words (John 14:6–11). Paul is more specific in claiming "[God] has given proof of this to all men by raising [Jesus] from the dead" (Acts 17:31). As Craig Blomberg has said, "No religion stands or falls with a claim about the resurrection of its founder in the way that Christianity does."[17] But can we accept the idea that one event is so important as to affect the whole world in such a marked way? The church has believed this over the centuries, but can we hold this view in today's pluralistic environment?

The key to the answer to that question is for us to remember who Jesus is. The Christian claim about the uniqueness of Christ is closely associated with the belief that Jesus is God Himself. Any standard evangelical book of theology or apologetics will include the arguments about that. It is significant that pluralists like John Hick were in the forefront of the present-day denial of the orthodox Christian understanding of the Incarnation.[18] If you hold to the doctrine of the deity of Christ, then a corollary of that is the uniqueness of Christ.

The Bible says that Jesus is the Creator and absolute Lord of the whole universe (John 1:1–3; Ephesians 1:19–21; Colossians 1:15–20). We believe that God, the Creator of the universe, presented Jesus as the ultimate answer to the problems of the world He created. His sacrifice was not the sacrifice of an ordinary man. At the cross the spotless God Himself bridged the infinite gap that exists between heaven and the sin of the world. How could we fathom the immensity of a sacrifice in which the immortal and eternal God died? This is why we call it an eternal sacrifice. Surely such a sacrifice would suffice for the sins of the whole world.[19]

If this is true, then it is not a big problem for us to accept that this answer of the Creator of the universe is the universal solution to the malady of the world. The Bible teaches that the malady of the world is caused by human rejection of the lordship of God (Romans 1:18–32). If this is so, we can see how, if Jesus is God, the way to restoration for a fallen world is by acknowledging His lordship.

Because Jesus is God incarnate and Lord of the universe, then it is not strange for us to accept that He is the only Lord and Savior of the whole world. When a whole nation elects a national president in a way that is compatible with that nation's constitution, then there is no question about the fact that he or she is the president of the whole nation. Others may stake a claim to be regarded as president of the nation, but one cannot oust the legitimately elected president by any means contrary to the constitution. This is what we are saying about Jesus. He is not the elected leader, but He is the Creator. By virtue of that fact He is the Lord of the whole universe.

Sometimes people may oust an elected president through a coup. But although Jesus has given people the freedom to reject Him on a personal level, that does not take away His lordship at the cosmic level. We may reject Him, but we are powerless to overthrow Him. Our rejection of his lordship does not negate the fact that He is Lord. A person may reject the leadership of a president and migrate to another country. But that does not disqualify the president from holding office. It is the same with Jesus. People may reject Him and try to leave His kingdom. But that does not stop His kingdom from existing, nor does it change the fact that this kingdom will finally rule the universe.

Today many people think about Jesus only as a loving Savior who gently woos people to Himself and weeps over those who reject Him. This is a true picture of Jesus, but it is not a complete picture. If this is the predominant picture we have of Jesus, we could accommodate the idea that Jesus is not the Lord of the universe, that there may be others whose lordship Jesus permits. But there is another side to Jesus. Paul admonishes us: "Consider therefore the kindness and sternness of God: sternness to those who fell, but kindness to you, provided that you continue in his kindness. Otherwise, you also will be cut off" (Romans 11:22). We often forget that the original context in which the statement that every knee shall bow and every tongue confess that Jesus is Lord is the context of judgment (Isaiah 45:23; Romans 14:11; Philippians 2:10–11). Those who spurn His lordship will be judged, and then they will be compelled to bow to Him and confess His lordship.

If we take into account the full biblical picture of the person of Jesus, we would have to conclude that Jesus is indeed absolute Lord of all. We would realize that we do not need to modify the belief about the uniqueness of Christ that the church has held through the centuries. Paul said:

> Therefore God exalted him to the highest place and gave him the name that is above every name, that at the name of Jesus every knee should bow, in heaven and on earth and under the earth, and every tongue confess that Jesus Christ is Lord, to the glory of God the Father. (Philippians 2:9–11)

Incarnation and Avatar

Perhaps we should say something about Hinduism's concept of the incarnations of the gods, because some people could consider these equal to the incarnation of Christ and thus detract from His absolute uniqueness. In popular Hinduism there is an idea that Vishnu, the pre-server god, comes down to the world, when order or righteousness has been lost, to help restore order and protect the good and destroy evildo-ers. Hinduism's best-loved scripture, the Bhagavad Gita (which is part of the third- or second-century BC epic, *The Mahabharata*), says, "Whenever righteousness declines and unrighteousness grows powerful, then, O Bhārata, I manifest myself. I come into being from age to age to protect the good, destroy the wicked and establish righteousness" (4:8–8).[20]

There is a common idea in Hindu literature that there will be ten avatars of Vishnu, some of whom are still to come. (The word *avatar* means "a descent.") Rama and Krishna are the most famous avatars. Some schol-ars include the Buddha and/or Jesus in this list of ten. Some modern gurus also claim to be avatars. Sai Baba is the most famous of the modern gurus, and he is unusual in that he claims to be an incarnation of the god Shiva, the god of contrasts who is viewed both as creator and destroyer.

Several scholars have pointed out the similarities and points of con-trast between the incarnations of the avatars and that of Jesus.[21] In some ways devotion (*bhakti*) to some of the avatars, such as to Krishna, is the closest that Hinduism comes to the Christian concepts of salvation by grace and faith in and devotion to a personal God.[22] When George Harrison sang his song of devotion and commitment, "My Sweet Lord," the devotion was addressed to Krishna. This could be a point of contact when we communicate the gospel to the Hindus. But it is also a problem because, given their pluralistic approach, they could simply add Jesus to their list of gods, especially if they get the idea that He is another incar-nation of Vishnu.

Some of the avatars "are depicted as falling very far short of what we should regard as moral perfection."[23] This was what Tal Brooke, one of the chief Western disciples of Satya Sai Baba, discovered about his mas-ter. That led Brooke to question Sai Baba's credentials and finally to faith in Christ.[24] The moral dimension of divinity is not so important in some Eastern cultures, as we saw in our discussion of spirituality (chapter 11).

But because of a universal commitment to human rights and justice, what seem to be the unjust actions of the avatars will begin to pose a more serious challenge than before. Stories about the abuse of children and other atrocities by a very popular "god-man" guru have been spreading recently. This ought to make people who now regard these as terrible crimes to have second thoughts about their attraction to him.

The biggest difference between the Hindu idea of incarnation and the Christian one is that in Hinduism the incarnations are repeated several times. They come when things have deteriorated so much that there is a special need to save the world. As there is no universally accepted doctrinal basis for Hinduism, the approach to the idea of the avatars varies among Hindus. Some view the avatars as mythical figures whose historicity is doubtful. Some view them as not being totally involved in humanity with its struggles and experiences, somewhat like the Docetists' understanding of Christ's incarnation.[25] Others view them as real historical beings who lived complete lives on earth. Some see them as "manifestations of the divine suitable for those not yet at the highest stages of spiritual growth."[26]

To add to this is the guru phenomenon that is popular in Hinduism. The word *guru* can mean a lot of things; in many languages in the Indian subcontinent it is the basic word for teacher. But there is the phenomenon of the Indian teacher who is regarded as an especially holy man. Many are regarded as gods or as possessing the attributes of God in a special way.[27] Then there is the belief of Hindu pantheists that we are all part of God. All this makes the avatar idea different from the Christian idea of the incarnation of Christ, which was a never-to-be-repeated event that has eternal ramifications.

The *bodhisattvas* of Mahayana Buddhism are also often considered equal to the gods. The bodhisattvas, who have delayed attaining *nirvana* so that they can help others to salvation, lack an absolute and universal character as to their place in the religion.

The Christ event was a once-and-for-all event. The contrast in Hebrews between Jesus' sacrifice and the Jewish sacrificial system applies to our discussion too: "Unlike the other high priests, he does not need to offer sacrifices day after day. . . . He sacrificed for their sins once for all when he offered himself" (Hebrews 7:27). He saves us "through the blood of the eternal covenant" (13:20). This brings us back to the point that the work of Jesus is absolute and universal in its application.

This chapter on the uniqueness of Christ has highlighted the claim that Jesus is the Lord of creation—God's answer to the problems of the world He created. As such He is unique in an absolute sense. Pluralists say there is no such thing as absolute truth. We cannot say that, for the Creator of the world has given humanity a unique and once-for-all message in the person and work of the Lord of the universe: Jesus Christ.

Chapter 12 endnotes

[1] Ajith Fernando, *The Supremacy of Christ* (Wheaton, IL: Crossway Books, 1995).

[2] What follows in the next few paragraphs is a summary of what I have argued for in several chapters of my book, *The Supremacy of Christ*.

[3] For a description of a few more ways see Frederick W. Schmidt, "Jesus and the Salvation of the Gentiles," in *Through No Fault of Their Own? The Fate of Those Who Have Never Heard,* William V. Crockett and James G. Sigountos, editors (Grand Rapids, MI: Baker Book House, 1991), 97–105. M. Thomas Thangaraj describes four ways in which people who reject the absolute uniqueness of Christ interpret John 14:6 in *Relating to People of Other Religions: What Every Christian Needs to Know* (Nashville: Abingdon Press, 1997), 101–106. The following books are a representative sampling of the many that have been published recently that reject the uniqueness of Christ as understood by the church over the centuries: Wesley Ariarajah, *The Bible and People of Other Faiths* (Geneva: World Council of Churches, 1985; reprinted by Maryknoll, NY: Orbis Books); John Hick, *God and the Universe of Faiths* (London: Macmillan, 1973; reprinted by Chatham, NY and Oxford: Oneworld Publication, 1993); *The Myth of Christian Uniqueness: Toward a Pluralistic Theology of Religions,* John Hick and Paul F. Knitter, editors (Maryknoll, NY: Orbis Books, 1987); Paul F. Knitter, *No Other Name? A Critical Survey of Christian Attitudes Toward the World Religions* (Maryknoll, NY: Orbis Books, 1985); S. J. Samartha, *One Christ, Many Religions: Toward a Revised Christology* (Maryknoll, NY: Orbis Books, 1991).

4 John 6:35; 8:12; 10:7, 9; 10:11; 11:25; 14:6; 15:1.

5 Ariarajah, *The Bible and People of Other Faiths,* 21 –27.

6 Ariarajah, *The Bible and People of Other Faiths,* 24–25.

7 Fernando, *The Supremacy of Christ,* chapter 6, "Are the Gospels Historically Accurate Accounts?" For more comprehensive treatments of this issue, see F. F. Bruce, *The New Testament Documents: Are They Reliable?* (Leicester and Downers Grove, IL: InterVarsity Press, 1960); and Craig Blomberg, *The Historical Reliability of the Gospels* (Leicester and Downers Grove, IL: InterVarsity Press, 1987).

8 George Eldon Ladd, *A Theology of the New Testament,* revised edition, Donald A. Hagner, editor (Grand Rapids, MI: Wm. B. Eerdmans Publishing Co., 1993), 147.

9 See, for example, John A. T. Robinson, *The Priority of John* (London: SCM Press; Philadelphia: The Westminster Press, 1986). Evangelical defenses of the historical value of John are seen in Craig Blomberg, *The Historical Reliability of the Gospels,* 162–89; D. A. Carson, *The Gospel According to John* (Leicester: InterVarsity Press; Grand Rapids, MI: Wm. B. Eerdmans Publishing Co., 1991), 40–68; Leon Morris, *The Gospel According to John,* revised (Grand Rapids, MI: Wm. B. Eerdmans Publishing Co., 1995), 35–42.

10 I have done this in *The Supremacy of Christ,* 95–97.

11 Lesslie, Newbigin, *Truth to Tell* (Grand Rapids, MI: Wm. B. Eerdmans Publishing Co.; Geneva: World Council of Churches, 1991), 8–9.

12 See David E. Aune, The New Testament in Its Literary Environment (Philadelphia: The Westminster Press, 1987).

13 Thangaraj, *Relating to People of Other Religions,* 101–102.

14 Thangaraj, *Relating to People of Other Religions,* 102.

15 Thangaraj, *Relating to People of Other Religions,* 104.

16 See D. A. Carson, *The Gagging of God: Christianity Confronts Pluralism* (Grand Rapids, MI: Zondervan Publishing House, 1996), 270–72.

17 Blomberg, *The Historical Reliability of the Gospels,* 77. For an extended reflection on this, see my *The Supremacy of Christ,* chapter 15: "The Resurrection is Proof"; and chapter 16: "The Evidence for the Resurrection."

18 See *The Myth of God Incarnate,* John Hick, editor (London: SCM Press, 1977); and John Hick, *God Has Many Names* (Philadelphia: Westminster

Press, 1982). For a response to Hick's approach see Ronald H. Nash, *Is Jesus the Only Savior?* (Grand Rapids, MI: Zondervan Publishing House, 1994), chapter 5: "Pluralism and the Christian Understanding of Jesus Christ."

[19] I have supported this claim that Jesus' sacrifice alone can atone for the sins of the whole world more fully in *The Supremacy of Christ,* 162–163.

[20] *The Bhagavadgita,* translated by Vrinda Nabar and Shanta Tumkur (Ware, Hertfordshire, Wordsworth editions, 1997), 20.

[21] See Sir Norman Anderson, *Christianity and the World Religions: The Challenge of Pluralism* (Leicester and Downers Grove, IL: InterVarsity Press, 1984), 56–60; Dave Burnett, *The Spirit of Hinduism: A Christian Perspective on Hindu Thought* (Tunbridge Wells: Monarch, 1992), 245–257; Richard de Smet, "Jesus and the Avatara," in *Dialogue and Syncretism: An Interdisciplinary Approach,* Jerald Gort and others, editors (Grand Rapids, MI: Wm. B. Eerdmans Publishing Co., 1989), 153–162; and Vinoth Ramachandra, *The Recovery of Mission: Beyond the Pluralist Paradigm* (Carlisle: The Paternoster Press, 1996), 240–244.

[22] See A. J. Appasamy, *The Theology of Hindu Bhakti* (Madras: CLS, 1970; and Stephen Neill, *Bhakti: Hindu and Christian* (Madras: CLS, 1974).

[23] Anderson, *Christianity and the World Religions,* 59.

[24] Tal Brooke, *Avatar of Night: The Hidden Side of Sai Baba* (Sahibabad, UP, India: Vikas Publishing House, 1982; US edition by End Run Publishing, 1999).

[25] "Docetic" comes from the Greek *dokein,* to seem. *Docetism* asserted that Christ only seemed to suffer. The death of the divine Christ was only apparent, not real.

[26] Ramachandra, *Recovery of Mission,* 241.

[27] For a study of the gurus of India by an Indian Christian scholar, see Vishal Mangalwadi, *The World of Gurus: A Critical Look at the Philosophies of India's Influential Gurus and Mystics,* revised edition (Chicago: Cornerstone Press, 1992; originally published by New Delhi: Nivedit Good Books, 1987).

13

REPENTANCE AND JUDGMENT? OR KARMA AND REINCARNATION?

We have seen that in Paul's ministry in Athens he was not reluctant to dialogue with non-Christians and agree with some of their religious teachings. He met them at their highest and used truth he could find in their own poets to buttress his claims about the nature of God. He was respectful of them and sensitive to their culture. But Paul never stopped with agreement. He went on to present a gospel that was so unique that he urged his hearers to leave their former ways of life to follow Christ and warned them of the consequences of failing to do that. This is seen clearly in the last three verses of his address to the Areopagus (Acts 17:29–31).

The Importance of Repentance

In Acts 17:29 Paul explicitly stated what he had been implying earlier: idolatry is wrong. In verse 28 he said that we are God's offspring. Then he said, "Therefore since we are God's offspring, we should not think that the divine being is like gold or silver or stone—an image made by man's design and skill" (17:29). In the next verse he described idolatry as ignorance. Paul has said in his speech that God is the source of life. If that is so, how can He be represented by lifeless things such as gold, silver, and stone? Besides, how presumptuous it is for mortals to think that they by their artistry can represent the eternal God! In chapter 2 we described this type of argumentation as part of the process of persuasion.

After arguing for the futility of idolatry, Paul urged his hearers to turn from it: "In the past God overlooked such ignorance, but now he commands all people everywhere to repent" (Acts 17:30). After appealing to his hearers' minds with arguments against idolatry, Paul appealed to their wills with a call to act on the truth and change the course of their lives. Truth is important; it is so important that what one does with it is vital. In all our witness our ultimate goal is to have the truth act upon the will. It is not enough to move people emotionally or have them give intellectual assent to what we say. Unless the effect travels from the emotions and the intellect to the will, there can be no lasting impact on the life.

Without repentance, then, there can be no conversion. This is why repentance is a key feature in the preaching of the Old Testament prophets, of John the Baptist, of Jesus, and of the apostles. Jesus begins His ministry in Galilee with the message, "The time has come. . . . The kingdom of God is near. Repent and believe the good news!" (Mark 1:14). After delivering the first Christian evangelistic sermon, Peter exhorted, "Repent and be baptized, every one of you, in the name of Jesus Christ so that your sins may be forgiven" (Acts 2:38 NRSV). A clear break from the past was called for, including baptism, which is a sign of incorporation into a new life and community.

There was a tendency among evangelicals, especially in the last century, to focus so much on the need to accept the facts of the gospel that repentance was downplayed. Emphasizing repentance was associated with works of righteousness, which in the New Testament are not required for salvation. Even today some evangelicals are reluctant to ask people to make Christ their Lord when inviting them to receive His salvation. They say all people need to do is to believe that Christ has died for their sins, to ask God to forgive them, and to accept the salvation Christ gives. Later we may preach on the lordship of Christ to those who have received His salvation.[1] In extreme situations, lordship is even regarded as an optional extra for Christians. But the Bible does not separate the lordship of Christ from His saviorhood. When we receive Him as Savior, we must also accept Him as Lord. This dual call must be reflected in our preaching.

The strength to live this life is given by grace through faith. God gives us the grace to even have faith. It is not living the life that saves us but entrusting ourselves to Christ in response to God's call and with His strength. This is a contentious issue in the church, and various books have been written about the issues pertaining to it.[2]

Many people are willing to pray to receive Christ into their lives when they are invited to do so. Yet this prayer may not represent a commitment of their lives to Christ as their only lord. An Asian may respond to such an invitation out of politeness or because he thinks that it is the response expected of him by those who have hosted him for the Christian program he is attending. He feels like a stranger at the meeting. When the preacher asks him to raise his hand, he does it. Others will try Jesus so that they can add a dimension of fulfillment that is missing in their lives. People say the born-again experience enriches one's life, so why not try it? A Hindu might pray to receive Christ and add Him to all his other gods. He will have pictures of Shiva, Krishna, and Jesus in his house, and he will read devotionally from the Bhagavad Gita and the Bible.

By calling for repentance Paul implied that if the Athenians were to come to Christ, they would have had to forsake Athenian religion. It is the same today. Some are saying that one can be a Buddhist Christian or a Hindu Christian. That idea is alien to the Scriptures. You cannot serve Shiva and Christ, or Buddha and Christ. For this reason, if I am leading a non-Christian in a prayer of commitment, I usually explain to him or her that this will mean that he or she will stop going to the temple and will not bow before idols any more. If that person shows some hesitancy, I will still pray with the person, but I will delay the prayer of commitment for a later occasion.

People need to repent of nonreligious idols too. A person's idol may relate to personal morality. When he comes to Christ, he resolves, and seeks God's help, to forsake his immoral actions. Another person's idol may be materialism. She has been ignoring some important principles in her quest for wealth. When she comes to Christ, she will need to give up some of her practices, such as lying to make a sale and underpaying her workers. Another person's idol may be racism. When he comes to Christ his attitude toward those of another race, with whom his race is in conflict, changes markedly. The fact that many Christians hold on to these idols without any sense of regret is an indication that the church has not presented this aspect of the gospel adequately.

One feature of the postmodern era has been a lack of moral criteria. That is, what society once considered evil is no longer considered evil, because people do not have standards by which to measure those things as evil. If this is a problem in society, the church should give more stress than before to moral issues so as to counter the wrong influences from society. Yet there seems to be less, not more, stress on moral purity in the church's proclamation. The result, as statistics show, is that the moral behavior of those in the evangelical church in the West is not very different from that of those outside the church.[3] The church has been so blinded by market considerations, which in ecclesiastical terms means increase in attendance, that it isn't going to take this challenge seriously. From the marketing perspective, preaching repentance, holiness, and morality has been relegated to the status of an undesirable practice.

All this brings great dishonor to Christ, and we in the East are embarrassed about the moral performance of the church in the West, especially because our newspapers delight in highlighting sad stories of moral lapses by Christian leaders. We are no better, and despite the growth of the church in the Third World, we too are faced with the huge problem of unholiness in the church.

Ultimately repentance is turning from our own way to God's way. The evidences that we are going our own way are manifested in religious, moral, material, or social spheres. We must repent specifically of these sins, for until repentance gets down to the specifics, it is not repentance. But our basic sin is that we choose our own way rather than God's. When we repent, we say to God that we hand over to Him the reins of our lives. We do what He wants us to do, not what we want to do. But most importantly we cease to work toward earning our salvation, accept our inability to save ourselves, and look to Christ alone to save us.

Baptism as a Crucial Step

After people from other faiths have committed their lives to Christ they need to take the step of baptism, which is their public witness that they have left their past life and identified with Christ and His family, the church. Jesus' statement of the Great Commission in Matthew 28:19–20 includes baptism: "Therefore go and make disciples of all nations, baptizing them in the name of the Father and of the Son and of the Holy Spirit, and teaching them to obey everything I have commanded you." The main verb in this verse is "make disciples." "Baptizing them" and "teaching them" are participles; that is, they describe what happens in the discipling process. Discipled people are to be baptized and taught to obey Christ's commands.

My experience has been that to a convert from another religion baptism is an enormously important step. The church needs to give baptism an important place in its program so that converts will sense that they have a warm welcome in their new family. It is traumatic to leave the religion in which one has grown up, especially if one's close relatives remain in the former religion. And the baptism ceremony is something like the final step of renouncing the past and identifying with the new community. So the church must work hard at making baptism meaningful to the convert.

In our work with youth we generally do not press for young people to be baptized until they have reached the age when they are legally considered majors, though we try to have them settled in local churches as soon as possible. This is because of family and national conventions that view the conversion of minors as a very serious thing. Another alternative is having baptism services that are not too public, as some cultures consider such a service a public affront to their religion. This may be a prudent course of action for converts in Muslim countries too.

Sometimes we can unwisely court opposition by public displays of our successes in evangelism. Those of other faiths could view this as a heralding of their defeat at the hands of Christians. We must avoid things that could be viewed as displays of one-upmanship. These are only suggestions of possible courses of action that could be taken in extreme situations. These suggestions need not be taken as principles for decision making about what one should generally do with converts from other religions. In most cases, people coming from other faiths should be baptized shortly after their conversion to Christ.

Retaining One's Original Culture

Although converts to Christianity renounce their former faith, they could still retain many of the cultural distinctives of their upbringing within that other faith. At one time Christians mistakenly regarded these as being opposed to Christianity and encouraged Christians to give up their former cultures. This became a hindrance to evangelism among the people of those faiths and also unnecessarily dislocated converts from their families and cultures. Here are some examples of practices that could be kept after conversion:

- A young Buddhist convert may delay his marriage by a few years so that he can save money to provide for his sister's marriage. This is a family obligation in many cultures where there are close family ties and where it is normal for family members to help each other at considerable cost to themselves. This may seem strange to missionaries coming from an individualistic Western culture. But they would be wise to consult Christians from within that culture before giving advice to new believers faced with the prospect of delaying their marriage.

- Parents usually have an important role to play in Buddhist wedding rituals but not in Christian marriage services that have been influenced by individualistic Western culture. I know of Christians in Sri Lanka who include as part of the wedding service a beautiful chant extolling the contribution of the parents to the lives of their children. While this is sung the children give gifts to the parents.

- Chinese converts to Christianity will buy gifts for their family members and celebrate the New Year with them. They will help in the special family responsibilities in connection with the New Year. But they will not participate in the religious ritual associated with the New Year activities that contradict their Christian beliefs.

- Respect for parents and ancestors is an important part of the Chinese culture. But Christians cannot participate in rituals involving ancestor worship that is part of Chinese popular religion. This has resulted in the charge that converts do not honor their ancestors. Chua Wee Hian lists ways in which they can counter this charge with positive acts that are compatible with Christianity. "They will always respect and honor their relatives while they are alive." he says. After they have died, "many are prepared to be the first in cleaning family tombs, and some Christians have even set up halls of remembrance for their forebears. Non-Christian relatives and friends may be invited to special memorial services where Christ is proclaimed as victor over the grave."[4]

- In some cultures there are New Year rituals that are aimed at persuading the gods and other forces to send blessings to the people. Similar things are done at the start of a farming or building project. Often small items made out of precious substances like gold are blessed and included in the foundation of a building at the foundation-laying ceremony. Instead of participating in these rituals, Christians can pray, in public if possible or otherwise in private, for God's blessings upon the farming, building, or other ventures that the family is involved in. Even if the family does not permit them to pray publicly, they can tell family members that they have prayed privately.

- Most of the cultural practices of the Jewish religion derive from the Old Testament. The early church decided that Gentile Christians do not need to follow many of these practices, so they went out of use in the Gentile churches. But Jewish Christians maintained many of them. In the same way, when Jews convert to Christianity they can retain many features of their Jewish identity without compromising their Christian faith. The description of Judaism in the appendix shows that festivals play an important part in Jewish community life. Christians can develop Christian versions of Old Testament festivals without much change from the present Jewish customs. Some of them, like the Passover, could be wonderful opportunities to present distinctively Christian truths and uphold the glory of the gospel. Jewish Christians must, however, reflect seriously about the dangers of legalism, which is a trap they could fall into, as Jewish Christians did in the first-century church.

- I know several converts from Buddhism and Hinduism who do not eat beef and pork because that is something they had grown to dislike and that their non-Christian family members find repulsive. Similarly converts from Islam can refrain from eating pork. At Youth for Christ camps we usually have a few special meals, and often pork is a delicacy served at such meals. But that is not the case if we have Muslim youths at a camp, for that would be unnecessarily insensitive to Muslim scruples. If some of them come to Christ, we may need to tell them that out of sensitivity to the scruples of their family members they would be wise to abstain from eating pork for the rest of their lives.

The Gospel Command and Warning

It is significant that Paul's call to repentance in Athens comes as a command. Paul said, "[God] commands all people everywhere to repent" (Acts 17:30b). We don't simply announce good news. We don't only invite people to accept Christ. We communicate a command to His subjects from the Lord of the universe. The gospel is good news to accept. But it is also a command to obey. So Paul said that those who "do not obey the gospel of our Lord Jesus" will be punished (2 Thessalonians 1:8).

After Paul communicated to the people in Athens God's command to repent, he gave a warning to support this command: "For he has set a day when he will judge the world with justice by the man he has appointed" (Acts 17:31). Receiving a new life is not the only result of repentance. One who repents also escapes punishment at the judgment. Every person must face God's judgment one day. The writer of Hebrews stated that "man is destined to die once, and after that to face judgment" (Hebrews 9:27).

Many people do not like to be confronted with the fact of judgment. To some it is a strange idea. In Sri Lanka we have recently had many angry articles in the papers written by non-Christians about the Christian doctrine of judgment. So it is not surprising that many Christians are hesitant to talk about it. It appears to be in bad taste to bring up such an unpleasant topic in conversation.

Yet evangelism without the message of judgment is not biblical evangelism. When we leave it out, we fail to give the whole message that God entrusted to us to take to the world. F. F. Bruce reminds us that "Greek thought had no room for such an eschatological judgment as the biblical revelation announces."[5] The majority of Paul's sophisticated listeners in Athens would have scoffed at what Paul said about judgment. But that did not deter Paul. This shows that we should dispel the idea that we can speak about judgment to unsophisticated people but not to sophisticated and highly educated people.

Many say that this type of doctrine is best introduced after people make a commitment to Christ. But judgment is part of the essential New Testament gospel. The writer of Hebrews lists it among the "elementary teachings about Christ" (Hebrews 6:1–2). We must preach about love, which is the bright side of the gospel. Love should be the primary focus of our evangelistic preaching. But we must not neglect to warn people about the coming wrath.[6] This, along with the call to repentance, constitutes the severe side of the gospel.

Paul urged us to consider "the kindness and sternness of God" (Romans 11:22). This combination of kindness and sternness must characterize all gospel proclamation. The German New Testament scholar Joachim Jeremias, in a book about the parables of Christ, talks of "the twofold issue of all preaching of the gospel." He describes this as "the offer of mercy and the threat of impending judgment inseparable from it, deliverance and fear, salvation and destruction, life and death."[7] May we too reflect this biblical combination of "the twofold issue" in our presentation of the gospel to non-Christians.

Tough Convictions Bring about Painful Feelings

We often hear people say that we must not try to convert everybody. "We will share the gospel," they say, "and leave the results to God." It is true that we always trust in the sovereignty of God to work in the people with whom we share the gospel. That is why we do not apply undue pressure on people when we invite them to respond to the gospel. But often I have found that people who say "We must not try to convert everybody" do not present a clear-cut and urgent call from God with the warning of judgment if that call is rejected. They will not make a determined effort to persuade people to leave their past ways. They will not forthrightly present the command of God as a matter of life and death. They don't have the passion for people's salvation we discussed in chapter 2.

Biblical Christians should be restless and broken when people they share the gospel with don't accept it. This is how Paul felt about the rejection of the gospel by the Jews. He said, "I have great sorrow and unceasing anguish in my heart. For I could wish that I myself were cursed and cut off from Christ for the sake of my brothers, those of my own race" (Romans 9:2–3). Paul believed that these people were lost, that gospel work was serious business that had to do with the eternal destiny of people. So his heart was broken when his people rejected the gospel. Today, however, such attitudes would be considered unhealthy and in need of correction. People are afraid of urgency and usually avoid it in the church. Elsewhere we have argued that entertainment has replaced urgency as a means of attracting people to the church.[8]

The problem is that the church is not strong enough to live with such tough doctrines as the uniqueness of Christ and the eternal lostness of people apart from Christ. There has been so much stress on the subjective, experiential aspect of the Bible that we have neglected to give Christians a strong sense of its authority and infallibility. Therefore Christians have lost the security and boldness that come from believing an infallible Bible. That is what provides us with the base for upholding and proclaiming such seemingly outrageous doctrines as the uniqueness of Christ and eternal punishment. If the Bible teaches it, then we will proclaim it, for the Bible is true. It is the very Word of God.

Jeremiah lived with this pain. He often complained about the terrible consequences in his life because the people rejected the message he gave (15:10–20; 20:7–18). Twice in the middle of his complaint he had to acknowledge the power of God's word upon his life that propelled him into his difficult ministry. Jeremiah 15:16 says, "When your words came, I ate them; they were my joy and my heart's delight, for I bear your name, O LORD God Almighty." Jeremiah 20:9 says, "But if I say, 'I will not mention him or speak any more in his name,' his word is in my heart like a fire, a fire shut up in my bones. I am weary of holding it in; indeed, I cannot." His foundation in the Word helped him to persevere with proclaiming such an unpopular message.

Another problem is related to the fact that we have found our joys so much from temporal things that we have missed out on fully experiencing the joy of the Lord. That joy remains unchanged for eternity and untouched by difficult temporal circumstances. It will give us the strength to embrace tough doctrines that produce inner turmoil. We belong to a generation in which people are so committed to feeling good that they find it difficult to handle the stress of holding to the absolute uniqueness of Christ with all the painful feelings that this brings. Charles Spurgeon spoke about Christians who said, "I could not rest comfortably if I believed the orthodox doctrine of the ruin of men." Spurgeon's response to them was, "Most true, but what right have we to rest comfortably?"[9]

Because many Christians are afraid of the bad feelings, conflict, and inward struggle that come when they believe in the absolute uniqueness of Christ, they don't like to face up to its implications. Instead they discard this doctrine or try to present it in a more palatable way. They see this as being relevant, but they forget that some of the most relevant preachers in the Bible were the Old Testament prophets. Part of their relevance was that they diagnosed the problem of the people accurately—it was a problem of sin. They also recommended the ideal solution—repentance and obedience to God, which involved the tough challenge of giving up the life they enjoyed living. When people are living in sin, among the most relevant messages given to them would be those that highlight their sin and its consequences and that call them to repentance.

Of course, many people don't like to hear such a message. The prophets were ridiculed and opposed by their contemporaries. This also happened to Paul in Athens: "When they heard about the resurrection of the dead, some of them sneered" (Acts 17:32a). Most of the people rejected what Paul said because they found his talk about resurrection outlandish. Absolute truth is so radical that it demands a response. Those who understand what we are saying realize that they can't be neutral about it. Watered-down, sugar-coated messages that pass for the gospel may not enrage people, but neither will they transform people. As radical a transformation as conversion calls for a radical message to trigger it.

While many people openly rejected Paul's message, some responded positively to it. Luke reports, "But others said, 'We want to hear you again on this subject.' . . . A few men became followers of Paul and believed. Among them was Dionysius, a member of the Areopagus, also a woman named Damaris, and a number of others" (Acts 17:32b, 34).

As I think of our work with youth, I often shudder to think of the reaction of parents when they realize that their child has become a Christian. We do a lot to soften that blow. We try to be friendly with the parents and do all we can to dispel the wrong ideas that people have about what happens when a child becomes a Christian. We urge our youth to be the best children to their parents that they could possibly be. But after all this, conversion is always a traumatic process in terms of the disruption caused. Yet we know that without Christ these people are lost. We know that although many will reject our message, some will accept. We know that this acceptance will mean a lot of pain for them because of the reaction of their loved ones. But it also means eternal salvation! That helps us to persevere.

Jesus said, "What good will it be for a man if he gains the whole world, yet forfeits his soul? Or what can a man give in exchange for his soul?" (Matthew 16:26). This is still true, and the way to help people find salvation is to proclaim the gospel to them. So we will be faithful in proclaiming it.

Karma

A major challenge to the Christian doctrine of judgment comes from the growth of belief in reincarnation and in *karma,* which lies at the heart of this belief. Karma is the Sanskrit word for "work" or "action." Karma is something like a moral law of cause and effect. Every action is said to have inevitable consequences that attach themselves to the doer, requiring reward or punishment.[10] Bad actions cause one to accrue bad karma or demerit, and good actions cause one to accrue good karma or merit. The situation of the person reborn with the soul of one who has died is determined by the karma that person's soul carries over to the next life. Those who believe in karma explain the inequalities of life as being a consequence of actions in previous lives.

The doctrine of karma is a helpful stepping-stone in presenting the gospel of Christ.[11] When we explain the work of Christ on the cross as paying the penalty for our sins, we can point out that every religion believes that people have to pay for their wrongdoing. The Buddhists call it karma, the Christians call it judgment, but the belief is universal. We may quote Galatians 6:7–8, "Do not be deceived: God cannot be mocked. A man reaps what he sows. The one who sows to please his sinful nature, from that nature will reap destruction; the one who sows to please the Spirit, from the Spirit will reap eternal life." Although there are significant differences from the Buddhist idea, there are significant parallels on which we can agree (e.g., reaping what you sow, pleasing the sinful nature, though with the latter Buddhists would use different terminology).

While we agreed that wrong, selfish acts reap bad consequences, we do not agree on how we can overcome those consequences. Those who believe in reincarnation say that they will have to pay for bad deeds in their next life and that they should accumulate good karma by doing good deeds and by avoiding bad deeds. We can point out that most people realize that it is virtually impossible to arrive at a net positive balance of merit over demerit. Then we can say that the God who created us and continues to love us, realizing our hopeless condition, provided a way out for us by having Christ pay for our wrongdoing. This brings up questions about the idea of one dying for another's sins, because this concept is at first quite strange. I have addressed these issues in *The Supremacy of Christ*[12] and tried to show that, explained in a certain way, these ideas are not as strange as we first think.

I know many people who, having come to understand what is meant by Jesus dying for their karma, have accepted the gospel. To them this has been a wonderfully liberating truth. This was the case for both my mother and grandmother, who are converts from Buddhism.

The idea that one can transfer merit to another dead or living person is found among many groups who believe in karma. In Mahayana Buddhism this may be done through a *bodhisattva;* thus prayers could be made to them. In Theravada Buddhism, people give alms and do other good deeds to transfer merit to dead relatives. This is called *Pattidāna,* which means "merit transference." This could be another stepping-stone to sharing the gospel with those who believe in karma,[13] for it shows that where there is love, the idea of transferring merit is not so strange. The problem is, who can effectively do this? We say that Christ alone can.

Reincarnation[14]

Reincarnation Described. Belief in reincarnation has been found even as far back as the time of the Greek philosopher Plato (427–347 BC), and it has taken different forms.[15] The word *reincarnation* comes from the Latin *re,* which means "again," and *incarnere,* which means "in flesh."[16] The meaning is "to come again in the flesh," and what comes again is the soul. This is why reincarnation is also called "the transmigration of the soul." More than 50 percent of the world population is said to hold to some form of this doctrine. It is a basic tenet of Hinduism,

Buddhism, Jainism, and Sikhism[17] and is found in the belief system of some Australian aboriginal societies too.[18]

Recently this belief has become very popular in the West. The New Age movement embraced it along with many other features of Hindu and Buddhist thought, and New Age propagandists like actress Shirley MacLaine have done much to popularize the belief in the West.[19] A 1985 poll of adults in the United States revealed that 44 percent of those sampled said they either believed (15 percent) in reincarnation or were not sure (29 percent) if they did.[20] A 1982 Gallup poll showed that 30 percent of Americans under thirty years said they believed in reincarnation,[21] and we can expect that the figures are higher today. David Burnett reported in his 1992 book on Hinduism that 27 percent of British adults believed in reincarnation.[22]

The Theravada form of Buddhism does not accept the existence of a soul and calls this doctrine *anatta,* meaning "no soul." Therefore Theravada Buddhists prefer to call their belief "rebirth" rather than reincarnation. They say that one's karma gathers energy to give birth to a new being who represents the net karma of the earlier being. The Venerable Nārada, a Sri Lankan scholar monk, compares the karmic force with the electric energy that lights up a bulb. When the bulb burns out, it lights up a new bulb. The bulb is equivalent to the being with a physical body who is born. He says, "The Kammic[23] force remains undisturbed by the disintegration of the physical body, and the passing away of the present consciousness leads to the arising of a fresh one in another birth."[24]

Rebirth does not have to always be in a human form. The Buddha is reported to have said that one who "cultivates thoroughly and constantly the practices, habits, mentality, and manners of a dog . . . upon the breaking up of the body, after death, will be reborn, amongst dogs."[25]

In Buddhism and Hinduism this seemingly endless cycle of birth, death, and rebirth is called *samsara* (a Sanskrit word meaning "going through" or "wandering"). The goal is to be freed from this cycle. In Buddhism this takes place upon attaining nirvana. The word *nirvana* means "blowing out" or "extinguishing," and the idea is that the flames of desire are no longer fueled. This is a state when the flames of desire (*tanha*) that cause suffering or frustration or unsatisfactoriness (*dukkha*, the most basic reality in life) are no longer fueled, and the desire to live on earth is gone. In some forms of Buddhism this is described as nothingness, but most forms see it as a state of bliss, with Mahayana Buddhism seeing it as being more like a heaven. In Hinduism the goal of the rebirth process is described as *moksha*, a Sanskrit word meaning "release" or "liberation," which is liberation from samsara, the cycle of birth, death, and rebirth. Here the end is generally viewed as absorption into the absolute God (Brahman or Paramatman). In both these systems the idea that most adherents have is that their goal (nirvana or moksha) is many, many lives away.

The Evidence for Reincarnation. Much publicity is given to the supposed evidence from people who are recalling their past lives and saying some accurate things about the person whom they were supposed to have been in their past life. This may take place without outside *inducement* (spontaneous recall), or it may take place in a hypnotic state when the subjects are led to delve into their past lives (*hypnotic regression*).

Many Christian authors have countered these claims.[26] Many of these cases lend themselves to natural explanations. Hypnosis is a direction of the mind and can result in a subject uttering thoughts that have been suggested to him or her. The capacity for memory is something that is not fully fathomed. Much of what we see and hear is said to be stored in our molecular memory bank in a process called *cryptoamnesia*. These details could emerge under special conditions. Some of the cases of past-life recall have been explained in this way. In an environment where belief in reincarnation is encouraged, we can imagine that cultural conditioning could result in instances of supposed past-life recall. This is highlighted by the fact that most accounts of past-life recall are from children, who are more susceptible to such conditioning and influences.

Yet in some cases there seems to be a supernatural element in which the subject shows knowledge that could not have been obtained through a natural process. These could be cases of demonic possession. Mark Albrecht has pointed out that "a great majority of cases [of past-life recall] exhibit features parallel with those of spiritism, seances, mediumship and demonic possession."[27] This should not surprise us.

Reincarnation is such a powerful tool to keep people from the truth that Satan, "the father of lies" (John 8:44), would use any means at his disposal to try to buttress the case for it.

Christian Reincarnationists? Many people, while claiming to be Christians, say they believe in reincarnation. The Gallup poll mentioned above found that 17 percent of those who said they went to church regularly believe in reincarnation. We had a European missionary in Sri Lanka who claimed to know what he and his wife were in their previous lives. The revered missionary doctor, scholar, and musician Albert Schweitzer is reported to have said that it was "a most comforting explanation of reality."

Various Scripture texts are quoted as giving evidence for this belief in the Bible:

- The statement of Jesus to Nicodemus about the need to be born again (John 3:3).
- The reference to Elijah coming back as John the Baptist (Matthew 11:14).
- The question of the disciples about whether the man born blind or his parents had sinned (John 9:1–3).
- The explanation of the resurrection (1 Corinthians 15).

If we study these passages in their contexts, we see that they do not support this doctrine.[28] The idea that reincarnation was present in the original Bible and was excised later by the church is speculative and without historical evidence.

The doctrine of reincarnation goes in a different direction from the Christian gospel, which proclaims that "man is destined to die once, and after that to face judgment" (Hebrews 9:27). Reender Kranenborg has done a careful study of the attempts of certain Christian reincarnationists to harmonize the doctrine with Christianity. At the end of his study he concludes that the Christian understanding of Jesus' work and person is incompatible with this doctrine "along with the role of substitutionary atonement and vicarious suffering, absolute grace and forgiveness." He says, "By accepting the notion of reincarnation, these beliefs are either changed or take on an altered meaning; and moreover, new elements are introduced, which were unknown to the early Christian tradition (karma, evolution)."[29] Kranenborg says that "many people in the Christian tradition who more or less accept the notion of reincarnation are unaware of such theological relations and connections."

The Attractiveness of Reincarnation. Given that the doctrine of reincarnation presents what seems to be an impossible goal that no one is close to achieving, it is surprising that it should be so popular. The key to its attraction is that it provides a way by which people can keep improving in their own strength. They don't have to bow in humble repentance and admit that they cannot help themselves. The West had moved strongly in a self-help direction even before it rejected Christianity. The Christian gospel became culturally unacceptable because it seemed to go against the direction in which Western society was moving. After secular humanism proved to be unsatisfying, the West, still in revolt against the transcendent and holy God of the Bible, needed a religious ideology to adhere to. New Age ideology, which focuses on spiritual things without requiring repentance and a confession of helplessness before God, seemed to satisfy this desire.

We must not forget the satisfaction that comes to humans, who have lost their reason for existence, from believing that they can save themselves. That attraction could blind them to seeing the dreariness of the seemingly unending cycle of rebirths. Students of the New Age movement, however, say that the Western forms of this doctrine have been infused with more hope and a more positive outlook than have the Eastern forms.[30]

Then there is the attraction of the pantheistic forms of reincarnation, under which we could classify most New Age and many Hindu forms, which believe that humans are divine. We don't need to bow before a transcendent God because we are God!

Reincarnation is also claimed as being a means by which human beings are able to achieve their fullest potential. Sylvia Cranston says, "It seems an inexcusable waste of resources" to restrict human beings to "but one sojourn on earth" because the earth "affords almost illimitable opportunities for growth of intelligence, talents and moral powers."[31]

However, there doesn't seem to be evidence that people who claim to be reborn are doing better with their successive births. If so, the world should be getting better, but many people think the world is deteriorating. We say that given the fallen nature of humanity, even a thousand lives would not suffice to help us out of our situation. Humans are born sinners. What they need is not more opportunities through more lives. They need a Savior who can redeem them from their bondage to their fallen nature and the effects this bondage has on them.

Still other people find reincarnation appealing because it is said to explain the inequalities and misfortunes of life. People are said to suffer because of what they have done in their past lives. But is it fair that people should be punished for things they know nothing about? If one has to bear responsibility for what another person did, surely he should at least know who that person is and what he did. As R. C. Sproul has pointed out, "Memory is a vital element of personal identity."[32] The newly born person has no conscious connection with the person he or she succeeds.

We must not forget that because of the belief in reincarnation, many people's rights have been suppressed and they have been exploited. This is especially so in the caste system, which for centuries has allowed the so-called untouchables in India to be deprived of their rights. By seeing birth into a lower caste as a punishment, higher-caste people are able to suppress the masses and exploit them. Recently there has been mounting opposition by supposedly high-caste Hindus to the conversion of supposedly low-caste Hindus and tribal peoples to Christianity. Some observers feel that this opposition could be a reaction to the social empowerment of these people as a result of their newfound identity in Christ and their consequent refusal to accept the exploitation to which they have been subjected for so long.

Vishal Mangalwadi describes an extreme case of how this belief can lull to inaction those who want to bring relief to suffering humanity. He says, "A professor of Hindi at Delhi University said that acts of compassion on behalf of the suffering were foolish." This is folly, because "if we did succeed in cutting short someone's suffering, he would still be reborn to complete his due term of suffering."[33] This is an extreme case, but it shows what can happen when this doctrine is taken to its fullest implications.

Some observers say that the Christian gospel and the example of service in India influenced the present emphasis on humanitarian activity that is found among Hindus. They say that Christianity helped refine Hinduism by causing it to add this dimension to its ethos.[34] The Indian ecumenical leader M. M. Thomas said that many of the great leaders who helped shaped India in the twentieth century "grappled with the person and teachings of Jesus Christ and assimilated the essence of Christian humanism into the religious and secular thought of modern India." He also says that the churches' model of Christian community, which transcends caste divisions, also influenced Indian religion, ideology, and philosophy.[35]

Recently Glen Hoddle, the manager of the England soccer team who had once claimed to be a born-again Christian, made an explosive statement coming from his belief in reincarnation. He said that disabled people are paying for sins of past lives. His statement resulted in a media frenzy. He tendered an apology stating that he had made "a serious error of judgment." But he lost his job. People saw that what he had said was very unfair to the disabled.

The Bible says that the suffering in the world has been ultimately caused by sin upsetting God's plan for the world. But it does not say that all those who suffer do so for sins they have committed. In fact, the servants of God are those who do all they can to counter the effects of sin and thus commit themselves to alleviating suffering. The Bible also says that God can turn suffering into something good and calls us to participate in this process of transforming suffering.

Stanley Jones tells the story of Japanese professor who was a Buddhist and who lost his sight because of a detached retina. This professor could not agree with what his religion taught about this tragedy: that it happened because of what he had done in a previous life. He was encouraged to look at the Christian answer to this problem. When reading the Gospel of John he found the story about Jesus and the man who had been born blind (John 9). Without accepting the typical karmic explanation for suffering, Jesus claimed that the works of God could be manifested through this man's blindness. The professor said, "Could the works of God be manifest through my blindness? Then that is the answer: I'll use this blindness." Not only did he become a Christian—he also became an effective evangelist. He went to Scotland for theological studies and then taught theology at Kobe Theological College in Japan.[36]

Chapter 13 endnotes

[1] Zane C. Hodges, *Absolutely Free! A Biblical Reply to Lordship Salvation* (Grand Rapids, MI: Zondervan Publishing House, 1989); Hodges, *The Gospel Under Siege* (Dallas: Redencion Viva, 1981).

[2] John F. MacArthur, Jr., *The Gospel According to Jesus* (Grand Rapids, MI: Zondervan Publishing House, 1994); MacArthur, *The Gospel According to the Apostles* (Dallas: Word Books, 2000).

[3] See G. E. Veith, Jr., *Postmodern Times: A Christian Guide to Contemporary Thought and Culture* (Wheaton, IL: Crossway Books, 1994), 16–18.

[4] Chua Wee Hian, "The Worship of Ancestors," *Eerdmans' Handbook to the World Religions,* Pat Alexander, organizing editor (Grand Rapids, MI: Wm. B. Eerdmans Publishing Co., 1994), 247.

[5] F. F. Bruce, "The Book of the Acts," *The New International Commentary on the New Testament* (Grand Rapids, MI: Wm. B. Eerdmans Publishing Co., 1988), 340–341.

[6] For a discussion about why and how we can practically present the message of judgment see my *Crucial Questions about Hell* (Wheaton, IL: Crossway Books, 1994), 125–180.

[7] Cited in Leslie Woodson, *What the Bible Says about Hell* (Grand Rapids, MI: Baker Book House, 1976), 91.

[8] Ajith Fernando, *The Supremacy of Christ* (Wheaton, IL: Crossway Books, 1995), 115–116; Fernando, "The Urgency of the Gospel," in *Telling the Truth: Evangelizing Postmoderns,* D. A. Carson, editor (Grand Rapids, MI: Zondervan Publishing House, 2000).

[9] In *Spurgeon at His Best,* Tom Carter, compiler (Grand Rapids, MI: Baker Book House, 1988), 99.

[10] *Eerdmans' Handbook to the World Religions,* 430.

[11] On the use of stepping-stones see chapters 4 and 5.

[12] Fernando, *Supremacy of Christ,* chapters 10–11.

[13] See Tissa Weerasinga, *The Cross and the Bo Tree: Communicating the Gospel to Buddhists* (Taichung, Taiwan: Asia Theological Association, 1989), 72–76.

[14] Many of the points given here are also given in greater detail in my *Crucial Questions about Hell,* chapter 7: "What about Reincarnation?"

[15] See Norman Geisler and J. Yukuta Amano, *The Reincarnation Sensation* (Wheaton, IL: Tyndale House Publishers, 1986), 27–56.

[16] Geisler and Amano, *Reincarnation Sensation,* 27.

[17] See Geisler and Amano, *Reincarnation Sensation,* 27–35, for a description of the various forms of this doctrine in the Asian religions.

[18] C. R. Taber, "Reincarnation," in *Abingdon Dictionary of Living Religions,* Keith Crim, editor (Nashville: Abingdon Press, 1981), 609.

[19] Shirley MacLaine, *Out on a Limb* (New York: Bantam Books, 1984); MacLaine, *Dancing in the Light* (New York: Bantam Books, 1986).

[20] From The Roper Center, University of Connecticut, cited by Russell Chandler, *Understanding the New Age* (Dallas and Milton Keynes, England: Word Publishing, 1988, the page number is from the British edition), 263.

[21] George Gallup, *Adventures in Immortality* (New York: McGraw-Hill, 1982).

[22] David Burnett, *The Spirit of Hinduism: A Christian Perspective on Hindu Thought* (Tunbridge Wells, England: Monarch Publications, 1992), 71.

[23] "Kamma" is the spelling derived from the Pali language. "Karma" is from the Sanskrit language. The most ancient Buddhist Scriptures to which Theravada Buddhism appeals were written in Pali, so Theravada Buddhists often use the Pali-derived spelling rather than the Sanskrit-derived spelling (e.g., *nibbana* rather than *nirvana*).

[24] Närada Maha Thera, *The Buddha and His Teachings* (Colombo: Lake House, 1980), 451.

[25] From the Majjhima Nikaya, Sutta no. 57. Cited in Närada, *Buddha and His Teachings,* 477.

[26] Mark Albrecht, *Reincarnation: A Christian Appraisal* (Downers Grove, IL: InterVarsity Press, 1982), 51–80; Geisler and Amano, *Reincarnation Sensation,* 57–86; Brad Scott, *Embraced by the Darkness: Exposing New Age Theology from the Inside Out* (Wheaton, IL: Crossway Books, 1996), 127–42. See also Fernando, *Crucial Questions about Hell,* 81–82.

[27] Albrecht, *Reincarnation,* 82.

[28] I have briefly discussed the meanings of the passages mentioned in my *Crucial Questions about Hell,* 79–81.

[29] Reender Kranenborg, "Christianity and Reincarnation," in *Dialogue and Syncretism: An Interdisciplinary Approach,* Jerald Gort and others, editors (Grand Rapids, MI: Wm. B. Eerdmans Publishing Co., 1989), 187.

[30] Mark Albrecht, *Reincarnation: A Christian Appraisal,* 15.

[31] In a letter to the editor, *Christian Parapsychologist* (June 1980).

[32] R. C. Sproul, "Reincarnation: A Second Time Around," *Eternity* (October 1988), 68.

[33] Vishal Mangalwadi, *When the New Age Gets Old: Looking for a Greater Spirituality* (Downers Grove, IL: InterVarsity Press, 1992) 194.

[34] See E. Stanley Jones, *The Christ of the Indian Road* (New York: The Abingdon Press, 1925), chapter 3: "The Growing Moral and Spiritual Supremacy of Jesus"; Vinoth Ramachandra, *Faiths in Conflict: Christian Integrity in a Multicultural World* (Leicester: InterVarsity Press, 1999), chapter 2: "Hinduism and the Search for Identity"; and *Christian Contribution to Indian Philosophy,* A. Amaldoss SJ, editor (Madras: CLS, 1995).

[35] M. M. Thomas, "The Christian Contribution to the Indian Philosophy of Being and Becoming Human," in *Christian Contribution to Indian Philosophy,* 217–218; cited in Ramachandra, *Faiths in Conflict,* 84.

[36] From E. Stanley Jones, *A Song of Ascents* (Nashville: Abingdon Press, 1968), 182.

14

THOSE WHO HAVE NOT HEARD

In the first chapter we described the view called inclusivism, which leaves room for people to be saved without hearing the gospel. The pluralist theologian John Hick says inclusivism "probably represents the nearest approach to a consensus among Christian thinkers today,"[1] and the list of esteemed evangelical scholars who espouse some form of inclusivism is growing. This topic requires a more comprehensive answer than can be offered in this book, and other writers have shown that the biblical base for inclusivism is a shaky one.[2] Here we will demonstrate the biblical insistence that the gospel must be preached for people to be saved and briefly touch on a few other issues and arguments relating to this important topic.

One Way to Salvation

In chapter 12 we said that the Bible clearly teaches that Christ is the only way to salvation. It also teaches that the salvation Christ offers is appropriated through faith in Him. When the Philippian jailer asked Paul and Silas, "What must I do to be saved?" they responded, "Believe in the Lord Jesus, and you will be saved" (Acts 16:30, 31). Acts 2:21 and Romans 10:13 summarize this teaching by proclaiming that "everyone who calls on the name of the Lord will be saved."

But what of those who have never heard? Will they be punished for rejecting a gospel they know nothing about? The Bible does not teach that they are lost because they reject the gospel. Rather, it says that people will be judged according to their response to the light they have received. But it also shows that no one lives according to the light he or she receives and that no one can be saved without the gospel. Paul explained this truth in Romans 1–3.

Light through Creation (Romans 1:18–25). While he was developing his case, Paul often touched on the topic of the light available to people apart from the gospel of Christ. He saw light as coming through creation, through the conscience, and through the law of Moses (Romans 1:18–3:8). His point is that people are unable to live up to the light they received. This is evidenced by the way he began this major section (1:18–3:20) of the epistle: "The wrath of God is being revealed from heaven against all the godlessness and wickedness of men" (1:18). This wickedness, he said, caused people to "suppress the truth," and the truth they suppress is the truth about God that is revealed in creation: "What may be known about God is plain to them, because God has made it plain to them. For since the creation of the world God's invisible qualities—his eternal power and divine nature—have been clearly seen, being understood from what has been made" (1:19–20). As C. K. Barrett explains, Paul was saying that by observing creation humans should arrive at the conclusion that "creation does not provide the key to its own existence."[3] They should realize that there is a God beyond creation.

People are held accountable to make an appropriate response to this message that comes from creation. Paul showed that because of this knowledge they "are without excuse" (Romans 1:20). He said that God would visit them with wrath (1:18) because, "though they have not had the advantage of hearing the gospel, they have rejected that rudimentary knowledge of God which was open to them."[4]

Paul described how humans rejected the knowledge of God available to them: "For although they knew God, they neither glorified him . . . nor gave thanks to him" (Romans 1:21). Their problem was not lack of knowledge. They had the opportunity to respond to God through the light they receive from creation, but they rejected this light and chose their own religious practices (1:18–21). Their problem was rebellion. This is the basic sin of humanity—independence from God. And that merits the wrath of God.

The next step in the human descent from God was idolatry. They "exchanged the glory of the immortal God for images made to look like mortal man and birds and animals and reptiles" (Romans 1:23). Paul concluded, "They exchanged the truth of God for a lie, and worshiped and served created things rather than the Creator—who is forever praised" (1:25).

Light through Conscience (Romans 2:12–16). The next source of light is the conscience. Paul says, "They show that the requirements of the law are written on their hearts, their consciences also bearing witness, and their thoughts now accusing, now even defending them" (Romans 2:15). All people experience a sense of right and wrong through the operation of their consciences. Because of its operation on a person's will, the conscience of each individual will one day accuse or defend him or her. This accusing and defending "will take place on the day when God will judge men's secrets through Jesus Christ" (2:16). Paul is saying that those who do not have the benefit of God's special revelation will be judged not for rejecting what they did not know but for rejecting their conscience. Paul summarizes, "All who sin apart from the law will also perish apart from the law" (2:12).

Below we will discuss the view that Paul's statement about the conscience defending Gentiles at the judgment (2:16) implies the possibility of salvation to the unevangelized.

All under Sin (Romans 3:9–12, 23). Romans 1–3 has an extended defense of the argument that all people in their natural state cannot be regarded as righteous before God because of their sin. Paul summarized his case by saying, "What shall we conclude then? Are we any better? Not at all! We have already made the charge that Jews and Gentiles alike are all under sin" (Romans 3:9). He then amplified: "As it is written: 'There is no one righteous, not even one; there is no one who understands, no one who seeks God. All have turned away, they have together become worthless; there is no one who does good, not even one'" (3:10–12).

Paul's purpose was to show how everyone in the human family is a sinner alienated from God. As Everett Harrison observes, Paul's language "is devastatingly clear and sharp," indicating that "no exception is allowed."[5] Paul asserted, "All have sinned and fall short of the glory of God" (Romans 3:23). By human standards, people may be righteous. But when they are judged by the standards of God's glory, all people fall hopelessly short. Even a comparatively righteous person such as Isaiah, when he had a vision of the glory of God, cried out in despair, "Woe to me! . . . I am ruined! For I am a man of unclean lips, and I live among a people of unclean lips, and my eyes have seen the King, the LORD Almighty" (Isaiah 6:5).

The fact that every person in his or her natural state is a sinner guilty before a holy God, and is therefore lost, has been largely forgotten. Much Christian preaching, teaching, and writing emphasize the blessings the gospel brings. The blessings are important, but there should be a corresponding emphasis on the seriousness of the separation from God in which people live apart from the gospel. This failure to emphasize both sides is one reason many people find it difficult to accept that without faith in Christ there is no hope of salvation for anyone. They see the born-again experience as a blessed extra to life. They don't see it as a transformation from death to life (Romans 6:23), from darkness to light (1 Peter 2:9), and from rejection by God to acceptance by God (Romans 5:9–11).

God's Solution (Romans 3:21–31). In Romans 3:21–31 Paul expounded God's solution to the problem of universal human sinfulness. He said that God's method of bringing people to a right relationship with Himself is not by their earning it through fulfilling the law (3:21). Instead, "this righteousness from God comes through faith in Jesus Christ to all who believe" (3:22). People must believe in Jesus. That is the only way to salvation.

And why is faith in Christ the only way? Paul answered this question in the next few verses. He first mentioned that all people are hopelessly lost: "For all have sinned and fall short of the glory of God" (Romans 3:23). We cannot save ourselves by our own efforts; therefore God acted in Christ to give us salvation. "And [we] are justified freely by his grace through the redemption that came by Christ Jesus. God presented him as a sacrifice of atonement, through faith in his blood" (3:24–25). These two verses exude an emphasis on grace. What we could not do for our salvation, God has done for us.

Here we see the flaw in the arguments of those who claim that a person's sincerity and religiousness can be a means of salvation. People are so lost in sin that they are incapable of enough sincerity to merit salvation. The effects of sin upon them and upon their relationship with God are so devastating that they cannot help themselves. Their only hope is the free gift of God's grace through Christ and His work. We are too sinful to do anything to merit our salvation. But our gracious God did everything that was necessary.

This passage also mentions over and over again that faith, or belief, is the way to appropriate the benefits of Christ's work.

- "This righteousness from God comes through faith in Jesus Christ to all who believe" (3:22).
- "[God is] the one who justifies the man who has faith in Jesus" (3:26).
- "For we maintain that a man is justified by faith apart from observing the law" (3:28).
- "There is only one God, who will justify the circumcised by faith and the uncircumcised through that same faith" (3:30).

Believing is not merely giving mental assent to what Christ did and then living any way we want. Saving faith has four important steps. First, we must decide to leave behind our past life. Second, we must admit that we cannot help ourselves. Third, we must accept what Christ has done on our behalf. Fourth, we must entrust ourselves to Him and His way; we accept His way as our way. This implies that when He becomes our Savior, He also automatically becomes our Lord.

Why is faith so important for salvation? Faith is the opposite of the basic sin that separates us from God. Genesis 3 tells us that the Fall took place when Adam and Eve chose to decide for themselves what is good and what is evil. They chose to build their own system of values. So the basic sin of fallen humanity is independence from God. Faith is the opposite of independence from God. When we exercise faith, we reject our own ways of saving ourselves and controlling our lives and submit to the way God provided for us in Christ Jesus. This way acquits us of our guilt so that we do not need to be punished and opens the door for us to live the way we were made to live, the way of dependence upon God. Now we let Him decide what is good and evil. Exercising saving faith is like giving back to God the fruit that Adam and Eve partook of.

Must They Hear?

Can those who do not hear the gospel exercise saving faith? Acts 4:12 says, "Salvation is found in no one else, for there is no other name under heaven given to men by which we must be saved." Some scholars say that verses such as this proclaim that Christ is the *ontological*[6] ground of salvation, that is, salvation is grounded in Christ. But they also say that this does not imply that He is the only *epistemological*[7] means of salvation. That means that salvation does not necessarily require knowledge of Jesus' name. They say that what is important about Christ are His qualities. To call on His name is to place one's trust in those qualities that one discerns to be worthy of allegiance. We who know Christ know that these qualities are the qualities of Christ. According to this view, those who repent of their selfishness and follow these principles of Christ will be saved even though they do not know Christ. Clark Pinnock, for example, says that Acts 4:12 "does not demand restrictive exclusivism."[8]

We have responded to this interpretation elsewhere, showing that use of the word *must* (*dei*) emphasizes necessity, that a response to the name is necessary.[9] In the ten occurrences of the "name" of the Lord in Acts 2–4, in all, except 4:12, clear, conscious acknowledgment of the name is undoubtedly implied, and that this is equally true of the other occurrences in the rest of Acts. In the evangelistic speech just before the defense in which 4:12 appears Peter said, "By faith in the name of Jesus, this man whom you see and know was made strong. It is Jesus' name and the faith that comes through him that has given this complete healing to him, as you can all see" (Acts 3:16). As Douglas Geivett and Gary Phillips point out, Peter is "indicating what must be acknowledged about Jesus before one must be saved."[10]

The many passages explaining the need for faith also present the object of faith as a person—Christ. More than the principles of Christ is intended here. These passages talk about asking a person to be Savior and Lord.

Other passages teach that we must hear the message of Christ before entrusting ourselves to Him. Jesus said, "Whoever hears my word and believes him who sent me has eternal life and will not be condemned" (John 5:24). Before believing comes hearing. The logic of this was clearly presented by Paul: "For, 'Everyone who calls on the name of the Lord will be saved.' How, then, can they call on the one they have not believed in? And how can they believe in the one of whom they have not heard? And how can they hear without someone preaching to them?" (Romans 10:13–14). Later Paul added, "Faith comes from hearing the message, and the message is heard through the word of Christ" (10:17).

Living According to Light Received: Romans 2
Some verses in Romans 2 are being described as teaching the possibility of salvation without hearing the gospel. These texts seem to suggest that if they do not hear the gospel, people can adequately respond to the light they receive and in this way be recipients of God's saving grace. Here we will examine the three such groups of verses used most (vv. 6–7, 9–10, and 14–16).

The Context Discourages Such an Interpretation. If these verses are divorced from their context, the idea of the unevangelized being saved is a possible implication. But it is not a necessary implication; that is, it is not the only way in which these verses can be interpreted. As we read on and sense Paul's point in this section of Romans (1:18–3:20), we realize that this interpretation contradicts what Paul has been arguing. As we saw, he is arguing that everyone in the whole human race, without exception, has sinned and fallen short of the glory of God.

In an article critiquing the inclusivist interpretation of Romans 2, Douglas Moo explains that Romans 1:18–3:20 "is intended to show why human beings need this 'revelation of the righteousness of God' and why it can be experienced only through faith." The reason for this is sin. "It holds every person, Jew or Gentile, under its power (3:9). And because of sin, no person can be justified before God by obeying the law or by doing any other good work (3:20)." Moo concludes, "Boiled down to its essentials, then, Paul is claiming that people must respond in faith to the revelation of God's righteousness because it, and it alone,

breaks the stranglehold of sin. And the revelation of God's righteousness occurs, he says, in the gospel."[11]

Some scholars have said that in the culmination of his argument
(Romans 3:20) Paul "does not state that no one is justified apart from having heard of Christ, but rather that no one is justified by the works of the
law."[12] Perhaps this is true, although it is implied that apart from hearing
the gospel there is no salvation. But the next paragraph states explicitly
that faith in Jesus is necessary for salvation. Consider these verses:

- Romans 3:22–24: "This righteousness from God comes through faith
  in Jesus Christ to all who believe. There is no difference, for all have
  sinned and fall short of the glory of God, and are justified freely by
  his grace through the redemption that came by Christ Jesus."
- Romans 3:25: "God presented him as a sacrifice of atonement,
  through faith in his blood."
- Romans 3:26: "He did it to demonstrate his justice at the present
  time, so as to be just and the one who justifies those who have
  faith in Jesus."

In the next paragraph (3:27–31) Paul refers to faith five times. In
the nine occurrences of "faith" and "believe" (3:22–31), faith in Christ is
intended. Later (10:13–17) Paul argued that the way such faith is born in
an individual is through proclamation of the gospel.

To see inclusivism in Romans 2 is to suggest that Paul contradicts
himself within the same book and also within the same section of this
book—a most unlikely possibility. Therefore it is best to look for alternate
explanations that avoid such an interpretation.

Romans 2:6–7, 9–10. Verses 6 and 7 say, "God 'will give to each person according to what he has done.' To those who by persistence in
doing good seek glory, honor and immortality, he will give eternal
life."[13] Some interpreters understand this text as implying that those
who have not heard the gospel could nevertheless do those works that
issue from God's grace (they have an attitude similar to the saving faith
of Christians) and thus receive eternal life. Verses 9 and 10 have also
elicited such an interpretation: "There will be trouble and distress for

every human being who does evil: first for the Jew, then for the Gentile; but glory, honor and peace for everyone who does good: first for the Jew, then for the Gentile." We will not discuss this text at length because what is said of verses 6–7 applies to verses 9–10.

An alternative interpretation of verses 6 and 7 is that in verses 1–16 Paul lays the foundation for his affirmation that the Jews also need the gospel. He does this by establishing that God is righteous in the way He judges people. Soon he will argue that Jews can't fall back on the fact that they are Jews and have the law, because they do not keep it in the way that pleases God (2:17–29). In Romans 4 he will show that the way Jews were saved in Old Testament times was the way of faith. In several places Paul teaches that after the Christ has come, the way for Jews to be saved is the way of faith in Christ (see Romans 3–4; 9–11). His insistence on the importance of obedience (Romans 2) shows us that Paul believes with the rest of the New Testament writers, especially James, that the evidence of saving faith is works (see also 1 Corinthians 6:9–11; 2 Corinthians 5:10; Galatians 5:21). For Jews the way of salvation is faith, and this faith must issue in works if it is saving faith. Paul would agree with other New Testament writers that at the judgment, the dual criteria, on the human side, of faith and works would be important. This point about judgment is demonstrated in the section on "Degrees of Responsibility."

That then is Paul's thought in Romans regarding the Jews. In Romans 2 Paul argues that the Jews need the gospel because in their present state they are headed for judgment. In verses 1–16 he argues that God is just in the way He judges. While building this case he presents various criteria that determine God's judgment. It is based on truth (v. 2), on what people have done (vv. 6–10), on whether or not those who had the law acted according to it (vv. 12–13), and on whether those who did not have the law acted according to their consciences, which is the law in their hearts (vv. 14–16). The discussion in 2:1–16 is not confined to a particular group of people. Paul brings in the case of Jews and Gentiles to buttress his case about the principles of God's judgment.

We cannot take individual statements in such a passage (Romans 2:1–16) as separate affirmations that give alternate ways of salvation. They are all intended to give weight to the affirmation that God's judgment is righteous. We cannot build a full-blown theology of salvation for those who have not heard from verses 6 and 7, which represent just one building block in a large structure. What then do we make of Paul's affirmation that God will give eternal life to those "who by persistence in doing good seek glory, honor and immortality"? Paul is saying that at the judgment only such people will be saved. But by noting the thrust of this section, we do not need to imply that this verse presents the only criteria for the salvation of those it describes. From Paul's thought in the rest of this book we infer that faith in Christ is also a necessary criterion for salvation at the judgment. According to our interpretation, then, verse 7 (and v. 10) is speaking of believers in Jesus Christ who do good works.[14]

One trusts that this argument about the message of Romans 2:1–16, including Paul's use of Jews and Gentiles, answers the objection that this interpretation "runs foul of the narrative flow of the epistle, in which the Christian gospel does not seem to be unpacked until 3:21."[15] It is true that the Christian gospel is unpacked only later, but here Paul brings different points to build his case that God's judgment is righteous. It would not be inconsistent for Paul to bring up the way that people are saved according to the gospel, even though he will unpack that only later. Perhaps that does not fit into the modern way of scholarly writing, but Paul was not bound by such restrictions.

A large number of distinguished and capable scholars interpret Romans 2:6–7 as presenting a hypothetical situation. They say that these verses describe how a Jew can be saved: by perfectly following the law. But, as Paul will go on to show, no one does this. Therefore in practice no one will be saved in this way. There is a good case for this interpretation.[16] But the sense when reading these verses is that the language in verses 7 and 10 is too firm to represent merely a hypothetical situation. Besides, as Thomas Schreiner has pointed out, "Paul elsewhere teaches that works are necessary to enter the kingdom of God (cf. 1 Corinthians 6:9–11; 2 Corinthians 5:10; Galatians 5:21),"[17] not as a means of salvation but because they are the essential result and therefore the evidence of salvation. Therefore the preceding interpretation is in harmony with Paul's teaching about the judgment. Although the case for the hypothetical explanation is a strong one, the case for taking those mentioned in verses 7 and 10 as believers in Christ is even stronger.

Romans 2:14-16. Verses 14–16 are also used to support inclusivism. These verses talk about Gentiles, who do not have the Jewish law, yet have the law of conscience. "Indeed, when Gentiles, who do not have the law, do by nature things required by the law, they are a law for themselves, even though they do not have the law, since they show that the requirements of the law are written on their hearts" (vv. 14–15a). This law of conscience is said to influence their condemnation and defense. "Their consciences also bearing witness, and their thoughts now accusing, now even defending them. This will take place on the day when God will judge men's secrets through Jesus Christ, as my gospel declares" (vv. 15b–16).

Paul says that the consciences of some people will defend them. Inclusivists interpret this statement as meaning that some who lived according to their consciences will be acquitted at the judgment even if they do not hear the gospel. Some inclusivists see this only as a faint possibility because Romans 3 suggests that all must respond to Christ in order to receive salvation.[18] Others are much more confident that large numbers of such people will be saved.[19]

In responding to the inclusivist interpretation of this passage we must reiterate that Paul's thrust in Romans 1–3 is that none live up to the demands of their consciences. We agree with the inclusivists that unbelieving Gentiles are intended in verses 14 and 15. But we need not imply that Paul is speaking of salvation in verse 15 when he says that sometimes people's thoughts will defend them. He is saying that when the law of conscience judges people's actions, some acts will be deemed acceptable whereas others will not be acceptable. At the judgment people will be judged according to how they responded to the light of their consciences. No one lives up to this light. Therefore conscience and our response to it will not suffice to save us. But some will be judged more severely than others because they violated the law of their consciences much more consistently than others did. In this view verse 15 says that the law of conscience sometimes accuses people and sometimes defends them.[20]

Douglas Moo explains that in verse 15, "the witness of the conscience consists in the mixed verdict of ones thoughts." Verse 16 points to the fact that though "the debate among the thoughts goes on constantly . . . , its ultimate significance will be revealed in the last judgment." Moo also points out that the use of the word "even" before "defending them" in verse 15 suggests that the thoughts have far more to accuse than to defend.[21]

Cornelius and Other Sincere Seekers

Clark Pinnock has argued that in the Bible there are numerous "pagan saints," that is, people who have not been exposed to God's special revelation but have come to trust in God and thus receive the grace of God's salvation. Among these are sincere seekers after truth who had no opportunity to hear the gospel. Foremost among the biblical examples is Cornelius, whom Pinnock calls "the pagan saint par excellence of the New Testament."[22]

Peter's statement to Cornelius that God "accepts men from every nation who fear him and do what is right" (Acts 10:35) is used to say that Cornelius was saved before Peter came to him. This passage, however, does not qualify for use in developing an inclusivist case. Cornelius was a God-fearer, a Gentile who worshiped the God of the Bible but who had not taken the step of becoming a Jew (proselyte).

Even after Cornelius had expressed an attitude that comes close to saving faith, "God's response," as Everett Harrison points out, "was not to save Cornelius by fiat, but to show him how he could learn of the appointed way."[23] The angel who visited Cornelius told him that Peter "will bring you a message through which you and all your household will be saved" (Acts 11:14). The message had to be heard for salvation to be granted. Therefore Acts 10:35 could not be implying that people such as Cornelius could be saved without hearing the gospel. We conclude with Harrison that when Peter said that God "accepts men from every nation who fear him and do what is right," he meant that even Gentiles "are suitable candidates for salvation." Harrison concludes, "Such preparation betokens a spiritual earnestness that will result in faith as the gospel is heard and received."[24]

From the story of Cornelius we learn that to a truly sincere person God will reveal the gospel, even if he has to work a miracle to do so. The only means we know of through which such a revelation can come is the proclamation of the gospel of Christ. J. Oswald Sanders gives two examples of such people that are worth noting.[25]

The first story was originally related by N. L. Niswander in *The Alliance Weekly* (July 2, 1958). While a missionary was preaching, he was impressed with a listener whose face expressed openness and interest. The subject of Christ as Savior brought him delight and joy. Later, when he talked with the missionary, the man spoke of three crises in his life. The first one was becoming aware of the perfection and wonder of the universe. Nature revealed to him the awesome wonder of the Mighty One. The next crisis was a serious condemnation and conviction of sin. His knowledge of the grandeur of nature brought to light his own imperfections. He realized then the close relationship between the physical laws and the moral law and the holiness of God. In the third crisis he became an earnest seeker for God's answer to this confusion in his heart and mind. He testified that when he sought God's forgiveness, he was conscious of a Savior's presence. And now, he continued, "Since I have heard you speak, I recognize in Jesus the Person who has made atonement for my sin." Here was a modern Cornelius. This person responded as best he could to the light he received until he was finally led to Christ.

A missionary nurse in Thailand related a story that Sanders gives:

A couple came to our home in Thailand about three o'clock in the afternoon. . . . The woman began to speak. "There is a matter which is troubling me, and I think you are the one who can help me. . . . I had a dream[26] about a man called Jesus. Could you tell me who he is?" The caller related her dreams and then asked what [they] could mean. She knew nothing of Jesus except that once she had heard this name. For five years she and her husband had been seeking peace, and together they had tried to live a holy life after the precepts of Buddha, but peace had not come. Their neighbors called them mad for seeking so earnestly. In a moment I asked the Lord for guidance and then for the next three hours we turned from passage to passage of Scripture, and the Holy Spirit guided and gave understanding. It was a thrill beyond telling to see this simple couple perceive the deep things of the Word of God. . . . The following Monday afternoon they came again. Their opening words in chorus were, "We have found peace and joy now as we never had before."

In both stories sincere seekers heard the gospel of Christ. Sanders quotes H. W. Frost, who described people "who have seen 'men in white' who have told them to go to certain cities or chapels and to believe the doctrine which they might hear there." Then Frost points out that "it took the going, the finding of the preacher, the hearing and believing to make them understand the full meaning of the vision."

Frost concludes, "It is conceivable that God might have ordained to preach the gospel directly to men through dreams, visions and revelations. But as a matter of fact he has not done this, but rather has committed the preaching to men, telling them to go and disciple all nations."[27]

The overwhelming majority of people do not seek God in this way. In fact, when the gospel is preached to them, many reject it. Most of those who have accepted the gospel would testify that they did not earnestly seek after it. My experience and that of many others working among non-Christians is that seekers like Cornelius are rarely found anywhere.

Salvation in Old Testament Times

A growing number of scholars are drawing a principle about salvation from the fact that there were Jews who were saved without the gospel before Christ came to this world. They say that in the same way people today may be saved before the gospel is presented to them if they fear the Lord as the Old Testament saints did.[28] These people are considered "theologically BC" even though they are not so chronologically.

Whatever may be the way that salvation was granted to Jews in Old Testament times, people today need to hear the gospel in order to be saved. This is a major point in Paul's discussion about the salvation of the Jews (Romans 9–11). The need for them to hear the gospel and for a preacher to be sent to them for this purpose is explicitly stated in Romans 10:8–17.

In Old Testament times two key features were necessary for salvation. Both features are keys to salvation in the gospel of Christ too. In every fundamental area, salvation in the Old Testament foreshadowed salvation in the gospel of Christ. The first feature of Old Testament salvation is that those saved received a special revelation of God and his ways. This revelation is now recorded in the Old Testament. The Jews often misunderstood this revelation. But, properly understood, it is essentially similar to the revelation in the gospel of Christ. It presents a covenant relationship between God and his people, which is mercifully initiated by God and received by individuals through faith.

Second, in the Old Testament times, there needed to be what Carl F. H. Henry calls "a divinely approved sacrifice . . . which focuses on the Mediator-Messiah . . . if only in an elementary and preparatory sense." Henry reminds us that "the God of the Old Testament is angry with mankind in sin; only the satisfaction of his righteousness and the expiation of sin by the perfect sacrifice of the Promised Mediator renders him propitiatory." The Old Testament sacrifices foreshadowed and looked forward to this sacrifice of Christ. They propitiated God. That is, they took away his wrath against sin. Henry concludes, "A religion that speaks of forgiveness without a doctrine of substitutionary mediation and atonement has nothing in common either with Old Testament or New Testament religion."[29]

In the Old Testament salvation involved a covenant relationship with God, which required accepting God's special revelation of Himself and His ways and also required offering sacrifices of atonement to God. The so-called saved BC non-Christians of today who have not yet heard the gospel cannot fulfill these two requirements.

Are exceptions to this method of salvation recorded in the Old Testament? Were people saved without the help of the covenant community, its revelation, and its sacrifices? Inclusivists say that the Bible does present such examples. Pinnock says, "No one can deny the fact that the Bible presents these holy pagans as saved by faith, even though they neither knew Israelite or Christian revelation." After giving some examples he says, "They all stand as positive proof that the grace of God touches people all over the world and that faith, without which it is impossible to please God, can and does occur outside as well as inside the formal covenant communities."[30] We will discuss five important Old Testament characters mentioned by inclusivists.

The first of these supposed exceptions is Abraham. He had to be an exceptional case because he was the founder of the covenant community, yet he fulfilled the two requirements mentioned above. That is, he accepted the special revelation of God, and he offered atoning sacrifices.

He did not receive revelation from a human source; God spoke directly to him. But because he was such an exceptional case we would do well to be cautious about concluding from his example that God speaks directly to others in bringing them to salvation.

The second so-called exception is Job. But we know so little of Job that it would be best not to arrive at conclusions about his religious background and how God revealed Himself to Job. We do know that Job too offered sacrifices to God (Job 1:5).

We know more about the background of the third so-called exception, Balaam. He was a non-Jewish prophet from Mesopotamia, and we know that God did speak through him. But, as Gordon Wenham points out, the Bible does not portray him as "a good man or true believer." Wenham reminds us that "throughout the Bible, prophecy and other ecstatic spiritual gifts are regarded as signs of inspiration, but not necessarily of holiness or of a right standing with God."[31] Balaam was among those killed when God asked the Israelites to take vengeance on the Midianites (Numbers 31:1–8). In the New Testament his name is a symbol of greed (2 Peter 2:15; Jude 11) and of participation in pagan worship and immorality (Revelation 2:14). Balaam is not portrayed in the Scriptures as a saved person.

The fourth example mentioned is Jethro, Moses' father-in-law, who is remembered for his advice on delegating the administration of justice (Exodus 18). We know that this man offered sacrifices to God (18:12). Although he was not a Jew, he did have close contact with the Jews and their revelation through his son-in-law, Moses. So he is not a good example to use as evidence for the view that the unevangelized could be saved. We are considering unevangelized persons who have no contact with the gospel, but Jethro had much contact with the Old Testament gospel.

The fifth example is Melchizedek, the priest-king of Salem, who blessed Abraham and received a tithe of the spoils from Abraham's victorious battle against neighboring kings. He seemed to have been in touch with God even though he was not a part of the covenant community. If he was saved, was he saved without contact with the Old Testament gospel? The text in Genesis 14 must imply that he was a friend of Abraham. An influential man like Abraham would know the king of neighboring Salem (probably Jerusalem). Could he have heard about God from Abraham?

This is possible, but we cannot be sure. Melchizedek appears so suddenly and then moves off the scene so soon that the writer of Hebrews uses this sudden appearance and disappearance as a symbol of eternity (Hebrews 7:1–3). We know too little about Melchizedek to develop a theology about the salvation of those not hearing the gospel.

The Bible does not make any clear statement about exceptional persons to whom God speaks directly and gives salvation without their hearing the gospel. This principle can be derived only from hints and questionable examples in Scripture. If God wants to save people without their hearing the gospel, I am not going to protest! Certainly God can directly do in a person what He does through an evangelist. But from what the Bible says, we do not have sufficient grounds to entertain a hope of salvation for anyone apart from hearing the gospel. We know that most people in the world do not seek after God as Cornelius did. We have no convincing evidence to expect that the few Cornelius-type seekers in the world can be saved apart from hearing the gospel. God would have us regard all people everywhere as lost and desperately in need of the message of the gospel.

Degrees of Responsibility

An important point in this discussion is that the Bible teaches that there will be degrees of punishment according to the degrees of responsibility of different individuals. This is a thought new to many Christians. They have learned that in God's sight sin is sin and that when it comes to the matter of salvation, there is no differentiation between big sins and small sins. In the Bible the individual sins are not of eternal consequence; it is the fact that we are sinners. Those who are dead in sin are dead whether they are good people in the eyes of the world or not. We heartily agree with all this. That is why we affirm that, apart from faith in Christ, there is no hope for salvation for anyone.

Yet, along with this body of biblical teaching, we must also consider the Scriptures that teach that at the judgment some will receive a harsher punishment than others. Two criteria determine the severity of this punishment: the light one has received and the works one has done.

Let us look at some texts that declare that the degree of light unbelievers receive influences the degree of their punishment. Matthew 11:20–24 says that Tyre, Sidon, and Sodom were destroyed for their wickedness. But they did not receive the light that Korazin, Bethsaida, and Capernaum had received. Jesus said that on the judgment day it would be more bearable for the wicked cities of Tyre, Sidon, and Sodom than for the other three cities not famous for overt wickedness.

Christ's words in Luke were even more explicit. He said that the "servant who knows his master's will and does not get ready [for his coming] or does not do what his master wants will be beaten with many blows" (Luke 12:47). He had much light but disregarded it. "The one who does not know and does things deserving punishment will be beaten with few blows" (12:48). He had enough light to be held accountable for his actions, so he was punished. But the master's will had not been explicitly communicated to him, so he received few blows. The principle is that "from everyone who has been given much, much will be demanded; and from the one who has been entrusted with much, much more will be asked" (12:48).

In Romans 2:11 Paul affirmed God's impartiality: "For God does not show favoritism." Then he illustrated how this impartiality is manifested in the judgment: "All who sin apart from the law will also perish apart from the law, and all who sin under the law will be judged by the law" (2:12).

Each of these passages states that those receiving less light will be punished. But those receiving more light will be punished more severely.

Hebrews 10:26–29 specifically states that the fate of those who reject the gospel will be worse than that of those who rejected the law of Moses:

> If we deliberately keep on sinning after we have received the knowledge of the truth, no sacrifice for sins is left, but only a fearful expectation of judgment and of raging fire that will consume the enemies of God. Anyone who rejected the law of Moses died without mercy on the testimony of two or three witnesses. How much more severely do you think a man deserves to be punished who has trampled the Son of God under foot?

From these passages we conclude that those who reject the gospel, after understanding what it is, will face severe punishment. Those who have not heard the gospel will be punished for not living up to the light they received. But their responsibility is less or diminished, to use a word from the law court. The law decrees that those with diminished responsibility (e.g., a person who is insane) are given a less severe punishment than are others. We can expect a similar situation to exist at God's judgment.

Another body of Scripture teaches that all people will be judged according to their works. We know that a person's works will not merit salvation. But evil deeds do merit punishment unless they have been for-given and washed away by the blood of Christ. The principle behind this fact is set forth vividly in Galatians 6:7: "Do not be deceived: God cannot be mocked. A man reaps what he sows." Revelation 20:12 describes the process of judgment: "And I saw the dead, great and small, standing before the throne, and books were opened. . . . The dead were judged according to what they had done as recorded in the books." Secret acts (Romans 2:16), careless words (Matthew 12:36), ungodly acts (Jude 14–15), in fact, all works will come under the judgment of God: "God will bring every deed into judgment, including every hidden thing, whether it is good or evil" (Ecclesiastes 12:14).

We should not expect a devout Buddhist who made some effort to live according to his principles to receive the same punishment as a cruel tyrant who broke whatever principles he needed to break in order to sat-isfy his evil desires. The Buddhist's religiousness, with its independence of God's way, was an affront to God's glory and thus will not merit salva-tion. But the tyrant's tyranny was a greater affront to God's glory.

The Bible does not give us enough evidence to speculate on the nature of the degrees of punishment and what form that will take. We can only say that all people are responsible for their lostness but that those with greater light and more severe wickedness will receive a more severe punishment. Here we find part of our answer to the questions relating to the fairness of God in saving only those who hear and respond to the gospel. Sin is such a terrible thing that no one deserves to be saved. In His mercy God saves some. Others will be punished. But those who tried to live up to the light they had will receive less punishment.

Unanswered Questions about God's Fairness

There may remain in the minds of readers some unanswered ques-tions about God's fairness and justice. When we are confronted with this problem, we must be careful not to try to fit God into our thinking by rejecting some things that the Bible teaches. Dick Dowsett has said,

"Human hunches do not give us right answers about God. Neither can we learn how God would behave by looking at the way nice people do things."[32] The Scriptures themselves say that God's ways and thoughts are higher than our ways and thoughts (Isaiah 55:8–9; see also Romans 11:33–34). We must approach these issues humbly, realizing that God has revealed His ways to us in the Scriptures and seeking to align our thinking with God's thinking as revealed in these Scriptures.

One aspect of scriptural truth that the contemporary human mind finds difficult to grasp is God's wrath. Our thinking about God's holiness falls so short of the complete truth that we have lost God's sense of the seriousness of sin and unbelief. We don't fully realize how much sin and unbelief affront God's glory. We don't realize what an awesome and serious act of rebellion against God is our independence. No one deserves to be saved. It is absolute mercy that causes at least some to be saved.

Although some questions may remain in our minds, we must affirm that the Bible clearly teaches the fairness of God's judgment (Genesis 18:25; Deuteronomy 10:17; 1 Peter 1:17). One day in heaven we will understand the justice of God's ways and even praise Him for His judgments as those in the courts of heaven do (Revelation 6:10; 11:17–18; 16:5–7; 18:20; 19:1–3). Paul reminded us that "now we see but a poor reflection" (1 Corinthians 13:12). In heaven our vision is unhindered by our weaknesses and wrong perceptions. Then we will understand the reasons for God's wrath and agree with them. Sanders says, "When from eternity's vantage point we learn what he has done, we will be amazed, not at His severity, but at His mercy."[33] Paul said that at the judgment seat every mouth will be silenced and the whole world will be held accountable to God (Romans 3:19). Everyone will realize God is just in His judgment.

Before we receive this full light about God's ways, we would be wise to accept, humbly and completely, what God has revealed in His Word. We should try to solve the problems arising from what is difficult to explain (see 1 Peter 3:15). This will be a lifelong task. Karl Barth is said to have stated that all theology is theodicy, the vindication of the ways of God.

Because questions on some topics may remain in our minds, we must not disregard what the Scriptures teach about them. People have discarded the passages that do not fit into their system of thought, and from other passages they have drawn conclusions that fit into their system of thought. But these conclusions read too much into the texts from which they are drawn. The conclusions are not necessary implications of these texts. It is far more appropriate for us to accept all Scripture and grapple with the problems we encounter in doing that rather than take the easier route of discarding some things the Scriptures teach because they do not fit with our understanding of God.

Lostness and Evangelism

It is often stated that the inclusivist approach to salvation would diminish the urgency of the missionary enterprise. Inclusivists have tried to deny this,[34] but a study by American sociologist James Davison Hunter suggests that inclusivism does diminish missionary and evangelistic urgency.[35] Some people say that this is a pragmatic argument against inclusivism, not a biblical one. Millard Erickson says, "We do not, as Evangelicals, adopt the most useful theological conclusions, but rather, those most faithful to Scripture."[36]

The Scriptures present lostness as a motivation for evangelism, although in a somewhat indirect way.[37] The lostness of the Jews lay behind Paul's "heart's desire and prayer to God for the Israelites . . . that they may be saved" (Romans 10:1). That desire arose from the fact that "they did not know the righteousness that comes from God" (see vv. 2–4). Their lostness was a source of "great sorrow and unceasing anguish in [his] heart" (Romans 9:2).

If we love people, our hearts will be broken over their lostness. This will produce in us a passion like that of Paul when he cried, "For I could wish that I myself were cursed and cut off from Christ for the sake of my brothers, those of my own race" (Romans 9:3). A little later he would go on to argue that it is by hearing the message that the Jews could be saved (10:12–18). The vision of lostness adds urgency to our task. If people are lost and headed for condemnation apart from the gospel, then we must hasten to share the gospel with them. Jude reflects this urgency when he writes, "Snatch others from the fire and save them" (Jude 23).

The lostness of humanity apart from faith in Christ has been a great motivation to evangelists throughout the centuries. The great missionary Hudson Taylor said, "I would have never thought of going to China had I not believed that the Chinese were lost and needed Christ." William Booth, the founder of the Salvation Army, said he would wish his workers might spend "one night in hell" in order to see the urgency of their evangelistic task. D. L. Moody told an audience in London, "If I believed there was no hell, I am sure I would be off tomorrow for America." He said he would give up going from town to town and spending day and night "urging men to escape the damnation of hell."[38]

While heeding Erickson's warning that we must not build our theology on the usefulness of a doctrine, we may be excused for describing the usefulness of a doctrine that is biblical: the doctrine of lostness. If this doctrine is true, then it places before us the huge challenge to do all we can to tell the lost about Christ.

I live in a nation where many citizens regard those doing evangelism with conversion in view as unpatriotic traitors who are dangerous to the stability of the nation. In response to the uproar that has followed the conversion of people of other faiths in Sri Lanka, some Christian leaders have publicly stated that they are not the ones who are trying to convert others. They say the fundamentalist Christians are doing this. It is painful for us to know that so many in our nation view us as being traitors. We too love our land and are willing to make whatever sacrifice is needed for its welfare.

In addition to the need for evangelism we are faced with so many other legitimate needs in the nation that we could spend all our time meeting those needs. Usually it is easier to raise funds for meeting social needs; vivid presentations of those to rich donors can cause emotional unrest and guilt that prompt immediate giving. Such service also generally wins us acclaim in society, whereas we dare not publicize our evangelistic work, as that will win us only trouble. (Christians in the West may think that they do not face such obstacles to evangelism. But hostility to evangelism and Christian convictions is growing there too.)

In this environment we find the doctrine of lostness a great spur to evangelism. We should present it regularly to all Christians, especially those who are doing social work. In an extended reflection on the nature of lostness, Paul urged the Ephesians to remember who they were before they came to Christ. He said, "Remember that at that time you were separate from Christ, excluded from citizenship in Israel and foreigners to the covenants of the promise, without hope and without God in the world" (Ephesians 2:12). Paul was saying that remembering lostness would help them understand the nature of salvation and incorporation into the body of Christ. Remembering this doctrine also gives us a sense of the urgency of the evangelistic task. This is not the only motivation for evangelism, nor is it the most important one. But when we are faced with the great cost of evangelism and are tempted to reduce evangelistic activity because of this, the stark reality of lostness will bring back the urgency and spur us to action.

Yet how little lostness is spoken of today! The spellcheck in my word processing program does not even have the word *lostness*. The Bible asks us to remember this doctrine. We trust this book will help some of God's people to rediscover the biblical doctrine of the lostness of people apart from Christ and through that motivate them to be faithful in the work of evangelism.

Chapter 14 endnotes

[1] John Hick, *The Metaphor of God Incarnate: Christology in a Pluralistic Age* (Louisville: Westminster John Knox, 1993), 88; quoted by Clark H. Pinnock, "An Inclusivist View," *Four Views of Salvation in a Pluralistic World,* Timothy R. Phillips and Dennis L. Ockholm, editors (Grand Rapids, MI: Zondervan Publishing House, 1995), 101.

[2] See, for example, D. A. Carson, *The Gagging of God: Christianity Confronts Pluralism* (Leicester: Apollos; and Grand Rapids, MI: Zondervan Publishing House, 1996), 279–314; Dick Dowsett, God, *That's Not Fair!* (Sevenoaks, Kent: OMF Books, 1982); Ronald H. Nash, *Is Jesus the Only Savior?* (Grand Rapids, MI: Zondervan Publishing House, 1994); Ramesh Richard, *The Population of Heaven* (Chicago: Moody Press, 1994); *Who Will Be Saved? Defending the Biblical Understanding of God, Salvation, and Evangelism,* Paul R. House and Gregory A. Thornbury, editors (Wheaton, IL: Crossway Books, 2000), 111–160; *Four Views of Salvation in a Pluralistic World,* Phillips and Ockholm, editors, contributions of R. Douglas Geivett and W. Gary Phillips; *Through No Fault of Their Own? The Fate of Those Who Have Never Heard,* William V. Crockett and James G. Sigountos, editors (Grand Rapids, MI: Baker Book House, 1991).

3 C. K. Barrett, *A Commentary on the Epistle to the Romans* (New York: Harper & Row, 1957), 35.

4 Barrett, *Romans,* 36.

5 Everett F. Harrison, "Romans," *The Expositor's Bible Commentary* (Grand Rapids, MI: Zondervan Publishing House, 1976), 38.

6 *Ontology* is the study of being.

7 *Epistemology* is the study of knowledge.

8 Clark H. Pinnock, "Acts 4:12—No Other Name Under Heaven," in *Through No Fault of Their Own?* 112.

9 See Ajith Fernando, NIV Application Commentary: Acts (Grand Rapids, MI: Zondervan Publishing House, 1998), 163–65. For more complete treatments see Richard, *The Population of Heaven,* 55–60; R. Douglas Geivett and W. Gary Phillips, "A Particularist View: An Evidentialist Approach," in *More Than One Way?* 230–33.

10 Geivett and Phillips, "A Particularist View," 232–33.

11 Douglas Moo, "Romans 2: Saved Apart from the Gospel?" in *Through No Fault of Their Own?* 140.

12 This is presented approvingly as James D. G. Dunn's position by Craig L. Blomberg in "Eschatology and the Church: Some New Testament Perspectives," in *Solid Ground: 25 Years of Evangelical Theology,* Carl R. Trueman and others, editors (Leicester: Apollos, InterVarsity Press, 2000), 89. However, I could not find this clearly stated in the pages cited by Blomberg in Dunn's commentary, "Romans 1–8," *Word Biblical Commentary* (Dallas: Word Books, 1988), 158–60.

13 See Klyne Snodgrass, "Justification by Grace—to the Doers: An Analysis of the Place of Romans 2 in the Theology of Paul," *New Testament Studies, vol. 32,* 1986, 72–93. This seems to be the implication of James D. G. Dunn in Romans 1–8, 85–86.

14 Thomas R. Schreiner comes to a similar conclusion in "Romans," *Baker Exegetical Commentary on the New Testament* (Grand Rapids, MI: Baker Book House, 1998), 112–15. See also Schreiner's "Did Paul Believe in Justification by Works? Another Look at Romans 2," *Bulletin of Biblical Research, vol. 3,* 1993, 131–58.

15 Blomberg, "Eschatology and the Church," 89.

16 For a description of this case see Moo, "Romans 2: Saved Apart from the Gospel?" in *Through No Fault of Their Own? The Fate of Those Who Have*

Never Heard; and Moo, "The Epistle to the Romans," *The New International Commentary on the New Testament,* (Grand Rapids, MI: Wm. B. Eerdmans Publishing Co., 1996), 136–142.

[17] Schreiner, "Romans," 115.

[18] Millard J. Erickson, *Christian Theology,* second edition (Grand Rapids, MI; Baker Book House, 1998), 197–98.

[19] See Clark H. Pinnock, *A Wideness in God's Mercy: The Finality of Jesus Christ in a World of Religions* (Grand Rapids, MI: Zondervan Publishing House, 1992), chapter 5: "Hope for the Unevangelized."

[20] Here, too, Schreiner (Romans, 119–124) comes up with a conclusion similar to mine.

[21] Moo, "Romans," 153.

[22] Pinnock, *A Wideness in God's Mercy,* 165.

[23] Everett F. Harrison, *Interpreting Acts: The Expanding Church* (Grand Rapids, MI: Zondervan Publishing House, 1986), 176.

[24] Harrison, *Interpreting Acts,* 182. For a fuller defense of this interpretation, see my Acts, 339–340.

[25] J. Oswald Sanders, *How Lost Are the Heathen?* (Chicago: Moody Press, 1972), 67–70.

[26] It is interesting that in recent years many people, especially those living in countries closed to the gospel (like Islamic countries), testify to having dreams and visions where they are confronted by Jesus.

[27] Sanders, *How Lost Are the Heathen?* 70–71.

[28] Pinnock, *A Wideness in God's Mercy,* 163; Sir Norman Anderson, *Christianity and World Religions: The Challenge of Pluralism* (Leicester and Downers Grove, IL: InterVarsity Press, 1984), 143–45.

[29] Carl F. H. Henry, *God, Revelation, and Authority: God Who Stands and Stays, vol. VI* (Waco: Word Books, 1983; re-issued by Wheaton, IL: Crossway Books), 369.

[30] Pinnock, *A Wideness in God's Mercy,* 162.

[31] Gordon J. Wenham, "Numbers," *The Tyndale Old Testament Commentaries* (Leicester and Downers Grove, IL: InterVarsity Press, 1981), 168.

[32] Dowsett, *God, That's Not Fair!* 4.

[33] Sanders, *How Lost are the Heathen?* 32.

[34] Pinnock, *A Wideness in God's Mercy, 176-180;* "An Inclusivist View," in *Four Views of Salvation in a Pluralistic World,* Dennis L. Ockholm and Timothy R. Phillips, editors (Grand Rapids, MI: Zondervan Publishing House, 1995), 120.

[35] James Davison Hunter, *Evangelicalism: The Coming Generation* (Chicago: The University of Chicago Press, 1987), 258.

[36] Erickson, *Christian Theology,* 197.

[37] See my *Crucial Questions about Hell* (Wheaton, IL Crossway Books, 1994), chapter 13: "Lostness as a Motivation to Evangelism," from which many of the points here are taken.

[38] Cited in Stanley N. Gundry, *Love Them In: The Life and Theology of D. L. Moody* (Grand Rapids, MI: Baker Book House, 1976 [reissued by Chicago: Moody Press]), 97–98.

APPENDIX: SKETCHES OF OTHER FAITHS

It is beyond the scope of this book to give a detailed description of the major world religions and ideologies. We have given some details when discussing various issues pertaining to these in this book and referred to some of these discussions in the body of this appendix. Therefore a brief introductory word is given about some of the major ideologies. You will notice that the descriptions of Buddhism, Hinduism, and Islam have fewer endnotes than the other descriptions. This is because I am more familiar with these three religions and less familiar with the others. The brevity of these descriptions may frustrate the reader. This frustration may cause you to secure a book describing world religions, some examples of which are given in the bibliography at the end of this appendix.

Descriptions of Native American religion and the Indian religion *Jainism* are not included. The former is included in the more general grouping, "Tribal or 'Primal' Religions" below. There are brief descriptions of these two traditions in Winfried Corduan's book *Neighboring Faiths* that is mentioned in the bibliography below.

Several tips for those seeking to witness to people of other faiths can be gleaned from various discussions in this book. In the bibliography below we have mentioned the books that present such tips. Here we will point out three of the most important features of witnessing to people whose beliefs are very different to Christian beliefs.

1. We need to be patient, as their approach to life (worldview) is very different from ours, and it may take time for them to become sympathetic to and to understand the gospel.

2. We need to listen to their ideas and objections carefully so that we can address them with the answers that the gospel gives to these ideas and objections.

3. When I talk with non-Christians about the gospel I always try to remember that, because the gospel is the answer provided by their Creator, only the gospel can fulfill their deep yearnings. All people are made in the image of God, and though this has been tainted through and through because of the ravages of sin, there still remains a thirst for God that the gospel alone can fully satisfy. This not only gives us confidence, it also gives us the encouragement to persevere without being discouraged by initial rejection of or disinterest in our message.

Atheism and Non-theism

The Christian witness often encounters atheists, who say there is no God, and non-theists, who say they do not need a God. These too are ideologies that we have to relate the gospel to. They are discussed in the last two sections of chapter 9.

Baha'i

Baha'i was founded in the eighteenth century by a Persian, Husayn Ali, who was from a Shi'ite Muslim background. He took the name *Baha'ullah,* meaning "the glory of God". He was banished to prison in Acre in modern Israel and lived in Constantinople, Adrianopole, and Acre after that. He launched a prolific writing program that spread his message everywhere. The present international Baha'i headquarters is in Haifa, Israel. Though a relatively new world religion, Baha'i has adherents all over the world. The impressive Baha'i temple in Wilmette, Illinois, is well known in North America.

Baha'ullah's message is one of unity. He believed that truth was revealed successively by manifestations of God or prophets such as

Adam, Moses, Krishna, Buddha, Zarathustra, Christ, and Muhammad. He saw himself as the latest and most important prophet. So Baha'i includes features from several religions. He saw the various religions as complementing rather than competing with each other.

The Baha'i religion emphasizes preparing the individual through personal devotion so as to be an agent of change in society. So there is a high emphasis on social action. John Boykin has given the following reasons for the appeal of this religion today:

> The Baha'i Faith brings a message of Unity: all religions are one, true science and true religion are one, all peoples are one. Baha'is advocate equality of men and women, a universal language and abolition of all forms of prejudice. It is, at first glance, a very attractive, very sensible religion.[1]

One can see how the emphasis on the unity of religions can appeal to many in this pluralistic age. The Baha'is organize a World Religion Day in several countries in which representatives of all the major religions participate.

Buddhism

Buddhism was founded in India by Siddharta Gautama more than 2,500 years ago, as a reform movement of Hinduism. After renouncing his princely comforts, Gautama launched a quest for truth, which included a period of asceticism. He received enlightenment about "the middle path" while meditating under a Bodhi (or Bo) tree. Thereafter he was called the Buddha, which means "the enlightened one."

Buddhism could be viewed as a reform movement of Hinduism with its strong repudiation of the caste system of Hinduism. It was virtually swallowed up in the land of its birth by Hinduism. But Hinduism was refined in the process. Now there are very few Buddhists in India.

As in Hinduism, Buddhism has a belief in *karma* ("work" or "action") and rebirth: the consequences of actions within one life flow into the next life and influence its character. Because of the Buddhist belief that there is no such thing as a soul (*anatta*), Buddhists do not refer to the transmigration of the soul, which takes on a new body (*reincarnation*). Therefore they prefer to call it rebirth rather than reincarnation. They say that one's karma gathers energy to give birth to a new being who represents the net karma of the earlier being. We have explained this in the sections entitled "Karma" and "Reincarnation" in chapter 13.

The Four Noble Truths. At the heart of Buddhism are the Four Noble Truths.

1. *Dukkha*. All life entails suffering. Suffering is something like the frustration or futility spoken of in Ecclesiastes. It has also been described as unsatisfactoriness and is the basic reality of life.

2. *Tanha*. The origin or cause of suffering is craving or desire for the wrong things or for the right things in the wrong way. This comes from a wrong sense of values—assigning value to earthly things or people that they cannot sustain.

3. *Nirodha*. The cessation of suffering occurs when craving is no more—even the craving to live on earth. Then one is freed from the cycle of rebirth (*samsara*) and attains *nirvana*. Nirvana means "blowing out" or "extinguishing." The flames of desire are no longer fueled. Many Buddhists have added a more positive feature to nirvana and view it as a blissful state. In *Mahayana Buddhism* (see below), nirvana is more like a heaven.

4. *Marga*. The way to the removal of desire is the Noble Eight-fold Path that has to do with wisdom, ethical conduct, and mental discipline: right views, right motives, right speech, right conduct, right means of livelihood, right effort, right mindfulness, right contemplation.

The Triple Gem—the Buddha, the *dharma* (teaching), and the *sangha* (the community of monks)—represents the three most important institutions of Buddhism.

Varieties of Buddhism. There are two main branches of Buddhism. *Theravada* (meaning "the doctrine of the elders") Buddhism is closer to the original teachings and is found in Thailand, Burma, Cambodia, Laos, and Sri Lanka. It could be described as a non-theistic (God is not necessary) ethical discipline. Though it is non-theistic in theory, many Theravada Buddhists have in practice kept old animistic and polytheistic practices side by side with Buddhism, sometimes even beside a Buddhist temple. We have discussed non-theism in the last section of chapter 9 and the theistic outlook of Buddhists in practice in the section "Help from the Gods" in chapter 10.

Mahayana (meaning "the greater vehicle") Buddhism has taken several different forms and is found in Nepal, Sikkim, Bhutan, Tibet, China, Taiwan, Mongolia, Korea, Japan, and Singapore, among other places. These forms have many more "religious" elements than in Theravada Buddhism. Often the Buddha is viewed almost as a god. Some (the *bodhisattvas*) hold back attaining nirvana in order that they may remain to help people. People pray to these bodhisattvas.

There are sects such as Rissho-Koseikai and Soka Gakkai in Japan. Soka Gakkai, the value-creating society of lay members, has about 20 million members. It is zealously evangelistic, exclusive, and highly organized. It runs its own political party and has schools and a university.

Zen Buddhism is prominent in and associated with Japan, though it originated in China. It is very different from other forms of Buddhism, and it said to have been influenced by the philosophy of Taoism. It "has been characterized as the world's most difficult religion to understand."[2] This is partly because it has no doctrine or creed. In fact it seeks to free people from bondage to doctrines and "the tyranny of words." It is growing in popularity in the West and fits well with the postmodern mood and its protest against the depersonalization of people through objective truth and rational principles.

A Zen master will give the devotee a riddle (*koan*) to meditate on, which is aimed at pushing one's thinking to the limit of the absurd. An example of a koan is, "When you clap both hands together a sound results. Now listen to the sound of one hand clapping." The aim is to arrive at enlightenment (*satori*) through this. This "is a spontaneous event, totally independent of concepts, techniques or rituals."[3] So enlightenment is available in this life. Alan Watts, whose books have helped popularize Zen in the West, says:

> The method of Zen is to baffle, excite, puzzle and exhaust the intellect until it is realized that intellection is only thinking about; it will provoke, irritate and again exhaust the emotions until it is realized that emotion is only feeling about; and then it contrives, when the disciple has been brought to an intellectual and emotional impasse, to bridge

the gap between second-hand conceptual contact with reality and first-hand experience.[4]

Zen aims at harmony in living and uses the arts to do that. This is expressed through the tea ceremony, judo, Ikebana flower arranging, landscape painting, calligraphy, fencing, and archery, among other things.

East Asian Religion

Julia Ching has observed, "A major difference between East Asian religious life and that of India and the West is that its communities are not completely separate." She points out that if you ask a Japanese "whether he or she is a believer in a particular religion, you may get the answer 'no.'" But, "If you ask whether he or she adheres to Shinto, Buddhism, and Confucianism, you may get the answer 'yes.'"[5] The same Japanese person could have a Shinto wedding and a Buddhist funeral.[6]

The religion of many Chinese is a mixture of many religious traditions, especially their traditional religions, Buddhism, Confucianism, and Taoism. In countries like Singapore and Hong Kong you will find Taoist and Buddhist temples, but the same people may go to both. Similarly, a Korean may be influenced by shamanism, Buddhism, and Confucianism. What we will do here is to present brief introductions to some of these religious traditions.

Harold Netland, out of his experience in Japan, has explained the above phenomenon in the following words:

> There is little interest in formal institutional religion; there is widespread fascination with "spirituality," the occult, and the very practical "this worldly" benefits of religion (healing, success in business, wealth, children, etc.). It is assumed that you can pick and choose from many different traditions indiscriminately, to see what "works." Beliefs and doctrines are minimized; practical benefits are what counts.[7]

Traditional Religion

Shamanism is a feature that has been prominent in the traditional religions of East Asian peoples for centuries. *Shamans* have been described as "specialists in mediating between the world of spirits and the world of men."[8] Usually through an ecstatic experience, like a trance, contact is made with gods, spirits, or souls of departed beings, and the shaman is able to perform things like exorcism, prophecy, fortune telling, rainmaking, interpreting dreams, and healing.[9] Korean Daniel S. Kim says, "At different times in Korean history Buddhism and Confucianism took over the dominant power as the national religion. But these foreign religions failed to dominate the gut level of the religious disposition of the Korean people."[10] Deep down it was shamanism that influenced people's thoughts and actions. Similarly Julia Ching says, "Shamanism persists in today's folk religious tradition wherever the Chinese live and thrive."

A related practice that is common in East Asian traditional religion is *divination*. Divination is the art of penetrating the unknown through a wide range of techniques that use spirit beings or powers. It is used for things like foretelling the future, finding the lost, or finding the best site for a building or well. Included are practices like I Ching and feng shui, which are described in the last section of chapter 10.

Important to Chinese and Korean thought is the idea of the *balance of nature*. The whole world is said to consist of "two opposing and complementary forces, *yin* and *yang*, which are optimally in perfect balance with each other." Winfried Corduan describes this with a helpful chart.[11]

Yin	Yang
Passive	Active
Earth-related	Sky-related
Cold	Hot
Moist	Dry
Mysterious	Clear
Dark	Light
Feminine	Masculine

Corduan explains, "It is important to recognize that neither force in itself is good or evil. Good is the balance between the two; evil is an imbalance in either direction."[12] Around this system have developed an abundance of practices and disciplines, ranging from health to ethics, such as acupuncture, which is described in the last section of chapter 5.

Confucianism

The name *Confucianism* is a Western invention attributed to seventeenth-century Jesuit missionaries.[13] Confucius is the Latinized version of the Chinese name *K'ung Fu-tzu* (meaning "Grand Master K'ung"). He was a Chinese civil servant and, for a short time, a minister who lived at a time (551–479 BC) of social collapse in China. He traveled extensively as a teacher, hoping to bring peace and security to the people through his teaching. He sought to influence the Chinese rulers, and his teaching soon became the imperial philosophy of China.

The most important writing attributed to him, *Lun-Yu,* is called the *Analects* or *Conversations* in English. Many scholars believe that this and other writings attributed to Confucius were edited and put into a somewhat systematic format by his disciples. Both Confucianism and Taoism are philosophies which only later developed into religions.

Confucius's teaching is based on the idea of *jen* (or *ren*), which means "humanity" but which refers to the "good nature" that resides in an individual. The good nature is the source from which virtues flow. The idea is that a person of *jen* achieves his or her full potential and thus manifests moral perfection. Basic to this is the attitude of seeking the welfare of other people. *Jen* provides the inner basis for this. "People should care for others and respect their humanity, allowing their aims to take precedence, if at all possible."[14]

Jen can also be viewed as a human process that includes "the practices of self-reflection, self-cultivation, and moral responsibility."[15] Thomas Leung says, "Confucius . . . was humanistic in his orientation in that he found the solution to the cultural crisis in humanity itself, not in anything religious or spiritual."[16]

So the original teachings of Confucius do not seem to have had what may be called new religious doctrines. Corduan says, "There are no new gods, acts of worship or revelations in his message. He concentrated entirely on the proper execution of duties. If those duties included ritual obligations toward departed ancestors, then they should be fulfilled punctiliously. But Confucius shied away from any further speculation about the spirit world or life after death."[17] However, there is no unanimity among scholars on the relationship between Confucius himself and the religious beliefs and practices of his time. It seems that he did not criticize these practices, but scholars disagree on how much of them he accepted and incorporated into his teachings.

Another important idea in Confucianism is *li,* doing the right thing at the right time. It can be translated as "propriety." From this comes the idea of "correct manners and conduct for all situations."[18] The combining of *jen* and *li* is said to lead to the model of an ideal human society. Very important here is *filial piety,* the respect and obedience that children owe to their parents. This extends to *ancestor worship,* which is described below. Related to all of this is *Tao* (pronounced "dow" and meaning "the Way"), which is important in both Confucianism and Taoism. In Confucianism it has an ethical content: it is "the Way in which an individual, a ruler or a state ought to go, the Way which heaven has made regulative for human conduct."[19]

Mencius (Meng-Zi, 372–289 BC) developed the ideas of Confucius further, giving even greater emphasis to the goodness of human nature. In the second century BC Confucianism became the official ideology of China. Buddhism was introduced to China in the second century AD and became the predominant Chinese religion. In the Sung Dynasty (960–1368) Confucianism resurfaced in a movement known as Neo-Confucianism, which included an integration of Buddhist teaching into Confucian thought. This became China's orthodox ideology until the early twentieth century. At this time there were questions as to whether Confucianism was responsible for China's failure to modernize. Into this situation communism came and finally captured China. With the waning influence of communism, Confucianism is once more becoming a major influence in China. "The rulers are not opposed to this resurgence because it emphasizes loyalty."[20]

Today among the Chinese people Confucianism, Buddhism and Taoism seem to have "worked out a kind of relationship in which all three were recognized as making their own contributions to religious life."[21] Confucianism has influenced the belief system of the Chinese, Japanese, Korean, and Vietnamese peoples. Thomas Leung estimates that about one-and-a-half billion people are consciously or unconsciously influenced by the Confucian worldview.

Taoism or Daoism

The lives of the two great teachers of Taoism—Lao-tzu and Chuang-tzu—are shrouded in mystery and legend. Generally, Lao-tzu is regarded as having lived around the same time as Confucius (around the sixth and fifth centuries BC) while Chaung-tzu is said to have lived in the fourth and third centuries BC. Lao-tzu was critical of Confucius because he felt that by emphasizing external laws he imposed a moral authoritarianism on the people.

Lao-tzu said the answer to the social chaos of the time is found in two principles. The first is Tao. We saw above that Confucius gave this word an ethical content. In Taoism, however, Tao is the underlying (metaphysical) principle of reality. The following description by D. Howard Smith is complex but helps us sense something of its nature.

> It is a first and all-embracing principle, whereby all things are produced. It is the unchanging Unity underlying the shifting plurality of phenomena, the impetus giving rise to every form of life and motion. It is that which exists of itself. It is formless, yet complete, existing before Heaven and Earth, without sound, substance or change, all-pervading and unfailing.[22]

This description helps us understand John Berthrong's words that the Tao is "a metaphysical absolute" and "appears to have been a philosophical transformation of the earlier personal God."[23] It is interesting that the term *Tao* is used sometimes in Chinese Bibles, for example in John 1, to translate the Greek word *logos* ("word").[24]

The second important principle is *wu-wei,* the principle of purposeful inactivity. Lao-tzu said that to realize harmony again, "our only 'action' should be to align ourselves with the natural flow of the Tao and to let it work its natural course through us. The less government is involved in this process, the better."[25] Wu-wei is sometimes translated "actionless action." It is "a condition of letting oneself become one with nature without trying to manipulate one's condition."[26] This is also described as "acting without intention" or as *quietism.*

The basic teachings of Taoism are found in the book *Tao Te Ching* (*Dao De Jing*), the origin of which is a matter of dispute. This name means "the book of the way and its power" implying that by following this way the power of a virtuous life can be realized. Corduan summarizes its teaching with the word *quietism*: "The solution to the problems of the empire lies in doing as little as possible." He says that the point of Taoism is that the Way "cannot be found, neither through words nor through actions. It must reveal itself. Anything that anyone does or says only obscures the Dao."[27] So while Confucius taught an ethical way with firm conviction and action, Lao-tzu taught a quietist way.

Chuang-tzu, who lived in the fourth century BC, was a popularizer of Taoism. When Confucianism became the state philosophy, those in the opposition adopted Taoism, and the book *Tao Te Ching* became like Scripture to some groups. Soon Taoism began to develop a religious side to it to add to the philosophical side of Lao-tzu and Chuang-tzu. Magical practices, spiritism, and superstition were added. Taoism was influenced by Mahayana Buddhism, with its belief in bodhisattvas (see the discussion on Buddhism above). Prescriptions for achieving long life and even immortality became popular.[28] Methods of meditation were developed to nourish "the yin and yang of the human body, uniting the two in an effort to recover the primordial energy (ch'i) that permeates and sustains all life."[29]

Julia Ching describes the development of the divine pantheon: "Taoism developed a pantheon of innumerable spiritual beings, gods, or celestials and immortals, as well as deified heroes and forces of nature. They make up a divine hierarchy resembling in its functions a state bureaucracy. The hierarchy includes mythical figures, as well as many who are divinized human beings, under the supremacy of the highest deity."[30]

Today there is a wide variety of expressions of Taoism. Often a distinction is made between "philosophical Taoism" (which follows Lao-tzu and Chuang-tzu) and "religious Taoism," which is less concerned with philosophical issues and concentrates on religious practices such as the search for immortality and the temporal benefits of wealth and health. As we have described in the section "Help from the Gods" in chapter 10, there are temples for various gods along with the corresponding priests. People go to different temples to get favors done, and the requests made range from success in studies to success in gambling.

Ancestor Worship

Harold Netland thinks that "the ancestor cult is the single greatest religious factor in East Asian Cultures. It was there before Confucianism in China or Buddhism or Shinto in Japan, and it is 'non-negotiable' in the sense that other Asian religions have all come to terms with it [by] accepting it." Netland says that only Protestant Christianity resisted the ancestral cult.[31]

Ancestor worship has been common in the Chinese culture for about three millennia, but it received added impetus when Confucius encouraged filial piety. The *Analects* says, "While [the parents] are alive, serve them according to the ritual; when they die bury them according to the ritual; and sacrifice to them according to the ritual."[32] Chua Wee Hian explains, "The Chinese believe that the soul of the deceased ancestor resides in three places. One part goes to heaven, the second remains in the grave to receive sacrifices and the third is localized in the ancestral tablet or shrine [which will be kept in the home]."[33]

Around this belief various practices have grown. There are elaborate funeral rituals with the help of a Taoist priest to assist the soul in its journey to heaven. The ancestral tablet usually has a photograph of the deceased, and *josssticks* (for incense) are burned and placed on it. Food is offered to it on feast days. For a Christian response to ancestor worship, see the section on "Retaining One's Original Culture" in chapter 13.

Shinto

Shinto is the name given to "a wide conglomeration of religious practices"[34] representing the "Japanese religious tradition that emerged out of prehistoric religious practices and such influences as Buddhism and Chinese religions."[35] Shinto (or *kama no michi*)—"the way of the gods"—is rooted in Japan's national history and therefore is closely connected to its culture.[36] Emperor worship was a part of Japanese life until the end of the Pacific war in 1945, and though this has been stopped, the imperial family is still an important part of the national identity of the Japanese people. Officially there is no state Shinto now, and the government cannot favor Shinto over other religions. But in reality there is a close collusion between the government and Shinto.

Harold Netland describes the relationship between Shinto and Japanese culture as follows:

It is often difficult to separate Shinto as a religion from the general Japanese culture, the two are so intertwined. But there is a distinct association of Shinto shrines, a priesthood, and some minimal beliefs that do identify Shinto as a religion. Also, it is unusual in that it is clearly an ethnic religion—it makes no sense to think of Shinto apart from the Japanese people. There is no general missionary thrust to Shintoism, no interest in having non-Japanese people embrace Shinto. It is for the Japanese.[37]

The Spirit of Shinto. Christian philosopher David Clark, who grew up in Japan, mentions three features that make up the spirit of Shinto.[38] We must remember that what he is describing is Japanese culture, and therefore some of the features mentioned here could have their origin in Buddhism, Confucianism, Taoism, and other cultural and religious influences.

The first feature Clark mentions is the social web, which includes "the moral values of loyalty and duty to the family, clan or group." Like many Asian societies, but in a more marked way, "Japanese society emphasizes community over individuality." There is the notion of indebtedness. When one receives something of value from another person that person is indebted to the other. This was evidenced after the election of J. R. Jayawardena as president of Sri Lanka in 1977. At an international conference on Japan shortly after the Pacific war, young Jayawardena had made an eloquent appeal for aid to and goodwill toward Japan. When he became president more than 30 years later, Japan aided in massive development schemes, spending hundreds of millions of dollars on Sri Lanka.

The parent/child relationship is also important, with children caring for their parents in old age and venerating them after they are dead. There are also some accepted social norms for relationships between people, such as giving gifts at certain occasions and seasons. These norms are strictly adhered to, and breaking them would be considered a serious error.

Clark's second point under the spirit of Shinto is that the Japanese highly value aesthetic sensitivity and refinement. The extraordinary graciousness and deference that the Japanese show in their conversations with outsiders is evidence of this. This is a cultural style that may mask the tough interior that those doing business with Japanese people have come to fear and respect. The Japanese may be vague and imprecise about the way they describe religious truth, unlike Westerners. "The Japanese way has its own rationale however," says Clark. "Anyone who would understand the logic should enter into it and seek to appreciate it aesthetically."

Reverence toward nature is an important part of Shinto. "The Japanese have a history of respect for physical beauty, perhaps because they live in one of the most beautiful parts of the world," says Clark. "Closeness to nature is a sacred component of Shinto devotion."[39] Shinto has therefore been described as a form of nature worship. The reverence for nature stems in part from the pantheistic and polytheistic worldview in which rocks and trees and mountains can be divine (called *kami*, described below).

The third feature is emotional depth and purity of heart. Shinto affirms the importance of physical cleanliness along with ritual and symbolic cleanliness. "One must be absolutely clean when one encounters the spirits and so must one's surroundings."[40] But there is also the emphasis on the pure *kokoro* (heart). This is something that must be lived out. Therefore truth is not a set of propositions. It is something that is experienced. Communicating truth "requires not explicit statements, but refined, allusive speech."[41] So the emphasis is on the quality of experience rather than precise theological statements.

Shinto Shrines and Their Gods. Shinto is explicitly polytheistic and there are innumerable Shinto gods known as *kami,* with shrines dedicated to them. The shrine may be built around an important natural object like a rock, and in that case the *kami* may be that natural object. There are shrines dedicated to the gods who are mentioned in their sacred books. Then there are legendary or historical persons who are *kami* for whom a shrine may be dedicated. Amarterasu, the sun goddess, is preeminent among the *kami* and is regarded as the source of the dynastic line of Japanese emperors.

Much Shinto religious life takes place in the Shinto shrine. These are marked off by one or more large sacred gates (*torii*), shaped like the Greek letter *p* but with two horizontal bars. There is much variety among the shrines. Each shrine has a reason for existence. This may be a natural phenomenon like a mountain, an event of significance in the history of a given community, or a god who is powerful in performing some task. People often go to shrines to make requests—"before a journey, before an examination, before some new enterprise, or perhaps because they just happen to be passing that way. . . . Family occasions also involve visits to the shrine. It is common, though not universal, to take a newborn baby there so that prayers may be said for his health."[42] It is also common to visit a shrine during the New Year time.

Festivals. Festivals (*matsuri*) honoring the gods or spirits have an important place in Shinto life. Each shrine will have one or more local festivals a year. This gives an opportunity "for people to congregate, socialize, and honor the particular spirit or spirits associated with the festival."[43] "A Shinto festival usually includes a procession or a fair with stalls and side-shows, and so it easily draws large numbers of people, many returning to visit relatives at the same time."[44] Sometimes in a procession a portable shrine "is taken from the main shrine to various points in the locality, symbolizing a journey made by the *kami*."[45]

Hinduism

Included under the name Hinduism are a wide variety of expressions of Indian religious traditions that have evolved over 5,000 years. It is difficult to describe Hinduism in a few words because the various traditions differ on many points. What is given here are some of the beliefs of some of the traditions. Other traditions will differ from these.

There is no fixed Hindu creed as such, but its most influential writings are the *Vedas* (beginning with the Rig Veda around 1500 BC and ending with the Upanishads around 800–400 BC) and the *Epics* (300 BC to 300 AD). The Epics were stories describing the Hindu approach to life that were later written down. The most popular are the *Ramayana* and the *Mahabharata*. In the Mahabharata is found the Bhagavad Gita, sometimes called the Bible of Hinduism owing to its popularity. It is a battlefield dialogue between the warrior prince Arjuna and his charioteer, who is Krishna, an avatar of the god Vishnu. Its theme is detached action: doing one's duty without the desire for reaping its fruit.

Karma and Reincarnation. Hindus believe in reincarnation or the transmigration of the soul, which is fueled by the operation of the law of karma, meaning "work" or "action". Karma is something like a moral law of cause and effect. The inevitable consequences of actions within one life are said to flow into the next life and influence its character. What is advocated is disciplined action performed in the right spirit, that is, action that does not arise from attachment or desire. The cycle of birth and death followed by rebirth is applied to both individuals and to the universe itself and is called *samsara,* meaning "stream of existence". Reincarnation is discussed in the section by that name in chapter 13.

In the Hindu caste system society is structured into groups according to the division of labor. In practice today, of course, Hindus do not necessarily follow the profession represented by their caste. One's caste is determined by one's karma, and there are different levels. Each caste is seen as symbolically emerging from different parts of the body of the creator God: Brahma.

- Brahmins, the priestly order, come from his mouth.
- Kshatriyas, warriors, come from his arms.
- Vaishyas, peasants, come from his thighs.
- Shudras, unskilled laborers, come from his feet. They probably descend from the people subjected by the invading Aryans. They were considered as having inferior (dark) color, in contrast to the Aryans, who were light-skinned. They could not hope for salvation in this life.
- Groups of no definite caste were regarded as untouchables and were banished from normal social life. Gandhi called them *Harijans*—children of God. They are also known as *Dalits*. The ruling Congress Party of post-independent India gave them many affirmative-action style concessions.

Liberation. The goal of Hinduism is *moksha,* which is liberation from the cycle of rebirth and attachment to the material world. Many view it as absorption into Brahman, the ultimate reality (see below). Three ways are said to help in this passage to moksha.

- The Way of Knowledge (*Jnana-Marga*). Release will be attained when knowledge replaces ignorance, when reality is understood, and the transient or illusory is rejected.
- The Way of Action (*Karma-Marga*). The performing of one's tasks in life and of ethical demands.
- The Way of Devotion (*Bhakti-Marga*). This could involve faith and even grace. It includes acts of worship, ritual acts and ceremonies, hymns of praise and veneration,and adoration of the gods at their statues. There are shrine rooms with statues or pictures of the gods in many Hindu homes. The Bhakti movements of Hinduism may involve personal devotion to Krishna somewhat akin to Christian devotion to Christ. Hare Krishna is a sect that emphasizes this.

Yoga is a way to union with god. Traditionally there are eight stages of Yoga: restraint, discipline, posture, breathing, detachment, concentration, meditation, and trance.

The Gods of Hinduism. A Hindu may be an atheist, a monotheist, or a worshiper of a few or many gods. The following is a list of some of the gods of Hinduism. Because of the variety of beliefs, the descriptions below do not represent a consensus about the nature of these gods.

- *Brahman* is the Absolute, the Ultimate Reality. Some schools see it as neutral and impersonal (hence the use of "it"), without form and name and therefore to be described only negatively (not this, not that). Some see Brahman as the origin, basis, and cause of all existence. Some say it is unknowable. Some describe Brahman as Pure Being (*sat*), Pure Intelligence (*chit*), and Pure Delight (*ananda*).
- Brahma is the creator. His female partner is *Sarasvati*.
- *Vishnu* is the preserver whose female partner is *Lakshmi*. He is said to come to earth as an avatar (meaning "descent") to help the world when order and righteousness is lost. The most popular avatars are Rama and Krishna. Avatars are discussed in the section "Incarnation and Avatar" in chapter 12.

- *Shiva* is the destroyer, the god of contrasts, presiding over creation and destruction, fertility and asceticism, good and evil. He is the original "Lord of the Dance" who dances out the creation of the universe. His symbol is the phallus-shaped pillar denoting procreation. His female partner is *Kali*. Brahma, Vishnu, and Shiva form the divine triad (*Trimurti*) of Hinduism.
- There are many other gods in popular Hinduism. *Ganesh* is a much-loved elephant-headed god—the god of good beginnings and symbol for luck and wealth in business and daily life.
- Some Hindus refer to 330 million gods!

Many Hindus are pantheistic, that is, they believe that everything is part of the divine. Chapter 8 of this book is devoted to the issue of pantheism.

Gurus (meaning "teachers," "masters") are common in Hinduism. They are spiritual guides who awaken disciples to a realization of their divine nature. Many are viewed as avatars. The most popular guru today is Satya Sai Baba, who was born in 1926. He is regarded as an incarnation of Shiva and of a previous Baba who lived earlier in the twentieth century. He is said to perform spectacular miracles.

Islam

Origin and Sources of Authority. Islam means submission to God, and *Muslim* means one who submits, that is, lives according to God's will. Islam was founded by Muhammad, who was born in Mecca in modern Saudi Arabia circa AD 570. Around 610 he came to believe that he was receiving messages from God (through the angel Gabriel) which he was to convey to the people. These messages or revelations were later collected to form what Muslims call the Holy Qur'an. According to the Muslim idea of inspiration, Muhammad was like a typewriter that recorded the exact words of God. His personality does not come into play in the writing process. The *Sunna* (meaning, "trodden path") represents the second most important source of authority in Islam and consists of the words and actions of Muhammad as recorded in the Traditions or Hadith.

Basic Beliefs

God. The Qur'an asserted that God—Allah—is one (Allah is related to *El*, the Hebrew word for God). There is a heavy emphasis on the transcendence of God (as described in the section "The Transcendent God of Islam" in chapter 9). He is all-powerful, controlling the course of events on earth. His mercy comes to the forefront in his relation to humans. On the last day he will judge people according to their acts and assign them to heaven or hell. The greatest sin in Islam is ascribing partners to God, or *shirk* (meaning "associating"). This is applied to the Christian doctrine of the Trinity.

The Confession of Faith (*shahada*) is the foundation of Islam and consists of two affirmations:

I bear witness that there is no God but God;

I bear witness that Muhammad is the Apostle (Prophet) of God.

The Five Pillars of Islam, along with an optional sixth feature, represent the marrow of Islam.

- The Confession of Faith (*Shahada*).
- Prayer five times a day (*Salat*). Prayer is preceded each time by ritual obligatory washing, and the prayer is done facing Mecca. All this emphasizes the importance of the Muslim community. In the mosque they follow the prayer leader or *imam*. Each set of prayers includes the repetition of "Allahu Akbar" ("God is greatest"), and at the end they pass the greeting, "*as-salamu alaikum*" ("Peace be upon you").
- Alms to the poor (*Zakat*). This is especially done on the festivals of the Muslim calendar and on the Muslim Sabbath (which runs from sunset on Thursday to sunset on Friday).
- Fasting (*Sawm*) in the month of Ramadan. Muslims abstain from food and drink from dawn to sunset during this month. Again there is the emphasis on community here.
- The pilgrimage to Mecca (*Hajj*). Hajj should be done if at all possible. Although pilgrimage can be done at any time of the year, the Hajj proper is to be performed only on the prescribed dates in the twelfth month—the Hajj season.

A sixth optional item is the holy war or *jihad* (meaning "striving") This word is used for war against worldly lust and against the infidel in defense of the faith.

Shari'a (meaning "the path") is the body of law for the Muslim community. It derives from the Qur'an, the Sunna, and other sources. In recent years fundamentalist Muslims (or Islamists) have instituted or are seeking to institute this in Muslim countries.

Varieties of Islam. The *Sunnis* comprise the large majority of the Muslim community. They are led by community consensus (*ijma'*). They accept the first four caliphs as the legitimate successors of Muhammad. They are the majority in the Arab countries, Africa, India, Pakistan, and Indonesia.

The *Shi'ites* (or *Shi'a*) have in common their distinctive belief in a spiritual leader or imam who is viewed as God's representative on earth. They consider Ali, Muhammad's son-in-law, to be the first Imam. Different groups have different views of the identity of the present-day Imam. Unlike the Sunnis, the Shi'ites have an institutionalized clergy who exercise great authority, as evidenced by the power of Ayatollah Khomeini and the present religious leaders in Iran. Shi'ites are in power in Iran and represent a large segment of the populations of Iraq, Bahrain, and Azerbaijan. They are smaller minorities in Lebanon, Pakistan, India, and several other countries. The Sunnis and Shi'ites have persecuted each other bitterly over the centuries.

Sufism (Sufi means "mystic;" *suf* means "wool"—what the early Muslim ascetics wore) is a mystical movement, which seeks direct personal contact with God. This tradition dates back almost to the seventh century. It was formerly considered unorthodox, but now it is accepted among Sunnis and Shi'ites. Considered the "charismatic movement of Islam," it emphasizes "the spirit and not the letter" of Islamic teaching. Its popularity is said to be waning with the rise of Islamic fundamentalism.

Islamic Community. There is great power in Muslim community solidarity! Muslims will generally help each other in a crisis. They pride themselves on the lack of discrimination in this community, and thus they are growing among people who have been discriminated against by Christians. This is one reason for the rapid growth of Islam among African-American people in North America.[46] Funds from the Middle East are being sent to poorer nations, especially to further the cause of Islam. This is evidenced in the large mosque buildings that are replacing earlier buildings in several poorer countries. The petrodollar has much influence in the political affairs of poorer nations, and the Muslim community has an influence greater than their numbers would usually produce, even where it is a small minority.

Judaism

Judaism is the religion that developed from the religion of ancient Israel. It is "the oldest of the world's three great monotheistic religions and is the parent of both Christianity and Islam."[47] Therefore it has many features in common with Christianity. "At the heart of Judaism is the belief that there is only one God who is creator and ruler of the whole world. He is transcendent and eternal. He sees everything and knows everything." The Jews have a strong sense that God chose them and revealed his will to them "so that they would be a light or example to all humanity."[48]

Sacred Writings. There are three main sacred writings of Judaism.

• The Jewish Bible has the same thirty-nine books as the Christian Old Testament, but it follows a different order and is divided into three sections. First comes the *Torah,* which includes the five books of Moses. Then comes the *Nevi'im,* the Prophets, which includes Joshua, Judges, 1 and 2 Samuel, and 1 and 2 Kings, Isaiah, Jeremiah, and Ezekiel and the twelve Minor Prophets. The third section is called the *Kethuvim,* and it includes what we call the Wisdom literature, Daniel and Lamentations, and the historical books which are not found in the Nevi'im.

• The *Mishnah* is a rabbinic commentary on the Law, which is intended to be a supplement to the Torah. The compilation of interpretations of the law that had grown over centuries took several years and it was completed around 200 AD.

• The *Talmud* is a massive tome, which includes the Mishnah and other teachings and commentaries that developed over the years. There are two Talmuds, the Palestinian Talmud, which was compiled while the Jews were under threat from the Christian church in the fourth century, and the Babylonian Talmud, which is more detailed and comprehensive and was completed in the fifth century. The Talmud is the authoritative source of Jewish law and tradition.

Special Days. As in biblical times, the Sabbath is an important part of Jewish life and identity. The biblical and other festivals have a major part to play in the lives of the Jews. These include

- three harvest festivals (Pentecost, Tabernacles, and Firstfruits at the end of Passover);
- the Day of Atonement (*Yom Kippur*), which is considered the holiest day of the religious calendar;
- the Festival of Lights (*Hanukkah*), around the Christmas season, which commemorates the victory of Judas Maccabeus over the Syrians and the rededication of the temple in Jerusalem in 164 BC;
- *Purim,* which commemorates the salvation of the Jews from massacre in Persia during Esther's time;
- New Year;
- the Festival that Rejoices over the Law (*Simchat Torah*); and
- the Day of Mourning, when the destruction of the temple by the Romans in AD 70 is remembered.[49]

When a male child is eight days old, he is circumcised, and at the age of thirteen he becomes *bar mitzvah* (literally, "a son of the commandment") and is considered an adult member of the community. Some groups also practice *bat mitzvah* for girls at this age.

Branches of Judaism. There are three main branches of Judaism. The most conservative are the *Orthodox* Jews, who are faithful to traditional Judaism and claim to be the ones who preserve real Judaism. They adhere closely not only to the Torah, which is God's Word, but also to the Talmud. The *Progressive* Jews relaxed some of the strict traditional practices of the

Orthodox Jews, such as the dietary laws. They tend to use the vernacular language in worship. The Conservative Jews stand midway between the Orthodox and the Progressive groups. In addition there is the ultra-orthodox wing known as the *Hasidim*. The synagogue (from the Greek meaning "a place of meeting") is not only the place of worship but also the center of Jewish community life especially for Jews living outside Israel. The different branches of Judaism have separate synagogues.

The "secular Jew" phenomenon is a distinct feature of the Jewish community. They are not religious and may even be atheists, but they honor their Jewish heritage and keep the Jewish festivals. Unlike in Christianity, entrance into the Jewish community is by birth for those born to Jewish parents.[50]

Sacrifice and Messiah. The Jews do not any more offer sacrifices even on the Day of Atonement, as they do not have a temple with the Holy of Holies as the Old Testament prescribes. But on that day there is prayer, fasting, and public confession, and they seek atonement through repentance. While Christians believe that the absence of the sacrificial system is a major acknowledged lack to the Jews, Winfried Corduan has shown that it is not so for most Jews, partly because their concept of religion is not so closely tied to gaining entrance to heaven as Christianity is.[51]

There were times in the history of the Jews when the expectation of the Messiah was an important factor. The twelfth-century rabbi, Maimonides, included belief in the coming of the Messiah as the twelfth of his "Thirteen Principles of the Faith." But today it is not a major concern of most Jews. Many interpret the Messianic idea in a symbolic way.[52] This presents Christian witnesses a challenge for which they may not have been prepared. The Jews reject the Christian doctrines of Christ and His deity, the Trinity, and the atonement in much the same way that the Muslims do.

New Age

Expressions and Sources. What is known as the New Age movement is staking a claim to be the most prominent religious orientation in the post-Christian West. New Age actually represents a network of organizations in North America and Europe that encompass many areas—religious and otherwise—but that have some common characteristics. Its name comes from the sense that these groups have that a New Age of spiritual awareness and of harmony and progress is dawning. Their teachings claim to revive the ancient spiritual traditions of the East and the West, and therefore they have many features in common with Hinduism and Buddhism; they could be considered Western adaptations of this Eastern religious tradition. The New Age approach to truth is generally pluralistic like in Hinduism.

Beliefs and Practices. Most New Age adherents believe in karma and reincarnation and are pantheists (everything is God). We described these concepts in the section on Hinduism above. Chapter 8 is devoted to the issue of pantheism and the final two sections of chapter 13 to karma and reincarnation. New Agers claim to be holistic in that they give due weight to every aspect of life, a feature they claim Christianity was defective in. The environment is emphasized, with a tendency to deify nature as a result of the pantheistic approach. Holistic health remedies, which seek not only to treat physical symptoms but also the spiritual and mental reasons that may lie behind physical ailments, are also common. This has brought alternative medicine into focus as these health systems claim to be holistic in their application. This is discussed in the section "Traditional Arts and Alternative Medicines" in chapter 5.

Spirituality is also very important in New Age, but New Age spirituality is generally more influenced by Eastern religions and occult practices than by the Bible. Meditation has an important part, and therefore transcendental meditation and yoga, both of which are Hindu in origin, have become popular in the West. In the words of New Age analyst Theodore Roszak, the goal of New Age spirituality is "to awaken the god who sleeps at the root of the human being."[53] The aim is to take away those factors which hinder our full experience of our essential divinity. This happens when one's consciousness is changed through disciplines like meditation and the awareness of who we really are and what life is.

New Age in the Arts. Many recent Western films and television serials have been reflecting this New Age approach to spirituality. So we see films and programs with good witches and wizards, with dead people appearing to speak to their loved ones, and with people acquiring knowledge through horoscopes, palm reading, psychic counselors, and the like. The jungles which Christians are said to have desacralized have been given their holy character again with the return of spirit beings to them. Science fiction has helped popularize New Age ideas tremendously, as is evidenced by the popularity of the catchphrase, "May the force be with you," from the *Star Wars* movies.

New Age music is one of the most popular categories of music in the Western world today. It is the name given for music composed by New Age musicians covering a wide range of styles and helping in some New Age practices like meditation and in achieving goals like self-actualization.[54]

New Age Science. Various factors have helped develop what may be called a New Age approach to science.[55] The *New Physics* gave what seemed like a scientific basis for New Age thinking. The quantum theory saw light and electrons as particles and waves, depending on how it is observed. But waves and particles exhibit qualities that are contradictory. So the quantum theory is interpreted as breaking the law of non-contradiction, though Christian authors have countered this interpretation.[56] Newton's way of looking at time and space from fixed laws which determined scientific thinking for so long also seem to be violated.[57] And the idea of a rationally ordered universe, which was considered synonymous with Christianity, came under fire.

Popular New Age author Fritjof Capra, who was a physicist at the University of California, found it possible to harmonize the findings of quantum physics with Taoism, Buddhism, and Hinduism, especially the idea that "all is one" (*monism*). He explains this is his influential book, *The Tao of Physics.*[58] He says that what the new physicists have recently found out, the mystics of old knew all along: that humans and everything else is one with the universal force. This is pantheism (everything is God). As John Newport explains, "Capra believes that because we cannot cut up the universe into 'independently existing smaller units' [as a result of the new physics], we must see its 'basic oneness.'"[59]

As most of the books in the bibliography at the conclusion of this section do not include discussions on the New Age movements, we will include here a brief bibliography of books written on the topic from a Christian perspective.

Ankerberg, John, and Weldon, John. *Encyclopedia of New Age Beliefs*. Eugene, OR: Harvest House Publishers, 1996.

Chandler, Russell. *Understanding the New Age*. Dallas: Word Publishing, 1988.

Groothuis, Douglas R. *Unmasking the New Age*. Downers Grove, IL: InterVarsity Press, 1986.

_____. *Confronting the New Age*. Downers Grove, IL: InterVarsity Press, 1988.

Hoyt, Karen, and others, *The New Age Rage*. Old Tappan, NJ: Fleming H. Revell Co., 1987.

Mangalwadi, Vishal. *When the New Age Gets Old: Looking for a Greater Spirituality*. Downers Grove, IL: InterVarsity Press, 1992.

Miller, Elliot. *A Crash Course on the New Age Movement*. Grand Rapids, MI: Baker Book House, 1989.

Newport, John P. *The New Age Movement and the Biblical Worldview: Conflict and Dialogue*. Grand Rapids, MI: Wm. B. Eerdmans Publishing Co., 1998.

Scott, Brad. *Embraced by the Darkness. Exposing New Age Theology from the Inside Out*. Wheaton, IL: Crossway Books, 1996.

Religious Pluralism

Religious pluralism is not a separate religion but represents the way many religions and people (including some who call themselves Christian) approach the issue of the nature of religious truth. The description of this under that name is one of the sections of chapter 1.

Postmodernism

Though postmodernism is a social phenomenon rather than a religious movement, it is important that we know something about this if we are to understand the religious landscape today. The description of this under that name is one of the sections of chapter 1.

"Primal" or Tribal Religions "

Many of the readers of this book will not encounter what are known as primal or tribal religions. These terms are used for the religious life of people living in cultures not heavily influenced by the technological progress of society and by the major world religions. Formerly these religions were described by the word *animism*, but that term has been dropped because its meaning, "spiritism," was felt to be misleading.[60] At the heart of this religious life are attempts to relate satisfactorily with the spiritual powers that are believed to be active in the world.

Expressions of this type of religious life are found among the jungle peoples of Africa, the Indians of the Americas, the so-called tribals in South and East Asia, the Aboriginal people of Australia, and the Melanesians and the Polynesians of the Pacific islands. Vestiges of these religious traditions are found in many of the technologically advanced cultures, and they often exist side by side with a major world religion. This is the case, for example, with Buddhist cultures where there are shrines to various gods, sometimes just beside a Buddhist temple or within the temple premises. In Roman Catholic communities in South America there are many animistic practices that have either been absorbed into the life of the church or permitted to exist alongside the church's activities.

We have given a description of this form of religion in the section "Help from the Gods" in chapter 10. There we said that the designation "primal" religion may be a misnomer if it is intended to give the idea that they are primary and therefore came prior to monotheism. But if "primal" is used in the sense of basic, then it is appropriate as they usually have "the main basic features that belong to all religions." We said that basic to these religions is "a belief in a spiritual world of powers or beings that are stronger than man himself."[61]

The Sikh Religion

The Sikh religion began at the end of the fifteenth century in Punjab, an area which now is in Northwest India and Pakistan, which at that time had both Hindus and Muslims. As most of the Sikh people are Punjabis this is sometimes called an ethnic religion. The founder is Guru Nanak (1469–1539).

The word *guru* essentially means "teacher." This idea is very important in the Sikh religion. Following Guru Nanak were nine other gurus who led the movement until 1708 and have a special place in the religion.

The tenth and last of these special gurus, Gobind Singh, did the final edition of the holiest book of the Sikhs, *Guru Granth* (*granth* means "book"). With that the authority was passed on to the sacred Scripture, *Guru Granth,* and to the Sikh community, *Guru Panth,* which continued the tradition set up by Gobind Singh. The ultimate guru is *Satguru,* the true and eternal guru.

The god of the Sikhs is one; he is the ultimate and is eternal and beyond description. But in his grace he has made it possible for humans to experience the divine. Humble and sincere devotees may experience god through worship and meditation. Hymns play an important role here. They are the means by which people's "hearts could reach out towards God and also by which God would move within their hearts."[62] Therefore mysticism has an important part to play in this religion, and this was the primary focus of the founder Guru Nanak. Pride and selfishness are considered the main hindrances to relating to God. Therefore to the Sikhs pilgrimage is not a physical journey but the journey from self to God. The end is to regard God and not the self as the center. When that is achieved there is a perfect love-union between God and the person. Until that end is achieved the soul will transmigrate in a process of reincarnation.

The more practical military and world-affirming aspects of the faith developed later as the Sikhs faced challenges from outside, especially conflict with the Muslims. Owing to the history of conflict, the Sikhs are often viewed as being a militant community. However, as Winfried Corduan observes, "The overwhelming majority of Sikhs . . . are gentle, peaceful people."[63] During the partitioning of India in 1947, the border between India and Pakistan went through Punjab. This resulted in turmoil within Punjab culminating in an armed struggle involving the quest for an independent state named Khalistan. The conflict claimed many lives. Once, when Indira Gandhi was prime minister, the Indian army occupied the most holy place of the Sikhs, the Golden Temple in Amritsar, and discovered a large cache of arms there.

Sikhs have a strong sense of community solidarity, and they consider theirs to be a society where caste differences are eliminated. Names had indicated the caste that one belonged to in India. The Sikhs eliminated this distinction by having all the males take the name Singh (Lion) and all the females take the name Kaur (Princess). Even in foreign countries, the

Sikh community has been successful in maintaining strong community solidarity.

The temple is very important to the community life. Each temple has a copy of the holy book, the Guru Granth, which is treated with great respect. Devotees must wash their hands and feet and cover their heads when they enter the temple. The temple looks like a mosque, and it has a large hall where the women sit on the left side and men on the right. Worship includes the use of devotional hymns. The worship is often followed by a communal meal that further accentuates the equality of all in this community.

Women are said to have a higher place of equality among the Sikhs than among the other Indian religious groups.[64] Male Sikhs are identified by the turban, which is related to the Sikh practice of not cutting the hair. Traditionally there have been five identifying features of adult males: uncut hair, a comb worn in the hair, knee-length underwear (breeches), a dagger, and a steel bracelet.

Bibliography of Christian Books on World Religions

There are many good books describing the world religions. A lot of the books that I have found useful were purchased from "secular" bookstores in Sri Lanka and abroad. There are good books on individual religions that have been written from a Christian viewpoint. Those are referred to in the endnotes. Here we will only mention a few good books that cover many religions and have been written from a Christian viewpoint.

Alexander, Pat, organizing editor. *Eerdmans' Handbook to the World's Religions*. Grand Rapids, MI: Wm. B. Eerdmans Publishing Co., 1994; Oxford: Lion Publishing, 1994. Lavishly illustrated, easy to read and always interesting, this is perhaps the standard non-technical Christian introduction.

Anderson, Sir Norman, Editor. *The World's Religions*. Fourth revised edition. Leicester: Inter-Varsity Press; Grand Rapids, MI: Wm. B. Eerdmans Publishing Co., 1975. Since the first edition was published in 1950 this has been a standard basic textbook.

Boa, Kenneth. *Cults, World Religions and You*. Wheaton, IL: Victor Books, 1977. Brief discussions on twenty-seven groups.

Braswell, George W. *Understanding Sectarian Groups in America*. Revised edition. Nashville, TN: Broadman & Holman Publishers, 1994. Covers religions and cults with a "Christian Perspectives" section at the end of each chapter.

Corduan, Winfried. *Neighboring Faiths: A Christian Introduction to World Religions*. Downers Grove, IL: InterVarsity Press, 1998. This excellent book has the advantage of having a section on "Relating the Gospel" to each religion.

Enroth, Ronald, and others. *A Guide to Cults and New Religions*. Downers Grove, IL: InterVarsity Press, 1983. This book focuses on Groups like Baha'i and Hare Krishna but does not cover the major world religions.

Halverson, Dean C., general editor. *Compact Guide to World Religions*. Minneapolis, MN: Bethany House Publishers, 1996. Each section in this helpful book has "Suggestions for Evangelism."

Hexham, Irving. *Concise Dictionary of Religion*. Downers Grove, IL: InterVarsity Press, 1993.

Mather, George A., and Larry A. *Dictionary of Cults, Sects, Religions and the Occult*. Grand Rapids, MI: Zondervan Publishing House, 1993. The breadth of subjects discussed, the brevity of the discussion, and the handy size makes this a valuable resource for laypeople.

McDowell, Josh, and Don Stewart. *Handbook of Today's Religions*. Nashville, TN: Thomas Nelson Publishers.

Tucker, Ruth A. *Another Gospel: Cults, Alternative Religions and the New Age Movement*. Grand Rapids, MI: Zondervan Publishing House, 1989. This book includes chapters on thirteen groups and smaller descriptions of twenty-one lesser known groups, but does not cover the major world religions.

Appendix endnotes

[1] John Boykin, "The Baha'i Faith," *A Guide to Cults and New Religions*, Ronald Enroth and others, editors (Downers Grove, IL: InterVarsity Press, 1983), 25.

[2] Ruth A. Tucker, *Another Gospel: Cults, Alternative Religions, and the New Age Movement* (Grand Rapids, MI: Zondervan Publishing House, 1989), 387.

[3] *Eerdmans' Handbook to World Religions,* Pat Alexander, organizing editor (Grand Rapids: Wm. B. Eerdmans Publishing Co., 1994), 452.

[4] Alan W. Watts, *The Spirit of Zen: A Way of Life, Word, and Art in the Far East* (New York: Grove Press, 1958), 19.

[5] Julia Ching, "East Asian Religions," *World Religions: Eastern Traditions,* Willard G. Oxtoby, editor (Toronto: Oxford University Press, 1996), 348.

[6] Michael Pye, "A Tapestry of Traditions: Japanese Religions," *Eerdman's Handbook to World Religions,* 255.

[7] In a personal letter to me, dated July 11, 2000.

[8] Eric J. Sharpe, "Shamanism," in *Dictionary of Comparative Religion,* S. G. F. Brandon, editor (New York: Charles Scribner's Sons, 1970), 571.

[9] From Julia Ching, citing Arthur Waley, "East Asian Religions," 359.

[10] Daniel S. Kim, "The Uniqueness of Christ and the Function of the Korean Shamanistic Worldview in the Christian Belief System," (unpublished paper presented at Trinity Evangelical Divinity School, 1999), 1.

[11] Winfried Corduan, *Neighboring Faiths: A Christian Introduction to World Religions* (Downers Grove, IL: InterVarsity Press, 1998), 282.

[12] Corduan, *Neighboring Faiths,* 282.

[13] John Berthrong, "Sages and Immortals: Chinese Religions," in *Eerdmans' Handbook to World Religions,* 246.

[14] Corduan, Neighboring Faiths, 293.

[15] Thomas I. S. Leung, "Confucianism," in *The Compact Guide to World Religions,* Dean C. Halverson, editor (Minneapolis: Bethany House Publishers, 1996), 72.

[16] Leung, "Confucianism," 73.

[17] Corduan, *Neighboring Faiths,* 293.

[18] Corduan, *Neighboring Faiths,* 293.

[19] D. Howard Smith, "Tao," in *Dictionary of Comparative Religion,* 601.

[20] Leung, "Confucianism," 70.

[21] Harold Netland, in a personal letter to me, dated July 11, 2000.

[22] Smith, "Tao," 601.

[23] Berthrong, "Sages and Immortals," 251.

[24] Harold Netland, in a personal letter to me, dated July 11, 2000.

[25] Kent Kedl and Dean C. Halverson, "Taoism," in *Compact Guide to World Religions,* 218.

[26] Corduan, *Neighboring Faiths,* 287.

[27] Corduan, *Neighboring Faiths,* 286.

[28] Taoism also influenced Buddhism. Zen is often regarded as a product of Chinese Mahayana Buddhism and Taoism.

[29] Ching, "East Asian Religions," 435.

[30] Ching, "East Asian Religions," 429–30.

[31] In a personal letter to me, dated July 11, 2000.

[32] Confucius, *Analects 2:5,* quoted in *Eerdmans' Handbook to World Religions,* 247.

[33] Chua Wee Hian, "The Worship of Ancestors," *Eerdmans' Handbook to World Religions,* 247.

[34] Pye, "A Tapestry of Traditions," 257.

[35] H. B. Earhart, "Shinto," in *Abingdon Dictionary of Living Religions,* Keith Crim, general editor (Nashville: Abingdon Press, 1981), 682.

[36] For a description of the historical development of Shinto, see David Clark, "Shinto," in *Compact Guide to World Religions,* 198–203.

[37] In a personal letter to me, dated July 11, 2000.

[38] Clark, "Shinto," 203–05. The quotations are from Clark's description.

[39] Brandon Toropov and Luke Buckles, *The Complete Idiot's Guide to the World's Religions* (New York: Alpha Books, 1997), 188.

[40] Toropov and Buckles, *The World's Religions,* 188.

[41] Clark, "Shinto," 205.

[42] Pye, "A Tapestry of Traditions," 260.

[43] Toropov and Buckles, *The World's Religions,* 188.

[44] Pye, "A Tapestry of Traditions," 261.

[45] Pye, "A Tapestry of Traditions," 262.

[46] See Wendy Murray Zoba, "Islam, USA"; and Carl Ellis, "How Islam Is Winning Black America," in *Christianity Today,* April 3, 2000, 40–53. See also Jane I. Smith, *Islam in America* (Columbia University).

[47] David Harley, "Chosen People: Judaism," in Eerdmans' *Handbook to World Religions,* 272.

[48] Harley, "Chosen People: Judaism," 272.

[49] I have depended on Harley, "Chosen People: Judaism," 274–77.

[50] See Corduan, *Neighboring Faiths,* 71–72.

[51] Corduan, *Neighboring Faiths,* 45–46.

[52] See H. D. Leuner, "Judaism," in *The World's Religions,* Sir Norman Anderson, editor (Leicester: InterVarsity Press; and Grand Rapids, MI: Wm. B. Eerdmans Publishing Co., 1975), 62–63.

[53] Theodore Roszak, *Unfinished Animal* (New York: Harper and Row, 1977), 225; cited in Douglas R. Groothuis, *Unmasking the New Age* (Downers Grove, IL: InterVarsity Press, 1986), 21.

[54] See John P. Newport, *The New Age Movement and the Biblical Worldview: Conflict and Dialogue* (Grand Rapids, MI: Wm. B. Eerdmans Publishing Co., 1998), chapter 12: "The Arts"; and Douglas R. Groothuis, *Confronting the New Age* (Downers Grove, IL: InterVarsity Press, 1988), 190–196.

[55] See Groothuis, *Unmasking the New Age,* chapter 5.

[56] See Douglas Groothuis, *Truth Decay: Defending Christianity Against the Challenge of Postmodernism* (Downers Grove, IL: InterVarsity Press, 2000), 77, n. 40. Groothuis directs the reader to Scott R. Burson and Jerry L. Walls, C. S. Lewis, and Francis Schaeffer: *Lessons for a New Century from the Most Influential Apologists of Our Time* (Downers Grove, IL: InterVarsity Press, 1998), 86–87.

[57] On the challenge from quantum physics to Christianity see Nancey R. Pearcey and Charles B. Thaxton, *The Soul of Science: Christian Faith and Natural Philosophy* (Wheaton, IL: Crossway Books, 1994), chapter 9: "Quantum Mysteries: Making Sense of the New Physics"; and Colin A. Russell, *Cross-Currents: Interactions Between Science and Faith* (Leicester: InterVarsity Press; and Grand Rapids, MI: Wm. B. Eerdmans Publishing Co., 1985), chapter 10: "Powerful Currents: Crisis in Newtonian Physics."

[58] Fritjof Capra, *The Tao of Physics* (New York: Bantam Books, 1984).

[59] Newport, *The New Age Movement,* 454.

[60] *Eerdmans' Handbook to World Religions,* 413.

[61] Harold Turner, "World of the Spirits," in *Eerdmans' Handbook to World Religions,* 130.

[62] Douglas Davies, "Religion of the Gurus: The Sikh Faith," in *Eerdmans' Handbook to World Religions,* 197.

[63] Corduan, *Neighboring Faiths,* 266.

[64] Corduan, *Neighboring Faiths,* 268.

ACKNOWLEDGMENTS

I am grateful to Dr. Robert De Vries of Discovery House Publishers, who first suggested this book and patiently endured many delays due to some responsibilities I had to take on unexpectedly for YFC. Those responsibilities involved supervising two ministries reaching out to those of other faiths. I believe that God planned that this should be the context out of which I write this book. It has been a joy to work on this book with the helpful and committed team at Discovery House Publishers, especially its managing editor, Tim Gustafson.

Many friends at home and abroad have helped me, through their generosity, with resources I needed for working on this book. I would like to mention particularly Dr. Ramesh Richard, Dr. Brian Stiller, Wightman Weese (who edited the earlier book which is replaced by this book), Albert Lee, Lim Chien Chong, Dwight Gibson, Dr. David Dwight, Donald and Charlaine Engelhardt, Loran and Merle Grant, Lester and Clara Finkbeiner, Cliff and Carol Johnson, Jack Yam, Lek Eng Kiang, Jito Senathiraja, Ray and Gyathrie Snell, Malcom Tan, the Northwest Baptist Church in Fresno, and my friends at Zondervan and Crossway Publishers.

I was blessed with the privilege of a week spent writing "in hiding" at Singapore Bible College. I am grateful to the dean there, Dr. Wayne Johnson, business manager Cathy Tan, the library staff, and others for all their kindness to me.

Several scholars helped me in different ways while I wrote this book. I am particularly grateful to Dr. Doug Groothuis, who read this book before I sent it to the publisher and made many helpful comments. Simon Fuller, Dr Harold Netland, and Ravi Ponnusamy read portions of this book relating to descriptions of the world religions. Drs. Charles Lowe, Tom Schreiner, and Benny Tan helped clarify my thinking on various issues. Bill Long gave helpful suggestions after reading some sections. My colleagues Mayukha and Roshan Perera read through most of my final manuscript when they were very busy and helped me improve the book in many ways. Linda Triemstra, whose editorial work gave shape to the final product, also deserves heartfelt thanks.

I am writing under the shadow of my seminary teachers whose lives and ministries helped send me along the path that I've taken as an evangelist, ministry team leader, Bible teacher, and writer. I must particularly mention three of them here. Dr. J. T. Seamands helped me appreciate my Asian culture and taught me the meaning of biblical contextualization. In *Tell it Well: Communicating the Gospel across Cultures,* his brilliant mind, his warm heart, and his practical experience as an evangelist in India combined to produce an eminently readable classic.

By teaching me and modeling in his life the truth that excitement over the gospel should not preclude careful, biblical theologizing, Dr. Robert Coleman became a spiritual father to me. Dr. Daniel Fuller was an ideal mentor for my graduate studies. He taught me to argue for the truth of the Word and to be willing to pay the price for that. Dr. Fuller told his students over and over again that theology must result in evangelism, and God used him to burn this message into my life.

People often wonder how I am able to write books out of a busy ministry. Indeed this has been a ministry combination that has resulted in fatigue. But it would not be possible if YFC had not given me the freedom to do this. I thank the board and staff of YFC for this. But I want especially to thank the two members of "my" little office staff. My secretary, Mrs. Srimali (Decko) Senn, helped out with many details relating to this book. Decko first came to a YFC club as a Buddhist teenager. Her testimony is a wonderful story of the transforming grace of the gospel. And I could never assess what life would be for us as a family without the ever-present help of Timothy Godwin, my assistant, who has now virtually become one of our family.

My wife, Nelun, reads everything I write and gives her layperson's response to it. The commitment to evangelism of my children Nirmali and Asiri remains one of the great joys of my life. The family suffers most when I write a book out of a busy ministry. Their suffering and mine would be so much more if they did not believe in what I write. They provide me the encouragement, joy and relaxation I need from a pressured life of ministry and writing.

As with all my books, I have relied on the prayers of my friends to mediate God's blessings to me. Often when I was unable to make any progress, I would send out an SOS for prayer to my family and friends. It was amazing how, soon after that, things would begin to fall into place and the thoughts would flow at a pace I sometimes found difficult to keep up with.

This long but partial list of those who have helped me demonstrates something I am convinced of. Christian literature is not the product of one individual but of the church. I regret that the earthly bibliographical details have only me as the author of this book. I know that in the annals of heaven a very different picture would be recorded, that is, if this work merits inclusion into such annals.

INDEX

ABOUT THE AUTHOR

Ajith Fernando, a native of Sri Lanka, says today's Christians must learn how to respond sensitively, compassionately, respectfully, and wisely to the cultures and beliefs of non-Christians of any nation. Yet they must do so while unequivocally presenting the absolute uniqueness and necessity of Jesus Christ.

In *Sharing the Truth in Love,* Ajith conveys these principles to a church that faces an increasingly pluralistic society. The author shows how believers must wisely and clearly oppose the wrong while allowing God's love to work in them to draw others to Christ.

Since 1976, Ajith has been the national director of Youth for Christ in Sri Lanka. Currently he is also active at Colombo (Sri Lanka) Theological Seminary and serves as a visiting professor at several foreign theological colleges.

Ajith considers his wife, Nelun, to be his most important ministry partner. The Fernandos have two children, daughter Nirmali, 21, and son Asiri, 17.

NOTE TO THE READER

The publisher invites you to share your response to the message of this book by writing Discovery House Publishers, P. O. Box 3566, Grand Rapids, MI 49501, USA or by calling 1-800-653-8333. For information about other Discovery House publications, contact us at the same address and phone number. Find us on the Internet at http://www.dhp.org/ or send e-mail to books@dhp.org.